POETIC MUSIC
RHYTHM AND HARMONY

POETIC MUSIC
RHYTHM AND HARMONY

Praveen Patnaik

Commonwealth

Poetic Music: Rhythm and Harmony

ISBN : 81-311-0001-4

Edition : 2026

Published by :
COMMONWEALTH PUBLISHERS (P) LTD.
4831/24, Govind Lane,
Ansari Road, Darya Ganj,
New Delhi - 110002
Ph. : 23272541, 23242541
e-mail : commonwealthpublishers2016@gmail.com

Distributed by :
ARJUN PUBLISHING HOUSE
4831/24, Govind Lane,
Ansari Road, Darya Ganj,
New Delhi - 110002
Ph. : 23272541, 23242541
e-mail : arjunbooks2001@gmail.com

Laser Typesetting by :
Dimple Computers
Delhi

Printed at :
Milan Enterprises
Delhi

Contents

Preface

As with anything, there is an elemental basis for the composition of music. The material essence of music lies with its melody, harmony, rhythm, and dynamics. Melody gives music soul, while rhythm blends the expression of harmony and dynamics with the tempo of the passage. All are necessary to create a recognisable pattern known as a song.

Harmony is the relation of notes to notes and chords to chords as they are played simultaneously. Harmonic patterns are established from notes and chords in successive order. Melodic intervals are those that are linear and occur in sequence, while harmonic intervals are sounded at the same time. Whether or not a harmony is pleasing is a matter of personal taste, as there are consonant and dissonant harmonies, both of which are pleasing to the ears of some and not others.

Rhythm is, by its simplest definition, musical time. The origin of the word is Greek, meaning 'flow'. Rhythm is indeed the embodiment of timely flow. As meter regulates and pulsates a poem, rhythm organises music in much the same way. The regular pulsations of the music are called the beat. Stronger beats are referred to as accented beats. Measures of music divide a piece into time-counted segments. Strong beats occur in patterns.

The present book discusses the nature and importance of rhythm and harmony in poetic music. It will enable the reader to understand the hidden design of these physical components of music, and their relationship to complex musical events. This work will of interest to composers, performers, teachers, students and lovers of music.

Praveen Patnaik

1

Poetry, Music and Rhythm

Poetry

Poetry is an art form in which human language is used for its aesthetic qualities in addition to, or instead of, its notional and semantic content. It consists largely of oral or literary works in which language is used in a manner that is felt by its user and audience to differ from ordinary prose. It may use condensed or compressed form to convey emotion or ideas to the reader's or listener's mind or ear; it may also use devices such as assonance and repetition to achieve musical or incantatory effects.

Poems frequently rely for their effect on imagery, word association, and the musical qualities of the language used. Because of its nature of emphasising linguistic form rather than using language purely for its content, poetry is notoriously difficult to translate from one language into another. In poetry, it is the connotations and the "baggage" that words carry (the weight of words) that are most important. These shades and nuances of meaning can be difficult to interpret and can cause different readers to "hear" a particular piece of poetry differently. While there are reasonable interpretations, there can never be a definitive interpretation.

Nature of Poetry

Poetry can be differentiated most of the time from prose, which is language meant to convey meaning in a more expansive and less condensed way, frequently using more complete logical or narrative structures than poetry does. A further complication is that prose poetry combines the characteristics of poetry with the superficial appearance of prose. And there is, of course, narrative poetry, not to mention dramatic poetry, both of which are used to tell stories and so resemble novels and plays. However, both these forms of poetry use the specific features of verse composition to make these stories more memorable or to enhance them in some way.

The Greek verb poieo (I make or create), gave rise to three words: poietis (the one who creates), poiesis (the act of creation), and poiema (the thing created). From these we get three English words: poet (the creator), poesy (the creation) and poem (the created). A poet is therefore one who creates, and poetry is what the poet creates. The underlying concept of the poet as maker or creator is not uncommon. For example, in Anglo-Saxon a poet is a scop (shaper or maker) and in Scots makar.

Sound in Poetry

Perhaps the most vital element of sound in poetry is rhythm. Often the rhythm of each line is arranged in a particular meter. Different types of meter played key roles in Classical, Early European, Eastern and Modern poetry. In the case of free verse, the rhythm of lines is often organized into looser units of cadence.

Poetry in English and other modern European languages often uses rhyme. Rhyme at the end of lines is the basis of a number of common poetic forms such as ballads, sonnets and rhyming couplets. However, the use of rhyme is not universal. Much modern poetry, for example, avoids traditional rhyme schemes. Furthermore, Classical Greek and Latin poetry did not use rhyme. In fact, rhyme did not enter European poetry at all until the High Middle Ages, when it was adopted from the Arabic language. The Arabs have always used it extensively.

Alliteration played a key role in structuring early Germanic and English forms of poetry (called Alliterative verse), akin to the role of rhyme in later European poetry. The alliterative patterns of early Germanic poetry and the rhyme schemes of Modern European poetry alike both include meter as a key part of their structure which determines when the listener expects instances rhyme or alliteration to occur. In this sense, both alliteration and rhyme when used in poetic structures help to emphasize and define a rhythmic pattern. By contrast, the chief device of Biblical poetry in ancient Hebrew was parallelism, a rhetorical structure in which successive lines reflected each other in grammatical structure, sound structure, notional content, or all three; a verse form that lent itself to antiphonal or call and response performance.

In addition to the forms of rhyme, alliteration and rhythm that structure much poetry, sound plays a more subtle role in even free verse poetry in creating pleasing, varied patterns and emphasizing or sometimes even illustrating semantic elements of the poem. Devices such as alliteration, assonance, consonance, dissonance and internal rhyme are among the ways poets use sound.

Poetry and Form

As it is created using language, poetry tends to use formal

linguistic units like phrases, sentences and paragraphs. In addition, it uses units of organisation that are purely poetic. The main units that are used are the line, the couplet, the strophe, the stanza, and the verse paragraph.

Lines may be self-contained units of sense, as in the famous To be, or not to be: that is the question. Alternatively a line may end in mid-phrase or sentence: Whether 'tis nobler in the mind to suffer. The linguistic unit is generally completed in the next line: The slings and arrows of outrageous fortune. This technique is called enjambement, and is used to create a sense of expectation in the reader and/or to add a dynamic to the movement of the verse.

Couplets, stanzas, and strophes are generally self-contained units of sense, although a kind of enjambement may also be used across these units. In blank verse, verse paragraphs are employed to indicate natural breaks in the flow of the poem.

In many instances, the effectiveness of a poem derives from the tension between the use of linguistic and formal units. With the advent of printing, poets gained greater control over the visual presentation of their work. As a result, the use of these formal elements, and of the white space they help create, became an important part of the poet's toolbox. Modernist poetry tends to take this to an extreme, with the placement of individual lines or groups of lines on the page forming an integral part of the poem's composition. In its most extreme form, this leads to the writing of concrete poetry.

Poetry and Rhetoric

Rhetorical devices such as simile and metaphor are frequently used in poetry. Or, maybe more accurately, rhetorics has learned these powerful ways of forging connections outside logical reasoning from poetry. Indeed, Aristotle wrote in his Poetics that "the greatest thing by far is to be a master of metaphor". However, particularly since the rise of Modernism, many poets have opted for reduced use of these devices, preferring rather to attempt the direct presentation of things and experiences.

History of Poetry

Poetry as an art form predates literacy. In pre-literate societies, poetry was frequently employed as a means of recording oral history, storytelling (epic poetry), genealogy, law and other forms of expression or knowledge that modern societies might expect to be handled in prose. Poetry is also often closely identified with liturgy in these societies, as the formal nature of poetry makes it easier to remember priestly incantations or prophecies. The greater part of the world's sacred scriptures are made up of poetry rather than prose.

Some writers believe that poetry has its origins in song. Most of the characteristics that distinguish it from other forms of utterance - rhythm, rhyme, compression, intensity of feeling, the use of refrains - appear to have come about from efforts to fit words to musical forms. However, in the European tradition the earliest surviving poems, the Homeric and Hesiodic epics, identify themselves as poems to be recited or chanted to a musical accompaniment rather than as pure song. Another interpretation, developed from 20th century studies of living Montenegran epic reciters by Milman Parry and others, is that rhythm, refrains, and kennings are essentially paratactic devices that enable the reciter to reconstruct the poem from memory.

In preliterate societies, all these forms of poetry were composed for, and sometimes during, performance. As such, there was a certain degree of fluidity to the exact wording of poems, given this could change from one performance or performer to another. The introduction of writing tended to fix the content of a poem to the version that happened to be written down and survive. Written composition also meant that poets began to compose not for an audience that was sitting in front of them but for an absent reader. Later, the invention of printing tended to accelerate these trends. Poets were now writing more for the eye than for the ear.

The development of literacy gave rise to more personal, shorter poems intended to be sung. These are called lyrics, which derives from the Greek lura or lyre, the instrument that was used to accompany the performance of Greek lyrics from about the seventh century B.C. onward. The Greek's practice of singing hymns in large choruses gave rise, in the sixth century B.C. to dramatic verse, and to the practice of writing poetic plays for performance in their theatres. In more recent times, the introduction of electronic media and the rise of the poetry reading have led to a resurgence of performance poetry and have resulted in a situation where poetry for the eye and poetry for the ear coexist, sometimes in the same poem.

Music

Defining music is as difficult as defining art. It is a problem that has been tackled at various times by philosophers, lexicographers, composers, teachers, students and various other musicians. The word has been used to mean various things from "any euphonious and pleasing sound" to a printed document showing how a piece is to be performed (as in sheet music). The question of what the art form we now call music actually consists and does not consist of is, however, something still argued about today.

The word itself comes from the Greek mousik by way of the Latin musica. It is ultimately derived from mousa, the Greek word for muse. In ancient Greece, the word mousike was used to mean any of the arts or sciences governed by the Muses.

Later, in Rome, ars musica embraced poetry as well as what we now think of as music. Our current understanding of music as being something which is abstract and has nothing to do with language (but something which may be combined with it in song) is relatively modern.

In the European Middle Ages, musica was part of the mathematical quadrivium - arithmetics, geometry, astronomy and musica. The concept of musica was split into three major kinds: musica universalis, musica mundana, musica instrumentalis. Of those, only the last - musica instrumentalis - referred to music as performed sound.

Musica universalis referred to the order of the universe, as God had created it in "measure, number and weight". The proportions of the spheres of the planets and stars (which at the time were still thought to revolve around the earth) were perceived as a form of music, without necessarily implying that any sound would be heard - music refers strictly to the mathematical proportions. From this concept later resulted the romantic idea of a music of the of the spheres.

Musica mundana designated the proportions of the human body. These were thought to reflect the proportions of the Heavens and as such, to be an expression of God's greatness. To Medieval thinking, all things were connected with each other - a mode of thought that finds its traces today in the occult sciences or esoteric thought - ranging from astrology to believing certain minerals have certain beneficiary effects. Rather than being ridiculed as unscientific, Medieval thought should be seen as a system that is constistent in itself, and is reflected in the religious or spiritual thought of many other cultures - for instance that of India- some of which are very much in vogue in Western society today.

Musica instrumentalis, finally, was the lowliest of the three disciplines and referred to the manifestation of those same mathematical proportions in sound - be it sung or played on instruments. The polyphonic organization of different melodies to sound at the same time was still a relatively new invention then, and it is understandable that the mathematical or physical relationships in frequency that give rise to the musical intervals as we hear them, should be foremost among the preoccopations of Medieval musicians.

An oft cited definition of music, made by Wynton Marsalis among others, is that it is "sound organized in time." Apart from objections that "organization" is not required, this definition is seen by many as being too broad. The fifteenth edition of the Encyclopaedia Britannica pinpoints the problem by saying that "while there are no sounds that can be described as inherently unmusical, musicians in each culture have tended to restrict the range of sounds they will admit." Organization would seem to be a crucial restricting criterium in this context, after all.

It might be added that as well as cultural background, historical era is also a determining factor in what is regarded as music. What would be accepted as music in Indonesia may be dismissed by many westerners as just "a din." What would today be accepted as music in the west without the blinking of an eye, would have been ridiculed in the 17th century. And what would be music to The Sex Pistols' Sid Vicious, who is said to have commented, "you just pick a chord, go twang, and you've got music," would almost certainly not have been music to William Congreve, who wrote that, "Musick has charms to sooth a savage breast". All of which is to say that there can be no absolute definition of music that will be accepted by everybody.

Many people do, however, share a general idea of music. The Websters definition of music is a typical example: "the science or art of ordering tones or sounds in succession, in combination, and in temporal relationships to produce a composition having unity and continuity" (Webster's Collegiate Dictionary, online edition). There are a number of potential objections to such a definition.

While some may find this definition too restrictive, arguing that "unity" and "continuity" are unnecessary, it is likely that more will find it too broad, thinking of music as being made of pitched sounds, and containing melody, harmony and rhythm. The idea that music must contain these elements is widespread, but there are several examples of what would be widely regarded as music, which lack one or more of them.

Plainsong for instance, or monophonic music in general, has no harmony. Much percussion music lacks both harmony and melody; it is true that drums are tuned, but their pitches are indefinite, and they cannot be said to produce a melody in the traditional sense. If one takes rhythm to mean a regular pulse underpinning music, then many kinds of modern electronic music can be said to lack rhythm.

Some attempts to define music concentrate on the method of producing it. Even though some of the first "instruments" in prehistory must have been rocks and bits of wood, it is only in the past one hundred years or so that the idea that music could only be produced by a singer or a traditional musical instrument (such as a violin in Europe, a sitar in India or a koto in Japan) has been challenged. Erik Satie challenged what constituted a musical instrument, and therefore a musical sound, when he wrote the ballet Parade which included a part for a typewriter. His justification was that since the typewriter made a noise, it was a musical instrument. In a lighter vein, Leroy Anderson also wrote music that included a manual typewriter, played with strict rhythm.

The composer John Cage challenged traditional ideas about music in his 4' 33", which is notated as three movements, each marked Tacet (that is, "do not play"). The implication, as expanded upon by Cage himself, is that the background noises which are normally a distraction from the music (the humming of the lights, the shuffling of the audience, the sound of traffic outside) are to be regarded as the actual music in this case.

This is contrary to the usual view that music is, if nothing else, deliberate. Furthermore, Cage does not state the length of the piece - the duration of the first performance (given by David Tudor seated at a piano) was arrived at by consulting the I Ching, but it is not stated in the score (although whenever the piece is performed nowadays, the original duration is usually maintained). The total time of silence is 273 seconds, which has a parallel in the temperature -273 degrees Celsius, absolute zero. This is pure coincidence, however.

Some people deal with the challenges posed by 4' 33" by simply refusing to consider it as music.

Of course, even in conventional music, the "silent" gaps between notes are part of the music. The pianist Artur Schnabel, when asked what made him a great pianist, said "The notes I handle no better than many pianists. But the pauses between the notes? Ah, that is where the art resides!" There is also at least one piece of music, a string quartet, in which the players stop suddenly while the sheet music shows a long rest at the end. When skillfully performed, the silence at the end is quite obviously part of the music.

The American composer La Monte Young took this line of thought to an extreme by suggesting that even sound itself was not necessary for a piece of music to exist. In Composition 1960 #5, one of a series of similar pieces, he instructed the performer to "Turn a butterfly (or any number of butterflies) loose in the performance area," the piece being considered complete when the butterflies have flown away. The choice of a butterfly is significant in that it is perceived as a silent animal. During the performance, there will be background noises, just as there are in a performance of 4' 33", but this is not the thrust of the piece. Rather, Young is interested in the theatrical element of music.

Young's point in this instance is that when one goes to a performance of a piece of music, seeing the musicians perform is as much a part of the music as hearing them, so why not remove the hearing element altogether? In this sense, his interest is similar to that of Mauricio Kagel, who carefully notates the theatrical element of performance in his works (although he usually maintains a significant sonic element also).

The academic discipline of ethnomusicology focuses on music as an act of performance - as opposed to classical western historical musicology, which is mainly concerned with analyzing "works", that is music in its abstract form as written down in a score or other mode of notation.

Rhythm

Rhythm is the variation of the duration of sounds over time. When governed by rule, it is called meter. It is inherent in any time-dependent medium, but it is most associated with music, dance, and most poetry. The study of rhythm, stress, and pitch in speech is called prosody; it is a topic in linguistics. All instrumentalists deal with rhythm, but it is often considered the primary domain of drummers and percussionists.

In Western music, rhythms are usually arranged with respect to a time signature, partially signifying a meter. The speed of the underlying pulse, called the beat, is the tempo. The length of the meter, or metric unit (usually corresponding with measure length), is divided almost exclusively into either two or three beats, being called duple meter and triple meter, respectively. If each beat is further divided by two it is simple meter, if by three compound meter.

Some genres of music make different use of rhythm than others. Most Western music is based on divisive rhythm, while non-Western music uses more additive rhythm. African music makes heavy use of polyrhythms, and Indian music uses complex cycles such as 7 and 13, while Balinese music often uses complex interlocking rhythms. By comparison, a lot of Western classical music is fairly rhythmically simple; it stays in a simple meter such as 4/4 or 3/4 and makes little use of syncopation. In the

20th century, composers like Igor Stravinsky, Philip Glass, and Steve Reich wrote more rhythmically complex music using odd meters, and techniques such as phasing and additive rhythm. At the same time, modernists such as Olivier Messiaen and his pupils used increased complexity to disrupt the sense of a regular beat, leading eventually to the widespread use of irrational rhythms in New Complexity. LaMonte Young also wrote music in which the sense of a regular beat is absent because the music consists only of long sustained tones (drones).

Clave is a common underlying rhythm in African, Cuban music, and Brazilian music.

A rhythm section generally consists of percussion instruments, and possibly chordal instruments (e.g., guitar, banjo) and keyboard instruments, such as piano (which, by the way, may be classified in any of these three types of instruments).

"Rhythm," wrote Tom Robbins in Another Roadside Attraction, "is everything pertaining to the duration of energy."

Riddim

The Jamaican-English term Riddim originates from the word rhythm. A riddim is a rhythm pattern, basically consisting of a drum pattern and a prominent bass line. Often a melody is associated with the riddim.

Riddims are the instrumental background of every Reggae, Lovers Rock, Dub, Raggamuffin (aka Ragga) or Dancehall Reggae composition. In other musical contexts a riddim would be called a groove or beat.

Different artists perform on one and the same of the hundreds of riddims with different lyrics and different vocal styles, ranging from singing to rapping (for example Beenie Mans? song "My Wish", Mr. Vegas' tune "Go Up" or TOK's "Man A Bad Man" are based on the "Juice Riddim"). Most riddims are named by a tune (as the "Satta-A-Masagana Riddim" is named by the song "Satta-A-Masagana" performed by the group "The Abyssinians").

In general riddims can be divided in three main sections. The oldest type of riddims is the classical riddim providing Roots Reggae/Roots Rock Reggae, Dub and Lovers Rock with instrumentals (for example: "Bam Bam Riddim" produced by Sly & Robbie).

Second type is the ragga riddims backing Raggamuffin/Ragga and Dancehall Reggae tunes (for example: "Juice Riddim" produced by Richard "Shams" Brown), just as the third and last type, the digital riddims (for example: "Sleng Teng Riddim").

Rhythmic Gesture

A rhythmic gesture is a durational pattern which, in contrast to a rhythmic unit, does not occupy a period of time equivalent to a pulse or pulses on an underlying metric level.

They may be described according to their beginnings and endings or as to the rhythmic units they contain. Beginnings on a strong pulse are thetic, a weak pulse, anacrustic, and those beginning after a rest or tied-over note are called initial rest. Endings on a strong pulse are strong, a weak pulse, weak, and those which end on a strong or weak upbeat are upbeat.

Rhythmic Unit

A rhythmic unit is a durational pattern which occupies a

period of time equivalent to a pulse or pulses on an underlying metric level, as opposed to a rhythmic gesture. Rhythmic units may be classified as:

— *Metric*: even-note patterns, such as steady eighth notes or pulses.

— *Intrametric:* confirming patterns, such as dotted eighth-sixteenth note and swing patterns.

— *Contrametric*: non-confirming, or syncopated patterns.

— *Extrametric:* irregular patterns, such as tuplets.

Rhythm and Blues

Rhythm and blues (or R & B) is a musical marketing term introduced in the United States in the late 1940s by Billboard magazine. It replaced the term race music, which was deemed offensive. To some extent, the kind of music it is attached to has changed to whatever form of contemporary music is popular with African-American pop musicians and audiences.

In its first manifestation, rhythm and blues was a black version of a predecessor to rock and roll. It was strongly influenced by jazz and jump music as well as black gospel music, and influenced jazz in return (hard bop was the product of the influence of rhythm and blues, blues, and gospel music on bebop).

The first rock and roll consisted of rhythm and blues songs like "Rocket 88" and "Shake, Rattle and Roll" making an appearance on the popular music charts as well as the R&B charts. "Whole Lotta Shakin' Goin' On", the first hit by Jerry Lee Lewis was an R&B cover song that made number one on pop, R&B and country and western charts.

Musicians paid little attention to the distinction between jazz and rhythm and blues, and frequently recorded in both genres. Numerous swing bands (for example, Jay McShann's, Tiny Bradshaw's, and Johnny Otis's) also recorded rhythm and blues. Count Basie had a weekly live rhythm and blues broadcast from Harlem. Even a bebop icon like arranger Tadd Dameron also arranged for Bull Moose Jackson and spent two years as Jackson's pianist after establishing himself in bebop. Most of the studio musicians in R&B were jazz musicians. And it worked in the other direction as well. Many of the musicians on Charlie Mingus's breakthrough jazz recordings were R&B veterans. Eddie "Cleanhead" Vinson was a one-man fusion, a bebop saxman and a blues shouter.

It was not in the US but through the thriving UK pop scene of the early 1960s that R&B reached the height of its popularity. Without the same kind of racial distinctions that refused it acceptance in the USA, white British performers and listeners adopted this novel style of music without question, and groups such as The Rolling Stones and Manfred Mann brought it to a wider audience.

The term fell into disfavor in the 1960s being replaced by soul music and Motown, but has re-emerged in recent years indicating black popular music encompassing pop heavily influenced by hip-hop, funk, and soul music. In this context only the abbreviation R&B is used, not the full expression. It is gaining popularity nowadays.

2

Poetic and Musical Rhythm: Theoretical Concepts

Poetry is an art or work of the poet; elevated expression of elevated thought or feeling in metrical or rhythmical form; quality (in any thing) that calls for poetical expression. It runs from tightly structured forms, such as the haiku or sonnet, to free verse and even prose poetry. Poetry is written on every subject possible and its subjects and images can be as varied as its structure. It is not a fixed and rigid discipline and poets break rules (usually for a good reason) as often as they follow them. This makes poetry a challenge to study and write about.

Defining characteristics of poetry are its compact form (compared to the equivalent prose to describe something) and the use of striking imagery. Poetry always tries to express something in a new and original way, be it an emotion, a scene or an opinion. It shows interesting use of language and often has a powerful effect.

Poetry and song are closely linked with the first exercise will have shown you how. The forms and devices (rhyme, rhythm, imagery etc.) used are often the same. Poetry's origins are in the oral tradition of storytelling and song. In the time when most people were illiterate, songs with definite rhyme schemes aided memory, keeping popular stories alive.

Poetry diverged along the lines of more formal structures and nowadays only the ballad is really song-like. Songs such as *Auld* Lang Syne, Jerusalem and The Star Spangled Banner began life as poems and this still happens today. Poets know that poems were meant to be heard, not just read on the page, and the oral tradition of poetry is not forgotten. It is preserved in tribal cultures and languages other than English.

Rhythm: Basic Concepts

Metre

The exact metrical scaffolding of a poem doesn't have to (and perhaps shouldn't) be in the forefront of consciousness of either the poet or the reader, any more than the exact key of a song. However, it is sometimes useful to have a vocabulary to describe rhythmical effects.

English Metre is normally based on the more or less regular alternation of a given pattern of stressed and unstressed syllables. The basic repeated unit is called a *foot*.

Lines can be *scanned*, using a notation such as *0* for an unstressed and / for a stressed syllable.

There are four feet in this line by Larkin:

... 0 ... / ...... 0 ... / ..... 0 .... / ...... 0 .... /
They *fuck* | you *up,* | your *mum* | and *dad*

Where words are of more than one syllable, word divisions don't always coincide with foot divisions, as in this line by Eliot is in the same metre:

... 0 ... / .... 0 ... / ..... 0 .... / ..... 0 .... /
The *win-* | ter *eve-* | ning *sett-* | les *down*..

Different metres are classified according to the kind of foot that predominates in a given piece of verse.

Common Metres

The most common metre is

iambic (*0 /* , unstressed followed by stressed, as in the above lines).

Others include

trochaic (*/ 0* , stressed followed by unstressed).

anapaestic (*0 0 /* , two unstressed followed by one stressed).

dactylic (*/ 0 0*, stressed followed by two unstressed).

Iambic and anapaestic are *rising rhythm* (rising to a stress), trochaic and dactylic as *falling rhythm* (falling from a stress) but few poems are wholly one or the other.

The following poem can be scanned as rising rhythm with extra syllables at the ends of lines or as falling rhythm with extra syllables at the beginnings of lines.

The *moun* | tain *sheep* | are *sweet*[er]
...scanned here as *rising* (iambic)
But the *vall* | ey *sheep* | are *fatt*[er];
...scanned here as *rising* (iambic/anapaestic)
[We] *there*fore | *deemed* it | *meet*er
...scanned here as *falling* (trochaic)
[To] *carry* | *off* the | *lat*ter.
...scanned here as *falling* (trochaic)

T L Peacock: The War Song of Dinas Vawr

A more significant distinction is between a predominantly *disyllabic* (iambic or trochaic) metre and one which is predominantly *trisyllabic* (anapaestic or dactylic). The stanza above, whether defined as rising rhythm or falling rhythm, is undoubtedly and consistently disyllabic (except for the trisyllabic foot at the beginning of line 2). Because no line ends with more than one unstressed syllable, while there are occasionally two at the beginning of a line, we would if you held a pistol to head class it as rising rhythm.

Tennyson's *Charge of the Light Brigade* is in a *trisyllabic* metre, predominantly dactylic (*/ 0 0*):

Half a league, | *half* a league,
Half a league | *on*ward,
All in the | *valley* of Death 1
Rode the six | *hund*red....
*Can*non to | *right* of them,
*Can*non to | *left* of them
*Can*non in | *front* of them
*Vol*leyed and | *thun*dered
[1 Notice the elision between adjacent vowels in line 3. Can *Death* be left unstressed?]

Extra syllables, like that in line 3, are always unstressed.

Stresses Matter More than Feet

Classical metre, based on syllable-*length* rather than stress, has a foot called the *spondee* (//)consisting of two heavy syllables, and one called the *pyrrhic* (00)consisting of two light syllables, but it can be argued that neither is possible in our stress-based metre, where the stressed syllable is like an atomic nucleus in every foot. Every alleged spondee is either two truncated feet or a normal foot with one syllable relatively stronger than the other.

Feet are useful to generalise with but tend to disappear when looked at close to. The following lines by Hopkins are more iambic than anything else, and each complete line may be divided tentatively into five feet, but *the number of stresses (5 per line) is what really matters.*

Oh the *mind, mind* has *moun*tains; *cliffs* of *fall*
*Fright*ful, *sheer,* no-man-*fath*omed. *Hold* them *cheap*
May who ne'er *hung* there. *Nor* does *long* our *small*
*Dur*ance *deal* with that *steep* or *deep*. Here, *creep....*

We would describe the first four syllables as a pair of fused iambs, rather than as a pyrrhic followed by a spondee. The second line begins with a *reversed foot* (trochaic rather than iambic), and it isn't easy to say which of the following words are stressed and which are unstressed. Stress has to be considered as relative rather than absolute.

Stress-based or Sprung Rhythm

The lines by Hopkins in the previous section could also be considered as *sprung rhythm,* the term he used for lines with a set number of stresses but a varying number of unstressed syllables.

Coleridge took a similar approach in *Christabel,* and some of Shakespeare's late blank verse at times almost struggles free of its basic iambic rhythm.

Not everyone will agree with the stress-placings in the examples below, and the foot divisions are not meant to be definitive; indeed the concept of the foot is not really applicable to this kind of verse, although there is no clear dividing line between verse that counts stresses and verse that measures feet.

'Tis the *midd*le | of the *night* | by the *cas*tle | *clock*

Christabel

If by | your *art,* | my *dear* | est *father,* | *you* have
Put the | wild *wat* | ers *in* | this *roar,* | al*lay* them.
The *sky,* | it *seems,* | would *pour* | down *stink* | ing *pitch*
But that | the *sea,* | *moun*ting | to th'*welk* | in's *cheek*
*Dash*es | the *fire* | *out.* | O! *I* | have *suff*ered 2
With *those* | that I *saw* | *suff*er; | a *brave* | *vessel....*

The Tempest

[2 *fire* could be scanned as two syllables]

Types of Line

Lines in metrical and sprung rhythm can be described according to the number of feet or stresses.

2. Dimeter: When *I* | de*scend* Hardy, The Robin)
3. Trimeter: When *I* | was *one*- | and-*twen*ty (Housman)
4. Tetrameter: *Had* we | but *world* | e*nough* | and *time* (Marvell, To His Coy Mistress)
5. Pentameter: To *be* | or *not* | to *be,* | *that* is | the *ques*tion (Shakespeare, Hamlet)
6. Hexameter: A *peri* | *phras*tic | *stu*dy | | in a *worn*-out | po*e*tical | *fash*ion (Eliot, East Coker)

All are predominantly iambic except the last, which is stress-based, but in no case is the actual rhythm fully defined by the notional metre. Metre is a digital analysis imposed on analog material. In each of the first two examples, the syllables of the first foot are almost equal in weight, causing the stress to hover. The second example has an extra syllable at the end. The tetrameter line has a reversed foot at the beginning. The pentameter has a reversed foot in the middle and an extra syllable at the end. In most of them the metre plays against the word-divisions and the syntactical or expressive pauses, as well as the differing weights and lengths of syllables. Longer lines, especially hexameters, tend to fall into two sections divided by a caesura.

As a test, the following lines contain examples of a) dactylic dimeter b) iambic trimeter c) iambic tetrameter d) trochaic tetrameter e) anapaestic tetrameter f) dactylic tetrameter g) iambic pentameter and h) iambic(?) hexameter, but not in that order.

1. Earth, receive an honoured guest! (Auden)
2. The stranger from the noisy inn (De La Mare)
3. Just for a handful of silver he left us! (Browning)
4. Tis the voice of the lobster; I heard him declare (Carroll)
5. The hop-poles stand in cones (Blunden)
6. Wondering, listening (Hodgson)
7. When I consider how my light is spent (Milton)
8. Pale flakes with fingering stealth come feeling for our faces (Owen)

Types of Stanza

A rhyme scheme can be defined by using identical letters for rhyming lines. Half-rhyme can be treated similarly.

— *Couplets* are always *aa,bb,cc,* etc.

— *Quatrains* may be *abab, abcb, abba,* etc.

— *Ballad Metre* consists of *abcb* quatrains with tetrameter for the first and third lines and trimeter for the rhymes.

— *Terza Rima has* interlaced triplets ending with a quatrain: *aba bcb cdc efe fgf ghg-h.*

— *A Petrarchan Sonnet* has an octave rhyming *abba abba* and a variously rhyming sestet (e.g.*cdecde*).

— *A Shakespearean Sonnet* has three quatrains (*abab cdcd efef*) and a couplet (*gg*).

Some poets, such as Donne and Hardy, invent their own intricately rhyming stanzas.

Poetic Rules

Metre is a contentious subject, and studies based on mechanical, musical, organic and linguistic analogies have shown how little is currently understood. Nonetheless, as defined as some pattern of phonological stress, pitch and/ or length, rhythm is an inescapable element of poetry. Cultural conventions and literary history select their varying requirements from the individual features of a language, but rhythm also arises naturally from the simple exercise of breathing and the desire for shape and regularity in human affairs.

Metre is a systematic regularity in rhythm. In western literature there are two great metrical systems — the quantitative (introduced by the Greeks) and the accentual (which appears in Latin of the third century AD) — but metre of some sort is found in all poetry, east and west.

Metrical skill comes from practice rather than any slavish following of rules, and rules indeed vary with the literary tradition and what poets are attempting to achieve. The ear is not the only judge. Swinburne and Chesterton appeal to the auditory imagination, but look bombastic on the page. The late blank verse of Shakespeare needs a trained actor to bring out its rough-hewn splendour, and the rhythmic subtleties of Geoffrey Hill are apt to vanish on public performance.

New metres are rarely created, but much more common is the importation and adaptation of metre from a foreign language, which is a good reason for reading beyond translations. Conventional English verse is usually (and confusedly) described in a terminology deriving from classical prosody: as iambic, trochaic, dactylic and anapaestic. On an elementary level it may be better to consider metre under two headings: whether the syllables or the stresses are being counted, and whether these counts are fixed or variable. Accentual verse has fixed counts of stress but variable syllables. Syllabic verse has fixed counts of syllables regardless of stresses. Accentual-syllabic is conventional metre with both stress and syllables fixed. Free verse has no restrictions on either. How readers recognize and respond to metre is unclear, but any particular metre seems to be a norm, a pattern intuited behind permissible examples. The examples are often irregular, and indeed the common iambic pentameter seems only to be exact in some 25% of cases overall.

Accentual verse is found in popular verse, ballads, nursery rhymes, songs and doggerel. Syllabic verse as exemplified by the French alexandrine is not strictly metrical, and twentieth century attempts to write a pure syllabic verse in English have not caught on. Accentual-syllabic was developed by Chaucer from Italian models, and became the staple for English poetry from Elizabethan times till comparatively recently. Free verse originated in France around the middle of the nineteenth century, was championed (briefly) by the founders of Modernism, and has ramified into various forms, some of them indistinguishable from prose.

Traditional verse is overshadowed by the achievements of the past. Chaucer, Spenser, Shakespeare, Milton, Pope and Wordsworth set standards difficult to emulate, and poets are nowadays hardly encouraged to try. Many of the better magazines, where the fledgling poet must start his publishing career, will not take traditional poetry, and those with more generous requirements may still lack readers or editors capable of telling the good from the merely facile. Nonetheless, strict verse enjoys periodic revivals, and has been a feature of several twentieth century schools: the Georgians, Neo-Romantics, the Movement poets and the New Formalists.

Free verse is very confused field, not properly understood or linguistically mapped. Adoption may be more about pamphleteering and cultural allegiances than poetic ends. Some of the speech rhythms claimed as "superior to metre" are not rhythms at all but an enviable dexterity in idiomatic expression. Some are loose assemblages of rhythmic expression to no constant base, and some an endearing tribute to their author's performance skills.

Why use the device? Because metre creates and organizes content, giving emphasis to words or elements that would otherwise escape attention: the tighter the metre, the more expressive can be small departures from the norm. Metre gives dignity and memorability, conveying tempo, mood, the subtle shifts in evidence, passion and persuasion beyond what is possible in prose. In the hands of great master like Shakespeare, metre provides grace, energy, elevation, expressiveness and a convincing approximation to everyday speech.

But metre is not diametrically opposed to free verse. Many contemporary poets write both, or served an apprenticeship in strict forms before creating something closer to their needs. Nonetheless, in the absence of this ability to highlight and compound meaning, free verse is often driven to expand in other directions. It prizes a convincing exactness of idiomatic expression, the line seeming exactly right in the circumstances: appropriate, authentic and sincere. It operates closely with syntax. It adopts a challenging layout on the page where line and syntax are rearranged to evade or exploit the usual expectations.

Poets write more by ear than rules. Rules govern many art forms — music, painting, choreography, etc. — and are seen as aids to creation once they are so thoroughly ingested as to be second nature. Indeed, without some rules, art fails to be art and becomes instead a perplexity to everyone, not least its practitioners.

Poetry is now fragmented into diverse schools, each claiming indisputable truth. As rhythmic expressions are often made into shibboleths, the sensible writer will want an understanding of the issues, so as to choose between the rival claims.

Study sharpens the ear, and will locate examples useful to the practising poet.

An understanding of rhythm will create links to other art forms, and open the door to current studies in human physiology and behaviour.

Rhythm in poetry can be treated in many different ways. In fact, there exist no fewer than sixteen different theories. Most are in use by literary criticism, and each theory adds depth and significance the others.

Foot Substitution

We start with the most popular theory, that of the foot substitution prosodists. The approach derives from classical scansion, and divides the line into feet. Each foot contains one dominant stress and a number of unstressed syllables. The metres are:

— *Iambic*: rising duple: The cúr | few tólls | the knéll | of párt | ing dáy.

— *Dactylic*: falling duple: Súm mer | ísles of | É den | lý ing | ín dark | púr ple | sphéres of | séa

— *Anapaestic:* rising triple: The Ass ý | rian came dówn | like a wólf | on the fóld

— *Dactylic:* falling triple: Tóuch her not | scórn full y

Verse is rarely completely regular, but if we a. add the pyrrhic (two unstressed syllables) and the spondee (two stressed syllables), and b. allow individual feet to be replaced (most commonly the iambic by a trochaic foot) then most verse can be scanned succinctly. The classification includes type of line (dimeter with two feet, trimeter with three feet, tetrameter with four feet, pentameter with five feet, hexameter with six feet and heptameter with seven feet), and groupings by stanzas of various types.

How real is this periodic stress? It is something instinctively felt on practice, but can be broken into amplitude (i.e. volume), duration and pitch — in that decreasing order of importance. Laboratory study on adults and children (and indeed unborn children) has substantiated the reality of the sensation, and some schools of linguistics recognize stress as a feature in everyday speech. In that sense, stress pattern is a reality of the English language, and not something imposed by outmoded literary conventions. If its intricate employment in verse is culturally determined, then so of course is language.

The foot substitution system has many advantages. It is:

1. Widespread in earlier literary criticism, and still very popular.
2. Simple to learn and apply.
3. Sufficiently flexible to cover everything from advertising jingles to Shakespearean blank verse.

Unfortunately, the system also has serious limitations:

1. The classification is artificial, the terminology and to some extent the practice being taken from the wholly different system of classical verse.
2. The classification does not distinguish degrees of stress.
3. Prosodists vary (sometimes very markedly) in their readings, and there seems no way of deciding between claims.
4. The system is somewhat rough and ready, and so not over-helpful to the poet. Only the trained ear will distinguish between a good and the merely correct line of verse, and that training exceeds what is needed to apply the system.
5. The system does not properly capture the experience of reading verse.
6. The system enforces correctness at a very elementary level, but metre is not integrated into an overall and illuminating view of a poem's structure.

Temporal Prosodists

The traditional rival to foot substitution has been temporal prosody. Under this approach, which derives from classical verse, the lines are divided into measures like a musical score. Each measure contains a major beat plus one or more subordinate beats. The beats are not marked by pitch or loudness but by the time taken to sound them. Some are long (major) and some are short (subordinate), but in total the beats make up measures of approximately equal duration. One measure may consist of one major beat lasting six intervals of time, for example, and another consist of three equal but subordinate beats, each lasting two intervals of time. Milton's famous opening to Paradise Lost could be scanned thus:

2 | 42 | 22 2 | 312 | 22 2 | 42

2 4 2 2 2 2 3 1 2 2 2 2 4 2

Of man's fir st dis o be di ence - and the fruit -

Many refinements are possible. Some prosodies, as in the example above, allow for pauses. Some would insist that the bar-lines fall always before the major beat. Many have indeed employed a musical notation.

One attraction of temporal prosody is its application to prose rhythm. Verse in this view is not something divorced from natural speech, but merely speech made more regular and pleasing. The same measures can be applied to both, and there thus exists a gradual progression from strict forms, through free verse and emotive prose into everyday, spasmodic conversation.

Yet the temporalist approach is not without its problems. Most telling is the complete lack of evidence that such measures actually exist. Decades of testing in speech laboratories have failed to substantiate the notion. Whether in everyday speech, narrative prose or verse, human beings do not linger over syllables in such a way that measures of equal duration can be recognized — not unless the lines are chanted, when all rhythmic subtlety is lost. Verse seems not to be a heightening of natural speech tendencies, but speech cultivated for a particular end. "What does not ripen with cultivation?" said Quintilian, and "that which is most natural is that which nature permits to be done to the greatest perfection." Verse allows the formal powers of language to release, inflect and modulate meaning, and so needs extensive training to write, to speak and to appreciate

Phrasalists

Phrasalists are not concerned with metre, but with rhythmic phrases, these phrases forming spatial patterns that give verse its aesthetic appeal. Lines are scanned for combinations of phrasal shapes — repetitions, variations, inversions, etc. — and the attraction of a poem ascribed to its figured harmonies of thought.

Some phrasalists ignore metre, or deny it exists at all, particularly in modern free verse, but the majority ascribe the effectiveness of verse to interplay between phrase and metre. Phrasal prosody may be directed to individual lines, stanzas, or to the poem as a whole. A few prosodists even extend the concept from units of sound to implied meaning, when their analysis encroaches on what has traditionally been considered rhetoric. Some of Whitman's verse, for example, can be analysed on four phrasal levels. Stresses combine into pause groups. Pause groups combine into lines. Lines combine into verse paragraphs. These three levels interact to form a fourth level, which is our experience of reading a poem as a whole.

Milton composed by verse paragraphs. The end of Paradise Lost, with its regular alternation of 2 and 3 beats phrases, is subdued and dignified: the only flourish of an extra syllable in wandering being echoed by solitary, strictly iambic but the ta taking only half a beat. The alternation is

3 I I 2 I I 3 I I 2 I 2 I 3 I I 2 I I 3 I I 2 I 3 :

Some natural tears they dropped I I but wiped them soon I I
The world was all before them I I where to choose
Their place of rest, I and Providence their guide: I I
They hand in hand, I I with wandering steps and slow, I I
Through Eden took I their solitary way. I I

The drawbacks with the phrasalist approach? Most obvious are those common to all such studies: knowing what is not knowing how. Findings cannot be applied as recipes, only as guides to self-cultivation. We also find ourselves recognizing the effectiveness of phrasal structures without entirely knowing why they are effective. Most of the phrasalist approaches until recently have indeed been limited, but the approach does form a basis for the sophisticated theory of rhythmic phrasing developed by David Cureton.

Prose Rhythms

The most ambitious study was George Saintsbury's A History of English Prose Rhythms, which extended the approach of foot substitution to prose paragraphs. Containing up to five syllables, these prose feet were longer than verse feet, however, and required a complex terminology: 22 types in all. The classification did not catch on, but Saintsbury was able to draw some lessons from the ordered variety. Juxtaposed feet were never of the same shape, but followed one or more of these patterns: grades moved from short to long and long to short; variations modified a common shape; shapes themselves reflected the content — rising for inspiration, for example, and falling for paragraph endings. Always there was opposition between verse feet (recurring feet with some variation) and prose feet (varied feet with some recurrence.)

Thomas Browne's celebrated passage in Urn Burial was analysed thus:

> Now since these dead bones | have already | outlasted | the living ones | of Methuselah, | and in a yard | under ground, | and thin | walls | of clay, | outworn | all the strong | and specious | buildings | above it; | and quietly | rested | under the drums | and tramplings | of three | conquests; | what Prince | can promise | such | diuturnity | unto his reliques, | or might not | gladly | say,
>
> Sic ego componi versus in ossa velim

The classification could be taken further. Croll, for example, proposed a system of ascending units. The lowest unit was a colon, a passage typically averaging some ten syllables that could be enunciated in one breath. The next unit was a commata, a melodic and rhythmic passage not necessarily contained by sense and syntax. Then came phrases, which were often twofold: a first phrase consisting of an appeal with modifying relative clause, and a second phrase of imperative clause or clauses. The highest unit was the period, defined as perfect in itself and easily comprehended by the understanding. Often these periods coincided with sentences, but they could include more than one sentence. This, from the English Book of Common Prayer, has two phrases and one period:

> Almighty and everlasting God who dost govern all things in heaven and earth;
>
> mercifully hear the supplications of thy people, and grant us peace all the days of our life.

Prose analysts were also interested in the cursus, a rhythmical formula that ended the commata or cola in liturgical writing. The cursus began with a strong accent, continued through a long span of unstressed syllables to a subordinate accent, and then tailed away in (optional) unstressed syllables. There was a recognized terminology for the various types: The planus had no subordinate accent and ended in one unstressed syllable: help and defend us. The tardus ended with two unstressed syllables: governed and sanctified. The velox had a subordinate accent: punished for our offences.

Another form of periodicity studied by prosodists was the overall shape of sentences. Periodic sentences place adverbial elaboration before the main clause. Loose sentences place them after. Balanced sentences have initial and final elaborations in equal proportions. Suspended or mid-branching sentences have elaboration between the mandatory elements of the main clause. The matter is complex, and the classifications even more so.

How does this affect poets? The exact terminology may not matter, but poetry of a high order was obtained by careful elaboration of such phrasing, and might be so again. The elaboration is inappropriate for demotic speech, as for writing of any naturalness or spontaneity, but fine prose shows that free verse is not bound to simple speech rhythms. French poets in particular have created marvels this century with such devices, though the prose poem is admittedly easier in loose hexameters than irregular blank verse.

Forster divided the rhythmic shape of an extended piece of prose into two categories. Easy rhythms were analogous to a musical motif. An event, action or scene recurred frequently, and each recurrence gained from previous incarnations, so that the prose was provided with a clear internal structure. Barthes formalized this in semic, symbolic and referential codes. Difficult rhythms are more analogous to the deep structural organization of a musical composition: they can be sensed but not tapped or spelt out. Most good prose belongs to the second category, of course: heterogeneous, unwieldy but somehow pleasing, which Barthes labelled as proaeretic and hermeneutic.

The advantages of such study? It gets us reading good prose, developing an ear for rhythmic subtleties and structural organization that are needed for the longer poem. We appreciate the poet's art better, understanding what Shakespeare did to Sir Thomas North's prose to arrive at The barge she sat in like a burnished throne...

But the difficulties are again legion. Saintsbury's terminology is daunting, and based on a never-substantiated temporal prosody. Scholars disagree on interpretation, very markedly, and even Saintsbury, in his usual disarming way, could not decide whether the Urn Burial piece quoted starts with a heavily weighted docmiac or four monosyllabic feet.

Free Verse

Free verse is the form most widely used in contemporary poetry, but is anything but new. Many of its features can be found in ancient Sumerian, Akkadian, Egyptian, Sanskrit and Hebrew literature. As a loosening of traditional metre, the form reappears in 17th century French poetry, and again in 19th century poetry throughout the European languages.

Pinning down the form has caused endless problems. Free verse has been defined as unmetered, metered but unscannable, non-conventionally metered, partially or loosely metered, complexly metrical verse, and so on. Perhaps all that the many studies have demonstrated is how readily the various forms of free verse evade any simple notation. Foot substitution in particular needs some metric norm to return to, but a norm is what free verse avoids. The lack of normative organization may indeed be the one defining characteristic of this complex and somewhat perplexing form.

Regardless of the facts, modern free verse sees itself as innovative, making a important break with the past. Two traditions run through American and British poetry. The first originates in Walt Whitman and comes down through Allen Ginsberg and Robert Bly. This is a personal style tending to use asymmetric and often long lines, parallelism, repetition of words and phrases, stresses in unexpected places and mixtures of idiom. The second is more tightly written, with lineation coinciding with grammatical units (D.H. Lawrence, Wallace Stevens and Carl Sandburg) or not so coinciding (William Carlos Williams, Carl Sandburg and Robert Creeley).

Freedom applies not only to freedom from traditional metre, but freedom to use visual and sound effects for surprise, thickening of meaning, symmetry, repetition, or simply for pleasure. Lines can be shortened for speed, or segmented into clots of words or syllables to slow down the reading or comprehension. Continuously long lines are more the preserve of Whitman (with David Jones, Robinson Jeffers and A.R. Ammons) but alternating long and short have been popular for long poems (Pound, Dorn, Reznikoff and others). Similarly the line breaks: some writers break their lines in unusual and sometimes arbitrary places (Williams), while others run them on (Lawrence).

Equally varied has been the disposition of the poem on the page. Eleanor Berry in The New Princeton Encyclopedia of Poetry and Poetics, for example, distinguishes some twelve ways in which such visual layouts may support the irony, openness, dissonance, anticlimax, tension, surprise, fragmentation, ambiguity and self-reference of modern poetry.

Those emphasizing the poem's autonomy or unity may:

1. Give prominence to the sound or structure in the text.
2. Indicate the juxtaposition of ideas or images.
3. Signal shifts in tone, meaning or perspective.
4. Frame a word or phrase.
5. Emphasize (foreground) the text as an aesthetic object.
6. Provide an abstract shape of energy.

The textural and disintegrative may:

1. Signal a reference to poetic tradition.
2. Allude to genres of printed texts.
3. Sustain interest through textural differences.
4. Create counterpoint between structures occupying the same words.
5. Heighten awareness of the reading process.
6. Defamiliarize certain areas or aspects of the text.

Behind these devices generally lies a belief that poetry should be a representation of lived experience. The poetry tries to replicate the perceptual, cognitive, emotional or imaginative processes which gave rise to the poem, and to do so in a manner that seems natural and everyday. Living and writing are matters not to be confused or fused completely, of course, but free verse at least tries to overcome the nineteenth century dichotomy between art and life.

Slavic Theorists

It is Russian and Polish theorists, the Slavic School, who have created the largest body of metrical analysis in the twentieth century. A few are well known in the west (Jacobson, Wellek, Tarjinskaya) but the work of others lies buried in foreign journals, where even here it was fortunate to survive the Leninist purges. From the sixties onwards, however, Slavic approaches have been applied to English verse, initially with considerable success. The approach is characterized by being

a) minutely attentive to the texts,
b) thorough and wide-ranging,
c) supportive of theoretical considerations that were later transported to the west: semiotics and structuralism
d) based on linguistics and
e) aimed at normative analysis: i.e. not the preferred reading of a particular line but the quantitative generalizations that could be made about all verse of a similar type.

Such studies do not make for easy comprehension, and their technicalities will not help the poet struggling with a particular line, since correct lines are not necessarily good lines. But some objectivity and clarity does emerge. We don't have to lay down rules in absence of the facts: we can analyse large bodies of poetry and see what actually happens. Tarjinskaya in 1976, for example, analysed the non-dramatic iambic pentameters of 30 major poets, from Chaucer to Swinburne.

The finding was that:

1. ictic (rhythmical or metrical) stress features in 75 - 87% of cases, that
2. non-ictic stress occurs three times more frequently in the first position of a line than elsewhere,
3. non-ictic stress declines progressively across a line,
4. ictic non-stress occurs most commonly with monosyllables and
5. lines having more than one non-ictic stress caused by polysyllables are generally avoided.

Not compelling reading, and not a revelation, but a prophylactic against any rigid imposition of rules. Verse types do indeed fall into normative patterns, but the patterns are derived from the analyses, not the other way round.

In their analyses, the Slavic metrists divided lines horizontally and vertically. In addition to rhythmical stress, for example, there is the part played by meaning, intonation, sound orchestration, syntax and visual form. These aspects are depicted vertically above the line, as secondary rhythmic features that are nonetheless important. Across the lines appear the sorts of findings noted by Tarjinskaya above. They give a horizontal shaping, so that a line of verse is not seen as an unvarying pattern of stressed and unstressed syllables.

Additionally, there is a hierarchical grouping, generally represented by syllable, word, phrase member, phrase and sentence (also called utterance or totality). The higher levels of syntax are also brought into the picture, so that these analyses merge with the structuralism of Levi-Strauss. How are analyses decided upon in the first place? They may be quantitative and objective, but someone has to decide on what is relevant and worth measuring, as indeed happens in all the sciences. So enters the speculative part, the theories that the evidence must support or refute. The Slavic metrists were often audacious theorists, and none more so than Ramon Jakobson. In his famous definition of poetry, the poetic function of language projects the principle of equivalence from the axis of selection into the axis of combination.

The idea is this. The order of words in a sentence is governed by syntax. In The dark night closed around them the syntax is quite straightforward: adjective subject noun, verb, adverb and object pronoun. We can replace the noun by another noun, an equivalent part of speech: The dark animal closed around them. Ditto for any other part of speech, or all of them together: The overpowering smell seeped into him. These replacements are in a vertical sense, along the axis of equivalence. Replacements in the horizontal sense are much more difficult. We can't write Around the night dark closed them, for instance, because words in this horizontal direction have to combine in certain ways. But we can in literary language carry out some replacements: Around them, the night was close and dark. The close night darkened around them. And so on: it is very typical of poetry, and imaginative literature generally.

Characteristics are one thing, but to make a definition of poetry in this way was preposterous. Poetry is an art, and art is governed by a good deal more than linguistics. There is no clear demarcation between literal and imaginative language, moreover, and the most compelling poems can include apparent statements of fact: witness The Divine Comedy and thousands more. A case can indeed be made for all language being metaphoric at base, so poetry and non-poetry cannot be distinguished on such a basis anyway. Jacobson's notion gained an undeserved currency in the sixties because it coincided with the obscurantism of Structuralism, and the hope that artistic creation could be placed on a scientific footing.

Jacobson did in fact elaborate the notion and provide detailed examples, but the moral should be clear. Poetry is the most subtle use of words, and the lumping together of reductionism destroys precisely what is worth distinguishing. To the extent that linguistics is a science, and science deals with propositions that must be falsifiable, linguistics does not provide a royal road to certainty in metrical analysis. The work of the Slavic metrists has been invaluable to clearing out dogma, however, and their stress on normative analysis is well worth preserving.

Intonationalists

Verse rhythm is not wholly to be represented by simple stressed and unstressed syllables. In their seminal work of 1951, Trager and Smith distinguished four levels in three elements: stress, pitch and juncture. Stress or loudness was denoted as primary, secondary, tertiary or weak. Pitch (as in music, technically the frequency of vibration of a column of air) was denoted as very high, high, mid or low. Juncture was denoted as open, sustained, rising or falling. All four levels of stress were needed to say elevator-operator, for example, and we indicate a question by raising the pitch at the end of a sentence. (I'm late. versus I'm late?). Open juncture allows us to distinguish nitrate from night rate. And so on. Other workers developed similar systems, using them to argue that

1. variation within regularity so characteristic of verse is elegantly captured by such systems,
2. verse rhythm is more easily seen an alternation of stress levels, and

3. the approach can be adapted to a normative approach: rhythm is best studied by statistical analysis of what seems acceptable to practiced readers.

Such systems can be extended vertically, moreover. Elizabeth Hewitt recognized what she termed metrical foot, measure, lower cadence and upper cadence in the poetry of T.S. Eliot, an analysis only possible with pitch and juncture as elements in the grouping. The pronunciation of American English is very different from that of British English, and has brought differences in approach. Americans tend to move from segment through phrase to meaning, where British intonationalists are top down, moving from overall meaning to phrase and segment.

Important to the British are tone units, which divide a text into informational segments. Each tone unit includes a prominent pitch movement (tonic syllable) that coincides with the information focus. Preceding the tonic syllable is information recoverable from context, and following is a short post-tonic element. Features making the pitch movement are tones that

1. rise,
2. fall,
3. remain level,
4. fall then rise and
5. rise then fall.

British linguists also divide the tone unit into rhythmic feet, comparable to prosodic feet, where the stresses can be implied rather sounded. Where does this lead?

British prosodists have used the tone unit and the melodic contour as alternatives to simple verse measures. Most poetic lines, it is claimed, end with a tonic syllable and a tone unit boundary. Unconsciously, readers expect lines to be intonationally delimited, unified and parallelled, and these are more practicable than standard rules of versification. More particularly, this approach finds patterns inherent in the many types of free verse that break the rules but are nonetheless pleasing. William Carlos Williams' "chopped-up prose" is often abrupt and jagged, for example, but has passages of stateliness when these deeper patterns are followed.

The approaches are technical and somewhat narrow, but Kenneth Pike on the American side, extended intonation into a larger study of rhythmic organization. Hierarchically, there are three 'standpoints': particles, field and wave. Any particle can have a nucleus, plus optional margins, and these margins can have a variety of roles: setting, denouement, action, etc. Each particle belongs to a class of waves in a vertical relationship with superordinate and subordinate waves. These waves in turn are associated with meaning and a field of structural and functional expectancies.

Poetic Closure

Less study has been given to movement among sentences, i.e. across the text as a whole. One exception is Barbara Herranstein Smith's work on poetic closure. Poems please us because they arouse our appetites and expectations, continually defer and evade those appetites and expectations, and then finally close when the structure is coherent, complete and stable. Smith believed that such processes give us psychological or even physiological gratification, and are of two types: formal and thematic.

Formal structures arise from the physical nature of words, and include such things as rhyme, alliteration, metre and stanza shaping. Thematic structures arise from the symbolic nature of language, and include syntax, genres, sense imagery and rhetorical figures. Formal and thematic structures interact to effect closure. Formal patterning depends on repetition, and can always be extended, at least until we feel an overwhelming need for change. These terminations are not random, moreover, but emphasize a thematic revelation at the close, antithesis, puns, hyperbole, aphoristic brevity and parallels often being employed for this purpose.

Thematic structures at their most basic are unordered and expandable, and can only be closed by adding some 'paratactic listing'. These may be a paraphrase of the opening line, a reference to natural stopping places in human experience (death, sleep, heave, etc.) or some element of narrative or dramatic ordering. Poetry uses these novelistic devices, but theme dominates plot: the poem usually comments rather than simply presents or portrays. Smith in fact recognized several types of thematic structure, which she termed paractic, temporal, sequential and associative/dialectical. The last are interior monologues, the wavering of minds on trains of thought that may not reach closure.

Generative Metrists

The success of Chomsky's generative grammar approach encouraged metrists to establish a similar system for well-formed verse. Comprehensive rules would specify what was acceptable and what was not acceptable as verse.

Various systems were proposed. Hall and Keyser demonstrated, for example, that iambic pentameters were specified by a set of correspondence rules operating on a metrical pattern of (W)SWSWSWSWS(X)(X) where ( )

indicates an optional element and X can only be occupied by an unstressed syllable. The correspondence rules are:

1. S, W or X corresponds to a single syllable or a sounded sequence of no more than two syllables.
2. Fully stressed syllables occur in all S and only in S positions, or

   Fully stressed syllables occur only in S positions but not in all S positions, or

Stress maxima occur in S positions only, but not in all S positions. (A stress maximum is a fully stressed syllable occurring between two unstressed syllables in the same syntactic constituent.)

Where does that take us? Well, firstly, the rules are specified. Then the rules can establish a norm and a hierarchy of departures from the norm. Thirdly, they emphasize the importance of word boundaries since monosyllabic words have metrical freedom whereas polysyllabic words usually have their lexical break in a strong position.

And so on: this early work has been much built on and modified. Kiparsky developed a concept of phonological word to examine metrical breaks that appear on syntactical and phonological grounds. (A phonological has lexical stress on a major category word plus syntactically associated unstressed syllables, a concept deriving from work of Chomsky and Halle in 1968. It is well known, for example, that poets tend to place stressed syllables in weakly stressed positions only after strong breaks, and Dillon suggested a sevenfold hierarchy of such phrasal breaks.

The drawbacks? The first is the difficulty with all generative grammars, that well-formed examples are not objectively derived. Second, the rules are not over-useful to practitioners. Like native speakers, poets construct their verses intuitively, not by following rules or blueprints. And finally, it must be admitted that disputes have frequently arise among generative metrists themselves, and that even their science has not escape radical transformations and schisms.

Reuven Tsur's Work

Rueven Tsur's cognitive poetics tries to fit the generative metrists approach into the larger framework of brain functioning. Literature has aesthetic effects when normal cognitive processing is interrupted or delayed. Something complex and irregular is therefore scanned for similarity, regularity and balance, and recoded into the simple, economical patterns the brain requires. Conversely, however, input which already has these properties (has what gestalt psychologists call strong shapes) is not immediately accepted. Indeed, these strong shapes stand out from the overall complexity of other inputs, and so (in the larger framework) constitute irregular or weak shapes. From this interaction between strong and weak arises the aesthetic phenomenon.

Some broad distinctions can be made. Convergent or conclusive styles are marked by clear-cut shapes, both in contents and structure. Divergent or suspensive styles have weak shapes: blurred, atmospheric and emotive. Into one of these styles can be placed most of English poetry, with very different consequences for rhythm. Misplaced stresses are not tolerated in iambic pentameters with convergent styles, for example, but can be acceptable in divergent styles provided they affect only certain positions, usually position. The brain, Tsur argues, integrates inputs into groupings on various levels based on word boundaries, syntactical breaks and pauses (caesurae). Some groupings are more common than others, and influence a good deal more than rhythm.

Derek Attridge

Attridge has united rhythmic experience with well-formedness and universals. The focus is on what the trained reader senses, and to this end Attridge identifies an underlying rhythm consisting of a small number of abstract patterns. Such patterns are given particularity by the verse traditions in question, and can be related to the language of the text by realization rules. The underlying rhythm is a perceived temporal pattern reinforced by repetition and periodicity. (The pulses of energy that make the rhythm itself are difficult to analyse further, but seem to have both cognitive and muscular components.) Strong pulses (beats) and weaker pulses (off-beats) set up patterns of expectation, which are heightened by deviations from regularity. Beats can be sensed but unrealized, as in Donne's

For I am every dead thing

Where the offbeat between dead and thing is not realized, but adds very powerfully to the metrical tension.

Art requires shapes or groupings. In English verse the most popular groupings are four- and five-beat lines. Four-beat lines are the most natural and popular, imparting a song-like quality. Five-beat lines are the more various, allowing the greater range of effects and are generally employed by serious poetry. Besides the underlying rhythm, however, experienced readers also recognize metrical patterns that particularize certain genres. These metrical patterns go well beyond rhythm, and include the shaping of lines, stanzas and the interplay of rhythm with content and syntax.

The theory uses a simple notation, is readily grasped, and overcomes the knotty problem of distinguishing between rising (iambic) and falling (trochaic) movement. Individual lines can be perplexing, as good line of verse commonly has both rising and falling sections. Attridge's theory regards the distinction as unimportant, the key features lying elsewhere. The problems? Attridge's realization rules are complicated enough (two-base rules, deviation rules, sets of conditions) but gloss over the finer points of verse structure. Syllables are either stressed or unstressed. Abnormally stressed syllables are called rhetorical stress, and phonetic elision is also oversimplified. Many theorists are also unhappy with the extensive use of unrealized beats, as this opens the door to regarding trimeter verse as tetrameter verse with a stress unsounded.

Metrical Phonologists

Why do we say The word is misspelt, but a misspelt word? What rules make us shift the stress? One approach to understanding is to construct a metrical grid. The grid is hierarchical and includes progressively larger elements upwards: syllable, word, phrase, sentence. At each level we recognize weak and strong elements (syllable level — mis spelt: word level — the word is misspelt). Then we can find the rules or constraints that apply to each level of the grid. It may be, for example, that an alternation of weak and strong at one level needs to be matched by a similar alternation at a higher level.

Such was the approach of Liberman and has been very influential, many workers refining and adding to the original notion. Hayes added three rules to that of simple alternation. One was that four syllables should occur between stresses at some highly salient level in the grid. A second required symmetrical division at a level below that of the highly salient level. The third required a strict polarization of stresses at the highest level. Hayes also identified five layers: word, clictic group, phonological phrase, intonational phrase and utterance.

How are these rules derived? Essentially by observation and induction, the scientific approach of trial and error. But they have some linguistic basis — i.e. form part of a larger set of linguistic rules — and aren't therefore purely arbitrary. Often the linguistic basis is that of generative grammar. Kiparsky for instance claimed that iambic pentameters had a structure like this:

Level 5: strong

Level 4: weak strong

Level 3: — weak strong

Level 2: weak strong — strong weak

Level 1: weak strong weak strong weak strong weak strong weak strong.

Constraints on metrical styles could then be derived by comparing well-formed verse instances with untrammelled possibilities. Hayes himself generalized a wide set of rules that governed the interaction of phrase with metre. Bounding rules governed stress peaks within a line. Right-edge rules forbade stress clusters at the end of phrases to appear in weak positions. Left-edge rules countermanded right-edge rules and allowed clusters of stresses at the beginning of phrases.

The importance? Much of this work confirmed the theories of the Slavic metrists that the beginnings of phrases are metrically lax and the ends of phrases are metrically strict. But they did so with greater precision, laying down rules for well-formed verse.

David Gil

David Gil and coworkers at Tel Aviv University underline an important aspect of the generative grammar approach, that of choosing examples of well formedness. We should not restrict ourselves to art forms, to the work of distinguished poets, they argue, but consider mankind's general competence at verse, what they call non-canonical verse. That competence, moreover, should extend from the smallest units of rhythm to texts as a whole, including nonlinguistic matters. Like Liberman, Gill and his coworkers employ a metrical grid, with constituents at each level composed of one strong unit and one or more weak units. These constituents are given the traditional labels of iambic (I), trochaic (T), anapaestic (A), or dactylic (D). Looking at the vertical organization of the grid, the central level is the line, labelled 0. The four levels below extend to the "sub-position" or 1/16 of the line. The four levels above extend to the "bi-super-stanza" or 16 lines. Individual constituents (I, T, A or D) are identified by superscripts for level and position within that level.

By analysing a good deal of material in this way, a number of unexpected features arise. Non-canonical verse operates as a continuous series of layers, with rules or constraints that control what can appear on adjacent lines. Depending on the verse type or genre, patterns appear in the syllables that can take strong or weak stresses, and there is also a patterning in the vertical sense. Most important of all, this patterning appears in the genres of other languages, and is a feature of broader linguistic features. Principles like "small precedes large" and "focus falls at the end of the unit" are well known in the phonological, intonational and narrative organization of language, but also apply to metre. Anyone who disputes the importance of metre, and most particularly its objective existence, has solid linguistic evidence to contend with.

Grammetrics

As should be apparent from these short notes (and would be overwhelmingly so on reference to textbooks or research papers) the linguistic analysis of rhythm has become a very technical subject, divorced not only from the writing of poetry but the study of literature as a whole. Donald Wesling's contention is that we need to look at the larger purposes of language, and be content with approximate answers to important questions. Linguistic prosodists have elaborated brilliant theories, but only related sign to sign, not sign to signifier: they have failed to ask what the signs mean. Literary critics have equally avoided reality by making a fetish of metrical regularity, recasting poetry in simplistic models that do not explain why poetry was ever written in the first place. For poetics to be useful today, we need to accept that contemporary writers are attempting to do away with stable forms, to dissolve genre and technique back into ordinary language. All aspects of a poem are now indexes of personality, a correlation between work and universe that Wesling calls "voice".

What does that amount to? We need to examine how voice is realized:

1. In the reader's experience of the poem.
2. In the language of the text.
3. In the relation between the two.

Wesling has a modernist conception for the first. Poetry defamiliarizes, defacilitates and retards our normal expectations in language, and does so because aesthetic and cognitive aspects interpenetrate.

He bases much of these contentions on the theoretical work of Jan Meijer, who recognized specific aesthetic and cognitive structures. The first create relations of equivalence and work towards self-perpetuation. The second create unequal relations of dependence and work towards closure. From the mutual interference of the two structures arises the artistic tension and the poet's individual voice.

And the language of the text? Wesling proposes a grid marking the intersections of syntax and a poem's structure. One axis of the grid has morpheme, word, phrase, clause, sentence and group of sentences. The other has syllable, foot, part-line, line, stanza and whole poem. The size of a circle drawn at each intersection can show its importance: an approach Wesling calls grammetrics.

How is that importance assessed? For an answer to question 3 above, Wesling uses the work of the Czech theorist Jiri Levy, who pointed to morphological analogies between prosodic forms and semantic effects. The linear flow in poetry, for example, follows three formative principles: continuity-discontinuity, equivalence-hierarchy and regularity-irregularity. Each plays its part in the formal aspects of poetry (pauses, intonation, rhyme, repetition and rhythm) but also impacts on the semantics. Each intersection can be used to form hypotheses about higher level interpretation (tone of voice, point of view) so that stylistic concepts can be loaded with semantic possibilities.

Henri Meschonnic

Henri Meschonnic also takes a broad, not to say speculative, view of rhythm. His Critique du Rythme encompasses language, society and the individual, and in much of its considerable bulk Meschonnic attempts to show how narrow, vague and wrong-headed are conventional views.

Rhythm is not binary, periodic or repetitive, but pervades all discourse. Rhythm is not valued for its mnemonic properties, but remembered because it is valuable. Rhythm is not decoration but a constituent of meaning. The essence of rhythm is form, not movement, as an examination of its etymology demonstrates.

What is Meschonnic's definition of rhythm? He doesn't really say, except to claim that rhythm is the most archaic part of language and human subjectivity, all those aspects of discourse that do not include signification. Rhythm is fragmentary and diverse, moreover, making definitions impracticable and unneeded.

Examples? Meschonnic postulates three sorts of rhythm: linguistic rhythms, rhetorical rhythms and poetic rhythms. Unfortunately, his Critique elaborates only the first, which does seem to involve just those matters that escape rigorous linguistic description. Here belong paralinguistic gesture, visual form, sound orchestration, metaphor, ambiguity, choriambic patterns and a host of others. Meschonnic's normalization of this category is standard but very elementary, its purpose being largely to demonstrate the inadequacy of traditional scansion.

Richard Cureton

Rhythmic Phrasing in English Verse, Richard Cureton's important book of 1992, brought together contemporary thought on verse rhythms, but did so in extensive and carefully thought out schemes. The inspiration was Jackendoff and Lerdahl's treatment of rhythm in western tonal music, which recognized three distinct but interacting components: a cyclic beating (metre), peaks of structural salience (grouping) and arrival at expected goals (prolongation).

Musical theorists had argued that what we call rhythm is the human ability to combine complex and diverse inputs into relatively simple patterns, and Cureton was equally determined not to oversimplify matters. Metre certainly existed, and consisted of duple or triple patterns. Grouping extracted more irregular shapes from structures inherent in the medium, and ordered these shapes in a hierarchical fashion over all levels. Prolongation was the reader's expectation of where the text was heading, and was therefore more general and subjective. Metre, grouping and prolongation were a feature of rhythm, but all three were not required for rhythm to exist.

An illustration may help. Cureton uses an extensive bracketing and tree notation, but here is a flavour of the metrical system, rather freely transposed into a scheme for web pages, the bold type indicating a beat. The text is from William Carlos William's Paterson:

Metre:

Level 5 Without invention nothing is well spaced

Level 4 Without invention nothing is well spaced

Level 3 Without invention nothing is well spaced

Level 2 Without invention nothing is well spaced

Level 1 Without invention nothing is well spaced

Grouping:

Level 10 Without invention nothing is well spaced

Level 4 Without invention | nothing is well spaced

Level 3 Without invention | nothing | is well spaced

Word   Without invention nothing is well spaced

Syllable   With out in ven tion no thing is well spaced

Readers will have to consult Cureton's book for a proper treatment. His scheme is relatively compact and simple, but daunting to those unfamiliar with linguistic notation. Moreover, by giving emphasis to grouping, Cureton's 1992 book rather neglected prolongation and metre, though work in progress . A Temporal Theory of Poetic Rhythm apparently corrects the imbalance. Language, literary convention and historical content are also to be brought into the new system, which is indeed the full set of metrical preference rules detailing how prosody and versification affect our metrical reading of a text. A fourth rhythmic component is also added (theme), and Cureton attempts wider correlations with cultural history, neurobiology, ethics and so forth.

Bracketed Grid Theory of Metrical Forms in Music and Poetry

There are similarities between metrical form in music and poetry, most notably the use of repeating binary or ternary rhythms. These similarities can be explained by using a similar theory: Bracketed Grid Theory. A fundamental difference between metrical poetry and metrical music is that in poetry metricality presupposes the division of the text into lines; this is not true in music. This shows that though they share a theoretical core, metrical form in music and in poetry also differ. Bracketed Grid Theory (BGT) is a theory of generative metrics which was introduced in Halle and Keyser, based on earlier work by Halle and Keyser and Idsardi; it is outlined in Fabb.

In English, there are four strict meters :

1. iambic,
2. trochaic,
3. anapaestic and
4. dactylic.

They are 'strict' because the heads of feet are evenly spaced apart in a binary or ternary pattern. In contrast, the 'loose' meters of English have variable numbers of syllables between heads of feet, as found in nursery rhymes, ballads, Coleridge's 'Christabel', Hopkins's 'sprung rhythm', and so on. The metrical forms of strict meters most closely resemble the binary- and ternarybased metrical structures proposed by Lerdahl and Jackendoff for western tonal music, and so we will discuss only the strict meters here.

In (1) We list the facts which must be explained about the strict English meters; (a-c) concern the relation between rhythm and meter, and (d-f) concern the relation between syllable counting and meter.

(1)

(i) There are general rhythmic tendencies towards either a binary or a ternary rhythm.

(ii) Some types of syllable (roughly: stressed syllables in polysyllabic words) are fixed in place relative to the rhythmic structure.

(iii) Notwithstanding (i) and (ii), there may be some rhythmic variation at one end of the line, most characteristically the 'inversion' which is common at the beginning of iambic lines.

(iv) The length of the line is predictable, in number of syllables.

(v) Notwithstanding (iv), there may be up to one syllable missing from one end of a line in a binary meter, and up to two syllables missing from one end of a line in a ternary meter. The end of the line is predictable, based on the meter.

(vi) Notwithstanding (iv), there may be up to one syllable extra at one end of a line in a binary meter, and up to two syllables extra at one end of a line in a ternary meter. The end of the line is predictable, based on the meter.

BGT proposes that a line of metrical verse has its metrical form mentally represented as a bracketed grid. Thus the last line of Milton's Paradise Lost is in the meter called iambic pentameter, and projects as a bracketed grid (2), a grid made of asterisks and brackets.

(2)	through	Eden	took	their	solitary	way.	
	)*	*)*	*)	*	*)* *)*	*)	gridline 0
			*	*)	* *	*)	gridline 1
	)		*			*)	gridline 2
						*	gridline 3

This grid is built step by step, first by representing syllables as asterisks on the bottom line of the grid by rule (3), with the result shown in (4).

(3) Projection

Project each syllable as an asterisk on gridline 0.

(4)	through	Eden	took	their	solitary	way.	
	*	* *	*	*	* * * *	*	gridline 0

The next stage is to apply a set of iterative rules as in (5).

(5) Iterative rules for iambic pentameters

(a) Gridline 0

From right to left, using right brackets,

- insert bracket

- skip a gap

...and repeat

Project to the next gridline the rightmost asterisk in each foot.

(b) Gridline 1

From right to left, using right brackets,

- insert bracket

- skip a gap

- skip a gap

...and repeat

Project to the next gridline the rightmost asterisk in each foot.

condition: final foot constructed is binary

(c) Gridline 2

From right to left, using right brackets,

- insert bracket

- skip a gap

..and repeat

Project to the next gridline the rightmost asterisk in each foot.

As an illustration of how the rules build structure, consider how (5a) applies to the line of asterisks which is gridline 0.

```
through   Eden   took   their   solitary       way.
   *       * *     *      *     * * * *         *      gridline 0
   *       * *     *      *     * * * *         *)
                                                ^      insert bracket
   *       * *     *      *     * * * *         *)
                                   ^                   skip a gap
   *       * *     *      *     * * *)*         *)
                                   ^                   insert bracket
   *       * *     *      *     * * * *         *)
                                   ^                   skip a gap
   *       * *     *      *     *)* *)*         *)
                          ^                            insert bracket
   *       * *     *      *     *)* *)*         *)
                          ^                            skip a gap
   *       * *     * )    *     *)* *)*         *)
                   ^                                   insert bracket
   *       * *     * )       * *)* *)*          *)
           ^                                           skip a gap
   *       *)*     * )       * *)* *)*          *)
   ^                                                   insert bracket
   *       *)*     * )       * *)* *)*          *)
   ^                                                   skip a gap
   )*      *)*     * )       * *)* *)*          *)
^                                                      insert bracket
   )*      *)*     * )    *     *)* *)*         *)
           *       *      *        *            *      project
```

The rules in (3) and (5) ensure that there are ten syllables in the line, thus explaining (1.iv). The rules build a structure which at its lowest level (gridline 0 and 1) is a binary structure, and this is the basis of explaining why there is a characteristic binary rhythm (1.i). We can add a condition to the rules, which holds of the grid, and is in two parts, the first part (7a) defining certain syllables, and the second part (7b) controlling the distribution of those syllables.

(7)

(a) Definition of maximum. (English strict metrical verse)

A maximum is:

The syllable carrying primary stress in a polysyllabic word, which is both preceded and followed within the same line by a syllable which does not carry primary lexical stress.

(b) Condition

Every maximum must project to gridline 1.

This now explains (1.ii), the fact that certain syllables (here defined as maxima) are fixed in place. The maxima are underlined in (8); in all cases they project to gridline 1.

```
(8)  through  Eden  took  their  solitary  way.
        )*     *)*   *)     *    *)* *)*    *)    gridline 0
                *    *)           * *       *)    gridline 1
 )                   *                      *)    gridline 2
                                            *     gridline 3
```

The definition in (7a) will also explain the variation (1.iii), which is illustrated by the second line of (9).

(9)

```
'How  sweet  is  mortal  Sovranty!' - think  some:
 ) *    *)    *    *)*     *) * *)       *      *)  gridline 0
        *          *)       * *                 *)  gridline 1
 )                 *                            *)  gridline 2
                                                *   gridline 3

Others - 'How  blest  the  Paradise  to  come!'
)* *)*     *)     *   *)* *)      *   *)  gridline 0
*          *)           * *           *)  gridline 1
```

```
)                    *                        *)     gridline 2
                                              *      gridline 3
```

Edward Fitzgerald 'Rubaiyat', in Karlin (1997: 117)

Here the first syllable in the second line is a syllable carrying stress in a polysyllabic word but it does not project to gridline 1, as such syllables normally do. This is because since it is at the beginning of the line it cannot be preceded by a syllable which does not carry primary lexical stress and thus by (7a) this syllable is not a maximum.

Lines in strict metrical verse can fall short at one end in all the strict meters. We illustrate this with lines in dactylic tetrameter, a ternary meter. The first line in (10) has twelve syllables, but the second has ten, the third eleven and the fourth ten; thus three of these lines fall short from the norm of twelve syllables.

(10)

```
Life's  night  begins:  let   him   never  come  back  to   us!
(*        *      *(*     *     *    (* *     *    ( *   *     *  (
*                 *                  *             *

    There  would  be   doubt,  hesitation   and   pain,
     (*      *     *    (*     * * (* *       *     (*
      *                  *          *                *

 Forced  praise   on  our   part  -the glimmer of  twilight,
  (*       *       *  (*     *     *     (* *   *    (* *
  *                    *           *            *

    Never   glad   confident   morning   again!
    (* *     *     (* * *      (* *      *(*
     *              *           *         *
```

Robert Browning 'The Lost Leader' in Karlin (1997: 221)

This can be explained in BGT by appealing to the way in which feet are constructed, with feet defined as in (11).

(11) Definition of Foot.

> A foot is a sequence of one or more asterisks to the right of a left bracket or to the left of a right bracket.

Note that the foot need not be closed off by another bracket; it requires only a bracket at one end. Thus all of the lines in (10) have four feet, and this is what makes the lines metrical examples of tetrameter. Note that only the lastconstructed foot can fall short because the iterative rule (12) for gridline 0 in a dactylic meter automatically inserts brackets after every third syllable until it runs out of syllables.

(12) Iterative rules for dactyls

(a) Gridline 0

From left to right, using left brackets,

- insert bracket

- skip a gap

- skip a gap

...and repeat

Project to the next gridline the leftmost asterisk in each foot.

This is illustrated in (13) which shows the final iterations of rule (12).

(13)

```
Forced  praise  on  our  part  - the  glimmer  of  twilight,
 (*       *      *   (*    *     *      (* *     *     * *
                                         ^
                                                  skip a gap
 (*       *      *   (*    *     *      (* *     *     * *
                                         ^
```

```
                                                  skip a gap
(*       *       *   (*      *      *     (* *    * (     * *
                                                  ^
                                                insert bracket
(*       *       *   (*      *      *     (*      * *    ( * *
                                                         ^
                                                  skip a gap
(*       *       *   (*      *      *     (*      * *    ( * *

                                                            ^
                                                  skip a gap
```

In dactylic verse, as here, it is the rightmost foot which can fall short (called catalexis) and this is because left brackets are inserted from left to right across the gridline. In anapaestic verse, it is the leftmost foot which can fall short (called acephaly) and this is because right brackets are inserted from right to left across the gridline. This is shown in (14), based on the gridline 0 rule for anapests shown in (15) and with the final iterations shown in (16).

(14)

```
   'What   had   I  given   to   hear   the   soft   sweep
     *)     *    *   *)*    *     *)     *     *      *)
     *      *    *   *

Of   a breeze bearing  life through that  vast realm  of  death!
)*   *   *)      * *     *)     *     *     *)    *     *    *)
*        *               *                  *

Thoughts  were  untroubled  and  dreams   were  asleep:
  *)        *     * *) *     *     *)       *     * *)
  *               *                *              *
```

```
The   spirit   lay   dreadless   and   hopeless   beneath.'
 *     *)*      *      *) *      *       *) *       * *)
        *               *                 *          *
```

Charlotte Bronte 'Diving' in Karlin (1997: 286)

(15) Iterative rules for anapaests

(a) Gridline 0

From right to left, using right brackets,
- insert bracket
- skip a gap
- skip a gap
...and repeat

Project to the next gridline the rightmost asterisk in each foot.

(16)

```
What  had  I  given  to  hear  the  soft  sweep
 *     *   *   * *   *    *)    *    *     *)
                     ^                              skip a gap
 *     *   *   * *   *    *)    *    *     *)
                 ^                                  skip a gap
 *     *   *   *) *  *    *)    *    *     *)
               ^                                    insert bracket
 *     *   *   *) *  *    *)    *    *     *)
           ^                                        skip a gap
 *     *   *   *)*   *    *)    *    *     *)
       ^                                            skip a gap
 *)    *   *   *)*   *    *)    *    *     *)
 ^                                                  insert bracket
```

Thus (1.v), the fact that lines can fall short in specific ways at specific ends of the line, is explained by BGT based on the construction and definition of feet. Finally, (1.vi), the fact that lines can be slightly extended at one end, is explained by BGT by exploiting the possibility of a variation in the iterative rules. In the rules for iambic pentameter (5), the iterative rule has an insert stage and a skip stage, in that order, repeated. If the order is reversed, the result will be an unfooted asterisk at the right edge of the line.

(17)

```
Who  were  the  builders?  Question  not  the  silence
 *    *     *     * *        * *       *    *     * *
                                                   ^
                                              skip a gap
 *    *     *     * *        * *       *    *     *)*
                                                   ^
                                            insert bracket
 *    *     *     * *        * *       *    *     *)*
                                            ^
                                              skip a gap
 *    *     *     * *        * *       *   ) *    *)*
                                       ^
                                            insert bracket
etc.
 Who  were  the  builders?  Question  not  the  silence
  )*   *)    *     *) *        *)      *   * ) *   *)*
                                                 gridline 0
       *           *)          *       *           *)
                                                 gridline 1
                   *                               *)
                                                 gridline 2
                                                    *
                                                 gridline 3
```

The rightmost asterisk in (17) is to the left of a right bracket (not a left bracket) and hence is not in a foot. In a binary meter only one syllable can be additional (because there is only one skip step in the binary rule), while in a ternary meter either one or two syllables can be additional. This was a brief overview of BGT as it applies to the English strict meters. The important features of the theory, for the present purposes, are as follows.

(18)

(a) The metrical representation is a grid consisting of asterisks and brackets.

(b) It is built step-by-step, largely by iterative rules which move from one end of the line to the other.

(c) The grid counts syllables by building a periodic structure; the periodic structure can explain the rhythm of the text by conditions which relate the structure to the text.

(d) Specific kinds of variation at one or the other end of the line are predicted by the theory.

One of the important characteristics of BGT is that it asserts the significance of a text's boundaries, and specifically line boundaries (left and right, or beginning and end) in enabling metrical representations to be built. This is because in BGT metrical representations are built from left to right or from right to left, from one line boundary to another. The fact that metricality in langage is found only where there is also lineation is strong support for BGT as a theory of meter in langauge; as we will see, metricality in music does not presuppose lineation and thus though it will be possible to apply BGT to music, this strong source of evidence no longer exists.

As an approach to meter in poetry, BGT competes with a 'traditional' approach, and with a different kind of generative approach. In the traditional approach, the metrical representation is built by by combining rhythmic components which directly represent the surface rhythm of the piece, these being 'feet' of different kinds which can be combined in any way to build a line.

BGT explains what the traditional approach only describes. This traditional approach to rhythm in poetry was borrowed by Cooper and Meyer in their theory of mental representation of music; Lerdahl and Jackendoff show that it cannot be true of musical meter.

BGT is a generative approach to metrical structure, but it differs from another tradition of explaining metrical structure associated for example with Hanson and Kiparsky and much other generative metrics in which the mental representation of rhythm is a template (for example, a complete tree structure) which is attached as a whole to the line of poetry, and attached to the linguistic material of the line by matching rules.

BGT in contrast builds the representation from the line, rather then taking the representation as a pre-existing template which is laid on top of the line; BGT thus closely associates metricality with lineation, which is the right result as in language metricality always presupposes lineation. Lerdahl and Jackendoff use something resembling this 'template' generative approach in explaining musical form; in the next section we show how their approach to music can be rethought in terms of BGT, thereby explaining some of its characteristics.

Rhythmic Regularities in Music

Lerdahl and Jackendoff represent the metrical structure of music by unbracketed grids, consisting of dots at different gridlines, where the dots express beats.

(19)

1 1|2 1 1 2 1 1| 2 2 [2]

```
 .  . . . .    .  .   . . . . . .    .   .   .    . .
 .    .      .    .    .     .     .
   .       .       .         .
   .               .
```

It is unproblematic as a first step to replace the dots in the grids by asterisks and to number the gridlines. (20) is a notational variant of (19).

(20)

```
• 1  1| 2      1  1  2        1  1| 2       2      [2]
  *   *  *  *   *  *  *  *     *  *  *  *    *   *   *  *

                                                  gridline 0
  *      *      *     *        *     *       *       *

                                                  gridline 1
         *            *              *               *

                                                  gridline 2
         *                           *

                                                  gridline 3
```

Three questions arise about the similarities and differences between poetic metrical grids and musical metrical grids, relating to (2.1) the relation between gridline 0 and the textual/musical material, (2.2) the use of brackets to control structure, and (2.3) the overall size of the grid (in terms of gridlines and hence overall length).

Gridline 0 and Textual/Musical Material

In poetry, the asterisks at gridline 0 each project from designated linguistic elements, usually syllables. The duration of the linguistic elements is rarely relevant in projection; for example a heavy and a light syllable may each project as a single asterisk, with the difference between them established by conditions on the grid. Poetry draws on a distinct domain - phonological form - which provides it with pre-existing and well-defined elements (syllables). In contrast, in music, there is no source of 'designated elements' which project as asterisks; instead we must treat the gridline 0 asterisks as projecting from musical time units. Consider for example sequence consisting of an eighth-note, a quarter-note, and an eighth-note-rest; this must project as four gridline 0 asterisks, with the quarter-note projecting two gridline 0 asterisks and the eighth-note and rest projecting one gridline 0 asterisk each.

The use of brackets to control structure L&J's grids consist only of asterisks, with no brackets. However, there is a role for iterative bracket-insertion rules in their theory: it would explain three of the metrical well-formedness rules.

(21)

MWFR 2 Every beat at a given level must also be a beat at all smaller levels present at that point in the piece.

MWFR 3 At each metrical level, strong beats are spaced either two or three beats apart.

MWFR 4 The tactus and immediately larger metrical levels must consist of beats equally spaced throughout the piece. At the subtactus metrical levels, weak beats must be equally spaced between the surrounding strong beats.

We can restate each of these rules in terms of a grid of asterisks at named gridlines, as in (22); We abstract away the issue of the tactus/subtactus from MWFR 4 here but return to it later.

(22)

MWFR 2′ An asterisk at gridline n+1 must project from an asterisk at gridline n.

MWFR 3′ Adjacent asterisks at gridline n+1 project from asterisks at gridline n which are separated from one another either (i) by one asterisk or (ii) by two asterisks.

MWFR 4′ At a given gridline, either option (i) or option (ii) of MFWR 3′ must hold; they cannot be mixed.

It is straightforward to derive MWFR 2′-4′ from iterative bracket-insertion rules which resemble those used for trochees (23) and dactyls (24) in poetry.

(23) Iterative rule for left-headed binary feet

Starting at the left edge of the gridline,

Insert a left bracket

Skip an asterisk

...and repeat.

Project heads left.

(24) Iterative rule for left-headed ternary feet

Starting at the left edge of the gridline,

Insert a left bracket

Skip an asterisk

Skip an asterisk

...and repeat.

Project heads left.

We illustrate this by applying rule (23) to gridline (25) which is a gridline 0 projecting from the musical time units which make up the beginning of the Mozart G-minor symphony.

(25)

```
                    * * * * * * * * * * * * * * * *
                                                      gridline 0
```

After the application of (23) we derive (26), which conforms to MFWR2'-4'.

(26)

```
                    (* *(* *(* *(* *(* *(* *(* *(* *(
                                                      gridline 0
                    * * * * * * * *
                                                      gridline 1
```

We now apply (23) to gridline 1, but we permit the skip stage to precede the insert stage at gridline 1, giving an unfooted asterisk (an anacrusis) at the left edge of gridline 1. (27)

```
                    (* *(* *(* *(* *(* *(* *(* *(* *(
                                                      gridline 0
* (* * (* * (* * (*
                                                      gridline 1
          * * * *
                                                      gridline 2
```

Now we apply (23) to gridline 2, thereby deriving the full grid (20), here represented as a bracketed grid (28).

(28)

```
                    (* *(* *(* *(* *(* *(* *(* *(* *(
                                                      gridline 0
* (* * (* * (* * (*
                                                      gridline 1
(* * (* *
                                                      gridline 2
    * *
                                                      gridline 3
```

The insertion of brackets ensures that the beats are evenly spaced in a binary pattern because the binary iterative rule (23) is used. Because the next gridline is built by projecting an asterisk as a head from one gridline to the next, MWFR'2 holds. This is evidence that the musical metrical grid is a bracketed grid.

L&J suggest that in some kinds of music MWFR3 and MWFR4 might not hold. If MWFR4 is dropped, the gridline would have variable binary or ternary feet within the line, as for example in some of Stravinsky's music. This could be explained by a rule (29) as a variant of rule (24). Here the second skip stage is made optional, as is symbolized by putting it in parentheses.

(29) Iterative rule for variable binary/ternary left-headed feet

Starting at the left edge of the gridline,

Insert a left bracket

Skip an asterisk

(Skip an asterisk)

...and repeat.

Project heads left.

The possibility of dropping both MFWR4 and MFWR3 such that beats are randomly spaced apart could be explained by a rule given in (30):

(30) Iterative rule for variable-sized left-headed feet

Starting at the left edge of the gridline,

Insert a left bracket

Skip an asterisk *

...and repeat

Project heads left.

Here, the skip stage could be repeated a random number of times (including zero) between each insertion, as symbolized by the asterisk. The rules given in (25) and (26) do not appear to have any direct analogues in poetic meters. There are poetic meters in which feet can vary in size, but they have a different explanation; these are the loose meters, discussed in Halle and Keyser, and Fabb.

Overall Size of the Grid

The problem of the upper and lower limits on the size of the grid clearly differentiates musical metrical form and poetic metrical form. L&J suggest that the hearer focuses primarily on several intermediate levels of the grid. Translated into our terms, we would say the hearer focuses on two or more adjacent gridlines. It is these gridlines which characterise the rhythm which is most dominantly heard by the listener: L&J call it the tactus. We can define the tactus in music as consisting of gridlines 0, 1 and 2 and possibly higher or lower gridlines. This raises the question of the height and 'depth' of the grid. We begin with the height of the grid. The musical metrical grid can in principle keep getting higher. There is no upper limit proposed by L&J on the number of gridlines above the tactus, though since they are increasingly unlikely to be perceived, the key evidence from perception for structure at higher gridlines is also increasingly weak.

The important point here is that unlike poetry, the musical metrical structure is not bounded by the edges of lines; in poetry line-boundaries define the edges of the grid and so prevent the grid ever getting higher than about gridline 3 or 4, but in music there are no such edges to constrain the overall size of the grid. Gridline 0 could in principle extend through the whole of a musical piece, with the iterative rules building a grid with a large number of gridlines. One way to understand this in terms of mental representations would be to make a change to the conditions on the grid.

We could say that the musical metrical grid does not have to have a single asterisk at its highest gridline. This could mean that the musical piece has a grid associated with it which extends from one end of the piece to the other, and has for example gridlines 0-3, with gridline 3 consisting of many asterisks which are themselves not bracketed into feet.

Musical metrical structure can also exist below the level of the tactus. L&J's MWFR 1 (21) states that 'every attack point must be associated with a beat at the smallest metrical level present at that point in the piece'. What this means is that if there were to be a marked section in which there were many attack points below the level of the tactus (e.g.. sixteenth-notes in a piece in common time), each of these attack points would be projected as an asterisk, grouped by the iterative rules into feet, projecting to higher gridlines etc. This metrical organisation might be below the level of the tactus - that is, below gridline 0. If a piece of music has quarter-notes projecting as asterisks at gridline 0, then a section in sixteenth-notes would have to project gridline -2 as its bottom line, and also a gridline -1. This has a major consequence for the difference between music and poetry when it comes to the relation between the text/piece and the lowest gridlines. The size of musical time unit which projects at the lowest gridline may vary at different parts of the piece. This is not possible in poetry, where gridline 0 is the only line of the grid which can project directly from linguistic form. Thus when it comes to the size of the grid, there are clear differences between music and poetry.

Metrical Form and Perceived Rhythm

Rhythm may be heard as 'rising' or 'falling'. L&J suggest that this should not be directly encoded in the musical metrical representation. Instead the experience of a rising or falling rhythm is an inference on the part of the listener, based on the relation between metrical form and other kinds of musical form; in particular it is the result of combining metrical form with grouping structure, which is a distinct kind of representation. The match between the two kinds of representation is governed by preference rules, and L&J explicitly link this with post-Gricean pragmatic theory. The combination of the two kinds of representation give rise to the experience of rhythms as 'rising' or 'falling'.

The metrical form of the line is determinately iambic or trochaic or some other meter as part of its mental representation as a bracketed grid; but metrical form is not directly experienced as rising or falling rhythm. Instead, the experience of rhythm is an inference, which takes the metrical form into account but can also be influenced by other factors.

Thus a text might be in a consistent iambic meter throughout (in terms of BGT representations) but sections of it might be experienced rhythmically as trochaic. In this light, it is worth noting that in musical metrical grids, the trochaic or dactylic (i.e. left-headed) feet which are constructed by the iterative rules (23) and (24) do not determine either a 'rising' or 'falling' rhythm. The function of the feet, constructed by the insertion of left brackets and the projection of leftmost heads, is to derive the Metrical wellformedness rules MWFR 2′, 3′ and 4′ (22) which govern musical metrical structures. The feet do not directly determine the experience of rhythm. Hence, the listener's experience of grouping and the metrical form of the music do not directly interact.

There is another relevant link between the experience of rhythm in music and in poetry, which is L&J's notion of the tactus. In music the metrical grid may have many gridlines but that only some subset of the gridlines correspond to experienced rhythm, the rhythm on which the hearer focuses; thus subset is the tactus. A similar notion might be useful in understanding the relation between the metrical grid and perceived structure in poetry. In iambic pentameter, there is a tendency towards a regular rhythm which is defined with reference to gridlines 0 and 1; while there is metrical organisation also at gridline 2 this is probably not perceived. Thus the tactus in most strict English meters would be gridlines 0 and 1. In 'dipodic' meter, favored by Kipling, iambic feet are perceived as alternatingly strong and weak, and we could understand this by saying that the tactus includes gridlines 0, 1 and 2. In syllable-counting meters such as those found in Welsh or French, there is a periodic grid but there is no perceived periodic rhythm; here the tactus involves just gridline 0. In accentual verse or perhaps the English 'loose iambic' tradition (found in nursery rhymes) it might be suggested that the tactus includes only gridline 1.

The Line

In linguistic texts there is a distinction between prose and verse, which is a matter of whether the text is divided into lines (verse) or not divided into lines (prose). An equivalent distinction does not exist in music, and in this section we explore some of the implications of this, particularly given that metrical texts are always verse: metricality in poetry presupposes the division into lines. A verbal text which is divided into lines typically has several characteristics, the most common in English being listed in (31).

(31) Characteristics of the line

— The final syllable in a line is the final syllable in a word, and is often the final syllable of a major syntactic constituent.

— The final syllable(s) in the line rhyme with the final syllable(s) in a nearby line.

— The line is the same length (approximately), counting syllables, as other nearby lines.

— The line can fall 'long' or 'short' at one specific end. The line shows different rhythmic characteristics in different parts (also lines are rhythmically more regular towards the end).

— The line is parallel to a nearby line, or the first half of the line is parallel to the second half of the line. Tthere are many other characteristics of the line, some of which are emergent or idiosyncratic; for example, in Milton's Paradise Lost and post-Miltonic poetry, the word 'of' appears frequently as the first syllable in a line, thus functioning as a weak cue to the location of the line boundary.

Three facts about lines are worth emphasising. First, the location of line boundaries is usually implied by several coinciding characteristics, which suggests both a stable lineation of the text and also the functional significance of multiply cueing the lineation of the text; the listener must be helped to determine line boundaries in order to build metrical structure, a grid for each line.

Second, lineation and metrical form are clearly related in that the 'measurement' of lines is based on meter (the metrical grid counts the number of syllables in the line), and also metrical irregularities cluster at line boundaries (because of how the grid is built).

Finally, while lineation of a text is reflected in the conventional writing down of texts, page layout does not alone define the text as verse: many other characteristics other than layout on the page also point to a particular way of lineating a text. Metricality in language always requires lineation. We know this because wherever we find metrical form (e.g. extended periodic rhythms) we also find evidence of the kinds seen in (31) for lineation. Tthere is no metrical prose; that is, there is no text which has metrical characteristics such as extended regular rhythms, but shows no evidence of division into lines.

It is possible to find various criteria for proposing a division of musical texts into lines. Lerdahl and Jackendoff suggest that musical texts are divided into groups (defined by the rules of Grouping Structure). Such a group might for example have a structural accent, such as a structural downbeat at its boundary , or a cadence. It is worth noting that parallelism is one way in which musical groups can be defined, and that this is also true of poetry: lines are characterised by parallelism in many kinds of verse (either parallelism between the two halves or parallelism between adjacent lines).

Groups are the closest that a musical piece comes to poetic lines, but there is a fundamental difference between them, which is that grouping structure is independent of metrical structure in Lerdahl and Jackendoff's theory: the interaction between them can be productive, but one type of structure does not determine the other. Thus musical groups are not like poetic lines, because poetic lines define metrical structure: the metrical grid is built from one end of the line to the other, measures the line, and permits metrical variation at the edges of the line. Metrical form in music thus does not presuppose a division into groups, unlike metrical form in poetry which does presuppose a division into lines.

Bracketed Grid Theory's account of meter in poetry shares with Lerdahl and Jackendoff's account of meter in music the assumption that the listener constructs mental representations of metrical structure. The metrical structure in both music and poetry is a bracketed grid: the iterative rules for the construction of bracketed grids in both cases explain why the rhythms are organised in pairs and triplets, and why at the edges of the representation there can be various kinds of rhythmic irregularity. Where music and poetry differ is in the size of the mental representation (the grid); in music a single grid may extend over the whole piece, while in poetry each line has a grid of its own. The bracketed grids constructed for poetic meter are limited in size, with the topmost gridline containing a single asterisk; this requires the division of the poetic text into lines as a prerequisite for the mental representation of metrical form. In contrast, the bracketed grids constructed for music are not limited in size; they may apparently have any number of gridlines, but more importantly there may be no constraint on the topmost gridline that it contain only one asterisk.

3

Musical Harmony

Harmony is the art of using chords (actual or implied) in music. It is sometimes referred to as the "vertical" aspect of music, melody being the "horizontal" aspect. Very often, harmony is a result of several melodic lines or motifs being played at once, creating counterpoint.

Harmony is based on harmonics and resonances. Notes may be considered to be in harmony with each other when some of the harmonics of each note, especially the louder harmonics (which are often the lower ones), share the same frequency (with a small margin of error). Some traditions of music performance, composition, and theory have specific rules of harmony, typically amounting to a simplified description of harmonics and resonances, which will be more or less appropriate depending on the instrument(s) to which they are applied.

Although most harmony comes about as a result of two or more notes being sounded simultaneously, it is possible to create harmony with only one melodic line. There are many pieces from the baroque period for solo string instruments for example, in which chords are very rare, but which nonetheless convey a full sense of harmony.

For much of the history of western classical music, including the common practice period, the conventions and rules of harmony were strictly enforced, often by the controlling influence of the Church, while folk music and non-Western music also developed often widely different notions of harmony. Church music was controlled by the churches in the Baroque and Classical periods, and music which had harmonies considered too dissonant were frowned upon. However, there was a general trend from the classical period to the 20th century in western classical music for harmony to become more advanced, with composers breaking many of the conventions which were once considered "rules".

Harmonic Series

Pitched musical instruments are usually based on some sort of harmonic oscillator, for example a string or a column of air, which can oscillate at a number of frequencies. The integer multiples of the lowest frequency make up the harmonic series.

The lowest of these frequencies is called the fundamental or first partial. This is the note created from normal bowing of a stringed instrument or from the lowest octave of a woodwind instrument. All of the other frequencies in the harmonic series are integer multiples of the fundamental. The difference in terms of frequency (measured in Hertz (Hz)) is the same between all partials, but the ear responds in a logarithmic fashion, so the partials sound 'closer' together. Put another way: since the harmonic series is an arithmetic series (1f, 2f, 3f, 4f...), and the octave, or octave series, is a geometric series (f, 2×f, 4×f, 8×f...), this causes the overtone series to divide the octave into increasingly smaller parts as it ascends.

The second partial is twice the frequency of the fundamental, which makes it an octave higher. On most woodwind instruments, for example the saxophone, oboe, or bassoon, there is an octave key which opens a small hole in the tube, prompting the instrument to oscillate at the second harmonic partial and giving the second octave of the instrument. On brass instruments, the second harmonic is the lowest playable note. The fundamental is called a pedal note or pedal tone and can be faked.

The third harmonic partial, at three times the frequency of the fundamental, is a perfect fifth above the second harmonic. Similarly, the fourth harmonic partial is four times the frequency of the fundamental; it is a perfect fourth above the third partial (two octaves above the fundamental). Note that double the partial number means double the frequency, which in turn means the 'pitch' is an octave higher. For example, the 6th partial G is an octave higher than the 3rd partial G.

After that the harmonics come thick and fast, getting closer and closer together. Some harmonics correspond very nearly to named pitches; others, for example the 7th harmonic, are significantly off from the equal tempered tones.

For example, given a fundamental of C′, the first 16 harmonics are:

— 1st C′

— 2nd C

— 3rd G

— 4th c

— 5th e (this, and the following odd-numbered partials are "out of tune" in terms of equal temperament)

— 6th g

— 7th b-sesquiflat

— 8th c′

— 9th d′- (the so-called 'major tone')

— 10th e′ - (the so-called 'minor tone')

— 11th f′-semisharp

— 12th g′

— 13th a′-semiflat (but out of tune)

— 14th b′-sesquiflat

— 15th b′ natural

— 16th c″

— 17th c-sharp″ but out of tune

In just intonation all notes are exact in regards to the harmonic series, and all intervals are based on ratios of the lower integers. In modern equal temperament, notes are approximate, so that music can be played in any key without retuning. See musical tuning.

Harmony in Western music, especially the major chord, is based on the lower pitches of the overtone series. Since it uses equal temperament, however, only the octave is exactly in tune.

The amplitude and placement of different partials determine the timbre of different instruments, and among a number of psychoacoustic factors, the separate envelopes of the partials two instruments playing in unison is what allows one to perceive them as separate. The placement of partials can also affect the perceived fundamental pitch. Not all musical instruments have partials that exactly match the harmonic partials as described here. The partials of Piano, and other, strings are increasingly sharper than perfect harmonics because the strings are stiff, leading to nonlinear, inharmonic effects.

INTERVALS

In music theory, an interval is the difference (a ratio or logarithmic measure) in pitch between two notes and often refers to those two notes themselves (otherwise known as a dyad). An interval class is measured by the shortest distance possible between its two pitch classes.

Intervals may be labelled according their pitch ratios, as is commonly used in just intonation. Intervals may also be labelled according to their diatonic functionality, as is commonly done for tonal music, and according to the number of notes they span in a diatonic scale. The interval of a note from its tonic is its scale degree, thus the fifth degree of a scale is a fifth from its tonic. For atonal music, such as that written using the twelve tone technique or serialism, integer notation is often used, such as in musical set theory.

Finally, it is also possible to label intervals using the logarithmic measure of cents, as is used to compare other intervals with those of twelve tone equal temperament. Intervals may also be described as narrow and wide or small and large, consonant and dissonant or stable and unstable, weak and strong, simple and compound, vertical (or harmonic) and linear (or melodic), and, if linear as steps or skips. Simple intervals are those which lie within an octave and compound are those which are larger than a single octave.

Thus a tenth is known as a compound third. Finally, intervals may be labelled with or modified by the addition of perfect, major, minor, augmented, and diminished before the number of notes apart (for instance, augmented fourth). Perfect intervals are never major or minor and major and minor intervals are never perfect. Major and minor intervals are one semitone above, or below, their minor and major counterparts, respectively.

Augmented and diminished intervals are raised or lowered a step and any interval may be augmented or diminished and may even be double augmented or diminished. Linear intervals are successive pitches while vertical intervals are simultaneous. Steps are linear intervals between consecutive scale degrees while skips are not. It is important to note that while intervals named by their harmonic functions, for instance, a major second, may be described by a ratio, cent, or integer, not every interval described by these more general terms may be described with the harmonic function name. For instance, all major seconds (in twelve tone equal temperament) are 200 cents, but not every interval of 200 cents is a major second.

Simple Diatonic Intervals

Below are listed the most commonly used harmonic function, ratio, integer, cents, and relative consonance or dissonance of common diatonic simple intervals. There are many other intervals and ratios, some of which follow.

Common simple intervals

— *Unison*: The ratio of 1:1 is a unison, two notes playing the same pitch. In integer notation it is a 0 and is also zero cents. It is the simplest and most consonant of intervals.

— *Octave*: The ratio of 2:1 is an octave, two notes, one of which is double or half the pitch of the other. It is 1200 cents and in integer notation it is a 0, like the unison. Octave equivalency describes the perception that octaves are the same note, that the same notes repeat throughout the pitch range. Thus C and C', C5 and C3, and C and any C any number of octaves above or below, are all the same note or pitch class. Thus the octave is slightly less or just as consonant as the unison.

— *Perfect fifth & perfect fourth*: The ratio of 3:2 is a perfect fifth, two pitches, one note 1.5 times the pitch of another. In integer notation it is 7 and is 700 cents in equal temperament, which is a ratio two (1.955) cents flat of 3:2. The inverse of a perfect fifth is a perfect fourth. A perfect fourth is the ratio 4:3, 5 in integer notation, and 500 cents in equal temperament, which is two cents sharp of 4:3. The unison, octave, fifth, and fourth are considered "perfect intervals" and thus the most consonant, in that order.

— *Major third & minor sixth*: The ratio of 5:4 is a major third. In integer notation it is 4 and is 400 cents, which is 13.686 cents sharp of 5:4. Its inverse is a minor sixth, 8:5, which is 8 in integer notation and 800 cents in equal temperament, 13.686 cents flat of 8:5. The thirds and sixths are considered the most dynamic and interesting of the consonant intervals, and are thus the least consonant, in the following order: major third, major sixth, minor third, minor sixth.

— *Minor third & major sixth*: The ratio of 6:5 is a minor third. In integer notation it is 3, and is 300 cents in equal temperament, which is 15.641 cents flat of 6:5. Its inverse is a major sixth, 5:3, which is 9 in integer notation and 900 cents in equal temperament, which is 15.641 cents sharp of 5:3.

— *Major second & minor seventh*: The ratio of 9:8 is a major second. In integer notation it is 2 and is 200 cents, which is 3.91 cents flat of 9:8. Its inverse is a minor seventh, 16:9, which is 10 in integer notation and is 1,000 cents or 3.91 cents sharp of 16:9. It is the first dissonant interval and is commonly used between chord tones such as in the dominant seventh chord, which features the minor seventh between the fifth and second degress of a major scale. A non-equal tempered minor seventh is also one of the blue notes used in the blues and jazz. The major second is also know as a whole tone or whole step.

— *Minor second and major seventh*: Like the above intervals, many ratios are used for the minor second, but 16:15 is the most common. In integer notation it is 1 and is 100 cents, which is 11.731 cents flat of 16:15, but fairly close to 18:17. Its inverse is the major seventh, commonly 15:8, which is 11 in integer notation and 1,100 cents. The minor second and minor seventh are the most dissonant intervals with the possible exception of the tritone, below. The minor second is also known as a semitone, half tone, or half step.

Augmented and diminished intervals

Along with all seconds and sevenths, all augmented and diminished intervals are considered dissonant. However, in twelve tone equal temperament, most intervals, when augmented or diminished, are enharmonically equivalent to another interval. For example, a diminished minor second is a unison and thus only the fourth and fifth are commonly altered.

Tritone: The tritone, which may be a diminished fifth or augmented fourth, is 6 in integer notation and 600 cents. It can be approximated by the ratio 17:12, whose inverse is 24:17 and is 6 cents flatter than 17:12. (Ideally, the tritone should equal its own inverse.) It is called "tritone" because it spans three whole steps. It exactly, symmetrically, divides the octave in half and was considered the most dissonant interval, literally "the devil's interval" (diabolus in musica). It plays an important role in the dominant seventh chord.

Generations of intervals

The intervals can be divided into five "generations", which correspond to negative powers of two:

1. Zeroth generation ($1+2^{-0}$): P1, P8.
2. First generation ($1+2^{-1}$): P4, P5.
3. Second generation ($1+2^{-2}$): M3, m3, M6, m6.
4. Third generation ($1+2^{-3}$): M2, m7.
5. Fourth generation ($1+2^{-4}$): m2, M7, p.

Each successive generation is more dissonant than the previous one. Here is the derivation of each generation from the previous one: Start with the octave's ratio, 2:1. Multiply each of its two numbers by two, viz. 4:2. Then stick the missing number in the middle, viz. 4:3:2. This breaks up into a pair of ratios — 4:3 and 3:2. The minor one is 4:3 and the major one is 3:2. These are the perfect fourth and the perfect fifth, respectively, and they are the first generation.

Now take the perfect fifth's ratio, 3:2. Multiply each of its two numbers by two, viz. 6:4. Then stick the missing number in the middle, viz. 6:5:4. This breaks up into a pair of ratios — 6:5 and 5:4. The minor one is 6:5 and the major one is 5:4. These are the minor third and major third, respectively. Their inversions are 5:3 and 8:5, which are the major sixth and the minor sixth, respectively. So these are the second generation: M3, m3, M6, m6. Now take the major third's ratio, 5:4. Multiply each of its two numbers by two, viz. 10:8. Then stick the missing number in the middle, viz. 10:9:8. This breaks up into a pair of ratios — 10:9 and 9:8. The minor one is 10:9 and the major one is 9:8. Both of these are whole-tones, i.e. major seconds. The inversion of 9:8 is 16:9, a minor seventh. So these are the third generation: M2, m7.

Now take the whole-tone's ratio, 9:8. Multiply each of its two numbers by two, viz. 18:16. Then stick the missing number in the middle, viz. 18:17:16. This breaks up into a pair of ratios — 18:17 and 17:16. The minor one is 18:17 and the major one is 17:16. Both of these are semitones, i.e. minor seconds. The inversion of 18:17 is 17:9, a major seventh. The last interval is the tritone. The tritone is ideally equal to the square root of two, which is irrational, but can be approximated by adding a semitone to a perfect fourth:

$$\frac{4}{3}\times\frac{17}{16}=\frac{1\times 17}{3\times 4}=\frac{17}{12}$$

or

$$\frac{4}{3}\times\frac{18}{17}=\frac{4\times 6}{1\times 17}=\frac{24}{17}$$

which is the inversion of 17:12. 24:17 has the same denominator as 18:17, and 17:12 has the same numerator as 17:16. So these are the intervals of the fourth generation: m2, M7, p.

Ordered and unordered pitch and pitch class intervals

In atonal or musical set theory there are numerous types of intervals, the first being ordered pitch interval, the distance between two pitches upward or downward. For instance, the interval from C to G upward is 7, but the interval from G to C downward is -7. Using integer notation and modulo 12, ordered pitch interval, ip, may be defined, for any two pitches x and y, as:

$$ip\ \langle x,y\rangle = y - x$$

and:

$$ip\ \langle y,x\rangle = x - y$$

the other way. One can also measure the distance between two pitches without taking into account direction with the unordered pitch interval, similar to the interval of tonal theory. This may be defined as:

$$ip(x,y) = |y - x|$$

The interval between pitch classes may be measured with ordered and unordered pitch class intervals. The ordered one, also called directed interval, may be considered the measure upwards, which, since we are dealing with pitch classes, depends on whichever pitch is chosen as 0. Thus the ordered pitch class interval, i<x, y>, may be defined as:

$$i\ \langle x,y\rangle = y - x$$

mod 12, of course.

Interval Cycles

Interval cycles, "unfold a single recurrent interval in a series that closes with a return to the initial pitch class", and are notated by George Perle using the letter "C", for cycle, with an interval class integer to distinguish the interval. Thus the diminished seventh chord would be C3 and the augmented triad would be C4. A superscript may be added to distinguish between transpositions, using 0-11 to indicate the lowest pitch class in the cycle. "These interval cycles play a fundamental role in the harmonic organization of post-diatonic music and can easily be identified by naming the cycle."

Interval Strength and Root

David Cope suggests the concept of interval strength, in which an interval's strength is determined by its approximation to a lower, stronger, or higher, weaker, position in the harmonic series.

Hindemith and David Cope both suggest the concept of interval roots. To determine an interval's root, one locates its nearest approximation in the harmonic series. The root of a perfect fourth, then, is its top note because it is an octave of the fundamental in the hypothetical harmonic series. The bottom note of every odd diatonically numbered intervals are the roots, as are the tops of all even numbered intervals.

The root of a collection of intervals or a chord is thus determined by the interval root of its strongest interval. As to its usefulness, Cope provides the example of the final tonic chord of some popular music being traditionally analyzable as a "submediant six-five chord" (added sixth chords by popular terminology), or a first inversion seventh chord (possibly the dominant of the mediant V/iii). According the interval root of the strongest interval of the chord (in first inversion, CEGA), the perfect fifth (C-G), is the bottom C, the tonic.

Other Intervals

There are also a number of intervals not found in the chromatic scale or labeled with a diatonic function which have names of their own. Many of these intervals describe small discrepancies between notes tuned according to the tuning systems used. Most of the following intervals may be described as microtones.

— A Pythagorean comma is the difference between twelve justly tuned perfect fifths and seven octaves. It is expressed by the frequency ratio 531441:524288, and is equal to 23.46 cents

— A syntonic comma is the difference between four justly tuned perfect fifths and two octaves plus a major third. It is expressed by the ratio 81:80, and is equal to 21.51 cents

— A Septimal comma is 64/63, and is the difference between the Pythagorean or 3-limit "7th" and the "harmonic 7th".

— Diesis is generally used to mean the difference between three justly tuned major thirds and one octave. It is expressed by the ratio 128:125, and is equal to 41.06 cents. However, it has been used to mean other small intervals.

— A schisma (also skhisma) is the difference between five octaves and eight justly tuned fifths plus one justly tuned major third. It is expressed by the ratio 32805:32768, and is equal to 1.95 cents. It is also the difference between the Pythagorean and syntonic commas.

— A schismic major third is a schisma different than a just major third, eight fifths down and five octaves up, Fb in C.

— A quarter tone is half the width of a semitone, which is half the width of a whole tone.

— A kleisma is six major thirds up, five fifths down and one octave up, or, more commonly, 225:224.

— A limma is the ratio 256:243, which is the semitone in Pythagorean tuning.

— A ditone is the pythagorean ratio 81:64, two 9:8 tones.

— Additionally, some cultures around the world have their own names for intervals found in their music.

Mystical Harmony

The great god Shiva once chanced upon his wife Parvati reposing most gracefully. Her breathing was like soft music; the exquisite bosom rising and falling in rhythm. Her arms and wrists laden with bangles caused music by their motion. Shiva was intoxicated by this ravishing vision, and watched her for a long time in silence. Such was the impression created in his mind that he found no peace until he discovered a way of making a permanent record of the beauty observed. The result was the veena, a musical instrument, whose long neck represents the straight lithe form of Parvati, and the two supporting gourds her breasts, the metal frets her bracelets, and the most expressive of all, the sound generated by this instrument is said to recreate Parvati's own, rhythmic breathing.

Indeed, this tale but echoes the belief inherent in all ancient traditions, that the first musical instrument was the human body itself, and the first created music, the human voice. Most stringed and wind instruments, which evolved with the human civilization, recall some quality or aspect of this voice.

From the music of his inherent voice, man graduated next to musical rhythms generated from his body externally. The age-old human yearning for adorning the physical form including the head, ears, arms, ankles etc is but a manifestation of the same. Ornamented in this way, the body is transformed into a musical instrument. The tinkling of the ornaments is not pre-planned; rather it arises spontaneously from the natural movements of the person. This is especially highlighted in classical Indian dance performances, where the elaborate jewelry adorning the dancer emphasizes her graceful movements, and also the rhythm that is laid down by the accompanying musical instruments.

As the dancer stamps on the ground with his feet, the bells on his ankles tinkle in time with his movements. Apart from the acoustic ornaments and jewelry worn to accentuate the rhythm of the dance, a whole range of tinkling accessories are used in conjunction with the apparel. These include small spherical bells sewn onto garments, charms, sequins, ornaments for the forehead and hair, acoustic rings, shards of glass, clinking chains for the arms or ankles to emphasize the movement of the body, not to mention the clacking of heels or sandals while walking. The last is reminiscent of the most primitive form of music, namely stamping on the ground. The deeply symbolic ritual act of treading the earth affirms the relationship of human beings to their native soil. In this act, man for the first time, shows himself capable of expressing and externalising the regular rhythm of his heart beat, utilizing his feet for a dynamic movement that is essentially an expression of joy translated into rhythm. Without the use of any type of instrument to mediate between him and the ground, the dancer thus communicates directly with mother earth, rooting his inner rhythms within her depths.

Over time, the ancients realized that a greater amplification was achieved by hollowing out the surface of the ground being stamped upon, and covering the space created with a floor. This was the natural precursor to the first drum. The drum is unique in the sense that though almost all musical instruments have their origin in the practice of ritual magic, it is the only instrument that has retained these associations even to the present day.

From a hollow ground covered with a floor, the drum progressed to a hollowed tree and then as the musical instinct of man evolved, developed into a cylinder or bowl made of wood, covered at both ends with a stretched membrane (like the 'floor' above).

It is not an exaggeration to say that of all implements capable of generating rhythmic music, the drum is the one imbued with the most mystery and potency. Not only the music it generates, but its entire structure and form is soaked in rich symbolism. Take for example its shape. The curvaceous form is representative of a woman, and the hollowness inside has a likewise similar significance. It is a receptive void, to be entered as a woman is, protective, cavernous, a shelter and hence a symbol of the womb. In contrast, its music is essentially thought to be masculine in nature. This ambivalence expresses a dualism that is inherent in human nature, and also signifies that the drum combines all the virtues of yin and yang in a harmonious whole.

Also, a drum is most often made of wood. In addition to enriching its acoustic abilities, the choice of this material has a metaphysical and indeed primordial significance. Wood is a metaphor for ascension to higher domains, which are experienced in the ecstatic states of psychic trance. There is a physical reason underlying this too. The tree, whose wood is used to construct the drum, is in itself a symbol of the Cosmic Tree, which connects the earth to heaven, and of which the earthly tree is but a microcosm. In primitive thought it was believed that a spiritually evolved person could climb the cosmic tree and journey back and forth from heaven. Such people were known as shamans. Indeed, the drum serves as a bridge between the two realms, terrestrial and heavenly, in more than one ways. Firstly is its round, outer form, suggesting the celestial spheres, while simultaneously the emptiness inside speaks of the inner void within each of us, and reiterates that they are both one and the same.

In his role as intermediary between the earthly world and the realm of the spirits, the shaman derives his powers from playing his frame drum, the vehicle by which he enters a state of trance.

According to scholar Mircea Eliade, a shaman is a man or woman who "journeys" in an ecstatic trance, usually induced by rhythmic drumming. In its widest sense, a shaman is someone who has the specialist techniques for communicating with the higher reality by entering into an alternative state of consciousness, and drumming is one of the most common means through which the shaman enters this state.

In ancient times, it was said to be the shaman's job to make sure that the relationship between the human and divine world was kept harmonious and balanced. His essential role was to search for the unifying connections between the two realms. This is the quest of the mystic too. In mysticism, everything is vibration. Not only are all material forms made up of vibrations; we as humans also live and move in vibrations - they surround us as the fish is surrounded by water, and we contain them within ourselves, as the pond contains water. The drum, through its rhythms, replicates these vibrations, and it is not surprising that when we move to the rhythms of a drum we feel as though we're being carried along by the beat - a feeling of effortlessness and harmony that defies synchrony. This is why that the rhythm of the drum seems to lift time out of the realm of the ordinary as we know it, and transmutes it into timelessness. Truly, one of the properties of instrumental or sung music is that it can make time appear to stand still, lulling the sense of the listener, or even literally inducing sleep. That indeed is the principle of the lullaby, whose slow rhythm and repeated words and phrases promote a state of soothing and calming drowsiness.

Another archetypal and natural human activity that gave rise to a musical instrument is the simple act of clapping. All over the world, this quasi-spontaneous gesture, the sound of which varies according to the position of the hands, provides the most common rhythmic accompaniment to the voice, and is also used to show enthusiasm in the form of applause. Clapping is an instinctive action that has an invigorating effect on the whole body by stimulating nerves residing on the palms of the hands. Due to this attribute, it is often a part of yogic therapy too. Truly, after or during a musical performance, this idiophonic beating brings the listener's body into the experience and helps to release the pent-up energy aroused by the music and the rhythm.

From clapping with his own hands, man graduated next to crafted clappers, which were held in both hands and were clashed together to produce sounds greater in intensity than those generated by the mere hands.

Such a pair of instruments, known as cymbals, continues to find use in religious rituals, including those of Hinduism and Buddhism.

These cymbals are used to punctuate sacred texts, whether read aloud, sung or chanted. In metaphysical terms, the beating together of cymbals is said to signify the symbolic union of opposites, wherein the naturally occurring male and female polar energies are combined, an activity which is necessary to maintain the harmony of the dynamic universe. Thus says an ancient Tibetan proverb: 'With only one wing, a bird cannot fly.'

As expressed in the example of the cymbals above, after deriving music from his own body, the next natural step for man was to devise instruments that were an extension of himself. Clearly, such implements had to be in close physical proximity to the musician. It is possible to imagine a variety of different such instrumental extensions. The breath, for example, is extended into pipes (flutes), and transformed into music when these are raised to the lips. Similarly, the tongue and its vibratory capability is extended by the means of the primitive reed that consists of a leaf or a blade of grass held by the fingers in front of the lips.

Fundamental to man's attempts to dominate, or at the very least placate the forces of nature, is the need to establish an analogy between nature and instrument, based on their common origin. Once the concept that all things are interrelated is acknowledged, and that each one affects the rest at every level in the relationship of cause and effect, then the magical principle is established which states that it is only necessary to influence one part of the whole in order to extend that influence to the totality. Thus a harmonious relationship existed, and continues to do so, between the human body and the musical instrument, for the one cannot operate without the other. Without his or her instrument, a musician may be likened to an amputee or a rider without his horse. Both are made up of body and soul, and together they become like two human beings, whose identities merge (as in the case of the cymbals mentioned above), in the playing of the instrument, giving rise to a higher reality. One only has to observe a sitar player in action to note the loving and energetic tenderness with which he or she seems to caress the instrument, speak to it, coax sounds out of it, making it vibrate and respond with sweet melodies and eloquent phrases.

In Tibet, the human cranium is used in making the damaru, a drum with whirling balls, here two skulls are combined and, according to the holy texts, it is preferable for these to be taken respectively from a boy of sixteen and a girl of twelve. Monkey skins are stretched over the skulls, and one end is decorated with an eight-petalled lotus smeared with a girl's menstrual blood, and the other end with a mandala. Sixteen pierced holes allow the skin to be attached using human hair. The whirling balls are made of bones taken from a waterbird's foot and encased in wax and cloth.

True to its character, Tantric philosophy takes this identification of man with instrument to its physical extreme, even to the extent of fashioning instruments out of different parts of the human body. For example, the Tibetan ritual trumpet 'rkang-gling' utilizes the male femur, the name itself means 'made of a man's leg.' This ideal is further expressed in the hourglass shaped drum with whirling balls, known in Sanskrit as 'damaru,' its shape echoing the inexorable passage of time. This drum is fashioned out of the human cranium, and is comprised of two skulls, taken respectively from a boy of sixteen and a girl of twelve. To consecrate it, and metaphorically infuse it with a magical life, the male side is smeared with sperm and female half with menstrual blood.

In the shape of an hourglass, it is also called a skull drum when made from human crania. Here the body is made of wood (carved in imitation of two skullcaps) and is decorated overall with paintings of religious scenes. The damaru is used in a variety of ceremonies, often in association with the rkang-gling. It is normally played inside Tibetan monasteries or by Bon monks.

Essentially, the damaru is composed of two inverted triangles with their apexes meeting at the center. The upward triangle suggests the fiery linga of Shiva, and the lower pointing triangle represents the female yoni. The point where they meet is of course once again the higher, transcendent reality, where all dualities merge giving rise to a refreshing oneness. This point is the primordial bindu, or the dimensionless entity that gives rise to all creation.

In the Indian tradition, the damaru drum is associated with the figure of Shiva, Lord of the Dance. In this context the playing of the damaru represents the diving act of Creation. The damaru is considered so sacred in Indian thought that rules are suggested even for the correct positioning of this drum when it is not being played. It is canonized that it should never be put down on its end, but positioned so that the male skull is to the musician's right, while the female skull is to his left. This arrangement follows the traditional established order of father/mother, right/left, and masculine/feminine.

The use of materials taken from human bodies has magical implications, linking the human, animal, vegetable and mineral worlds in an indissociable whole. By taking possession of these elements and controlling them in this way, man expresses his all embracing mystical and harmonious vision of the world.

Indeed, music has since time immemorial been the universal vehicle for man's attempts to reach out to a higher dimension of reality. The Upanishads state that this supreme domain is not a physical state of being, but is intangible and unsubstantial. Therefore, to gauge this supernormal state, man requires a symbolic medium that is similarly abstract, yet spiritually potent enough to withhold its essence, and is at the same time discernable to one or more of his sense organs. Music is the means by which he makes this leap into the unknown. To communicate with the intangible other world that lies just beyond our reach, it is necessary to transcend the material universe, so that no physical obstacle stands in the way of divine influence. Apprehending the material world solely in terms of its sounds has the effect of rendering it insubstantial, so that it becomes no more than a vibration in the air, intangible, yet graspable to a sense organ (ears). Hence does man fulfill his mystical destiny.

If any instrument retains its primal simplicity, it is the flute. Even today it is still the mere hollow stick through which Lord Krishna expressed himself with minimum adulteration.

It is not subject to complicated sets of rules, and anyone who wants to make music can fashion his own instrument. The flute is light in weight and easily transported. It is thus essentially nomadic, and hence naturally associated with Krishna, who is visualized as the divine cowherd. Krishna is said to have charmed his stock of cows with the music he composed with his flute.

Charming animals by means of sound is a common theme in world mythology, from Orpheus playing his lyre and attracting wild beasts to seat themselves at his feet to the snake charmers of India.

Orpheus provides a link between the human, animal and supernatural worlds, through the magic of his music. Animals, being supremely sensitive to sounds, becoming his willing slaves. The purpose of the cult of Orpheus is to liberate the soul by the grace of music, acknowledging in doing so the influence that each has on the other.

Harmonious Musical Forms

Sonata

Sonata (From Latin and Ital. sonare, to sound), in music, originally merely a piece "played" as opposed to cantata (Latin cantare, to sing), a piece sung, though the term is said to have been applied once or twice to a vocal composition. By the time of Arcangelo Corelli two polyphonic types of sonata were established, the sonata da chiesa and the sonata da camera. The sonata in its main classical significance is a work for one or two instruments consisting of a group of movements, four movements being the full scheme; the last movement in the same key as the first; each movement normally in one tempo, complete in design, independent from the other movements in themes, but aptly related to them in key and style; and constructed in the sonata forms.

Though, since the time of Bach (when trios were called sonatas), the term is not applied to works for more than two instruments, the full (and even the normal) characteristics of this most important of all instrumental art-forms are rarely revealed except in trios, quartets, &c., and symphonies. A movement is a piece of music forming a complete design, or at least not merely introductory; and within such limits as either to contain no radical change of pace or else to treat changes of pace in a simple and symmetrical alternation of episodes.

The first complete movement of a sonata seldom leads without break to the others, except in modern examples; but the later movements are often connected. The sonata da chiesa, generally for one or more violins and bass, consisted normally of a slow introduction, a loosely fugued allegro, a cantabile slow movement and a lively finale in some such binary form as suggests affinity with the dance-tunes of the suite. This scheme, however, is not very clearly defined, until the works of Johann Sebastian Bach and George Friderich Handel, when it becomes the sonata par excellence and persists as a tradition of Italian violin music even into the early 19th century in the works of Boccherini.

The sonata da camera consisted almost entirely of idealized dance-tunes. By the time of Bach and Handel it had, on the one hand, become entirely separate from the sonata, and was known as the suite, partita, ordre or (when it had a prelude in the form of a French opera-overture) the overture. On the other hand, the features of sonata da chiesa and sonata da camera became freely intermixed. But Bach, who does not use those titles, yet keeps the two types so distinct that they can be recognized by style and form. Thus, in his six solo violin sonatas, Nos. 1, 3 and 5 are sonate de chiesa, and Nos. 2, 4 and 6 are called partitas, but are admissible among the sonatas as being sonate da camera.

The sonatas of Domenico Scarlatti are a special type determined chiefly by those kinds of keyboard technique that are equally opposed, on the one hand, to contrapuntal style, and, on the other hand, to the supporting of melodies on a lifetess accompaniment. Longo's complete collection of Scarlatti's sonatas shows that, short of the true developed sonata-style, there is nothing between the old sonata da chiesa and Beethovenish experiments in unorthodox 'complementary keys' that Scarlatti does not carry off with a delightfully irresponsible "impressionism" that enables him to be modern in effect without any serious modern principle.

Great, however, as the variety of his forms is now known to be, and numerous as are the newly published slow movements, the normal Scarlatti sonata is that which the concerl-player popularizes; fireworks in binary form, with a perfunctory opening, a crowd of pregnant ideas in the complementary key, and, after the double bar, a second part reproducing these ideas as soon as possible in the tonic. The sonatas of Domenico Paradies are mild and elongated works of this type with a graceful and melodious little second movement added. The manuscript on which Longo bases his edition of Scarlatti frequently shows a similar juxtaposition of movements, though without definite indication of their connection. The style is still traceable in the sonatas of the later classics, whenever a first movement is in a uniform rush of rapid motion, as in Mozart's violin sonata in F, and in several of Clementi's best works.

A sonata's first movement is in sonata form, and is fast and lively. The second movement is slow and lyrical. It is traditionally in binary form or ternary form. The third movement is either a minuet or a scherzo. The fourth and final movement is either in sonata form or a rondo. Keep in mind, however, that the forms for the movements are traditional and composers always did and still do experiment with different forms.

Cantata

Cantata (Italian for a song or story set to music) is a vocal composition accompanied by instruments and generally containing more than one movement.

In the 16th century, when all serious music was vocal, the term had no reason to exist, but with the rise of instrumental music in the 17th century cantatas began to exist under that name as soon as the instrumental art was definite enough to be embodied in sonatas. From the middle of the 17th till late in the 18th century a favourite form of Italian chamber music was the cantata for one or two solo voices, with accompaniment of harpsichord and perhaps a few other solo instruments. It consisted at first of a declamatory narrative or scene in recitative, held together by a primitive aria repeated at intervals. Fine examples may be found in the church music of Carissimi; and the English vocal solos of Henry Purcell (such as Mad Tom and Mad Bess) show the utmost that can be made of this archaic form. With the rise of the Da Capo aria the cantata became a group of two or three arias joined by recitative. George Friderich Handel's numerous Italian duets and trios are examples on a rather large scale. His Latin motet Silete Venti, for soprano solo, shows the use of this form in church music.

The Italian solo cantata tended, when on a large scale, to become indistinguishable from a scene in an opera. In the same way the church cantata, solo or choral, is indistinguishable from a small oratorio or portion of an oratorio. This is equally evident whether we examine the unparalleled church cantatas of Bach, of which nearly 200 are extant, or the Chandos Anthems of Handel. In Johann Sebastian Bach's case many of the larger cantatas are actually called oratorios; and the Christmas Oratorio is a collection of six church cantatas actually intended for performance on six different days, though together forming as complete an artistic whole as any classical oratorio.

The essential point, however, in Bach's church cantatas is that they formed part of a church service, and moreover of a service in which the organization of the music was far more coherent than is possible in the Anglican church. Many of Bach's greatest cantatas begin with an elaborate chorus followed by a couple of arias and recitatives, and end with a plain chorale. This has often been commented upon as an example of Bach's indifference to artistic climax in the work as a whole. But no one will maintain this who realizes the place which the church cantata occupied in the Lutheran church service. The text was carefully based upon the gospel or lessons for the day; unless the cantata was short the sermon probably took place after the first chorus or one of the arias, and the congregation joined in. the final chorale. Thus the unity of the service was the unity of the music; and, in the cases where all the movements of the cantata were founded on one and the same chorale-tune, this unity has never been equalled, except by those 16th-century masses and motets which are founded upon the Gregorian tones of the festival for which they are written.

In modern times the term cantata is applied almost exclusively to choral, as distinguished from solo vocal music. There has, perhaps, been only one kind of cantata since Bach which can be recognized as an art form and not as a mere title for works otherwise impossible to classify. It is just possible to recognize as a distinct artistic type that kind of early 19th-century cantata in which the chorus is the vehicle for music more lyric and songlike than the oratorio style, though at the same time not exclude ing the possibility of a brilliant climax in the shape of a light order of fugue. Ludwig van Beethoven's Glorreiche Augenblick is a brilliant pot-boiler in this style; Carl Maria von Weber's Jubel Cantata is a typical specimen, and Felix Mendelssohn's Walpurgisnacht is the classic. Mendelssohn's Symphony

Cantata, the Lobgesang, is a hybrid work, partly in the oratorio style. It is preceded by three symphonic movements, a device avowedly suggested by Beethoven's ninth symphony; but the analogy is not accurate, as Beethoven's work is a symphony of which the fourth movement is a choral finale of essentially single design, whereas Mendelssohn's Symphony Cantata; is a cantata with three symphonic preludes. The full lyric possibilities of a string of choral songs were realized at last by Johannes Brahms in his Rinaldo, set to a text which Goethe wrote at the same time as he wrote that of the Walpurgisnacht. The point of Brahms's work (his only experiment in this genre) has been lost by critics who expected in so voluminous a composition the qualities of an elaborate choral music wIth which it has nothing whatever to do. Brahms has probably said the last word on this subject; and the remaining types of cantata (beginning with Beethoven's Meeres-stille, and including most of Brahms's and many notable English small choral works) are merely so many different ways of setting to choral music a poem which is just too long to be comprised in one movement.

Symphony

A symphony is an extended piece of music for orchestra, especially one in the form of a sonata. The word *symphony* is derived from the Greek *syn* (together) and *phone* (sounding), by way of the latin *symphonia*. The term was used by the Greeks, firstly to denote the general conception of concord, both between successive sounds and in the unison of simultaneous sounds; secondly, in the special sense of concordant pairs of successive sounds (i.e. the "perfect intervals" of modern music; the 4th, 5th and octave); and thirdly as dealing with the concord of the octave, thus meaning the art of singing in octaves, as opposed to singing and playing in unison.

In Roman times the word appears in the general sense which still survives in poetry, that is, as harmonious concourse of voices and instruments. It also appears to mean a concert. In the sense of "sounding together", the word appears in the titles of works by Giovanni Gabrieli (the *Sacrae symphoniae*) and Heinrich Schütz (the *Symphoniae sacre*) among others. Through the 17th century, the Italian word *sinfonia* was applied to a number of works, including overtures, instrumental ritornello sections of arias and concertos, and works which would later by classified as concertos or sonatas.

The form that we now recognise as the symphony took shape in the early 18th century. It is commonly regarded to have grown from the Italian overture, a three-movement piece used to open operas, often used by Alessandro Scarlatti among others. Another important progenitor of the symphony was the *ripieno concerto* - a relatively little explored form resembling a concerto for strings and continuo, but with no solo instruments. The earliest known ripieno concerti are by Giuseppe Torelli. Antonio Vivaldi also wrote works of this type. Perhaps the best known ripieno concerto is Johann Sebastian Bach's *Brandenburg Concerto No. 3*.

Early symphonies, in common with both Italian overtures and concertos, have three movements in the tempi quick-slow-quick. However, unlike the ripieno concerto, which uses the usual ritornello form of the concerto, at least the first movement of these symphonies is in some sort of binary form. They are distinguished from Italian overtures in that they were written for concert performance, rather than to introduce a stage work, although for much of the

18th century, the terms *overture* and *symphony* were used interchangeably, and a piece originally written as one was sometimes later used as the other. The vast majority of these early symphonies are in a major key.

Symphonies at this time, whether for concert, opera or church use were not considered the major work on a program, often, as with Concerti, they were divided up between other works, or drawn from suites or overtures. Vocal music was considered the heart of the musical experience, and symphonies were supposed to provide preludes, interludes and postludes to this. At the time most symphonies were relatively short - running between 10 and 20 minutes at the most.

The "Italian" style of symphony, often used as overture and entr'acte in opera houses, became a standard three movement for of a fast movement, the "allegro", a slow movement, and then a fast movement. Mozart's early symphonies are in this lay out. The early three-movement form was eventually replaced by a four-movement layout which was dominant in the latter part of the 18th century and throughout most of the 19th century. This symphonic form was influenced by Germanic practice, and would come to be associated with the "classical style" of Haydn and Mozart. The important changes were the addition of a "dance" movement was the important change, and the change in character of the first movement to becoming "first among equals".

The normal four movement form became, then:

- Quick, in a binary form or later sonata form
- Slow
- Minuet and trio (later developed into the scherzo and trio), in ternary form

— Quick, sometimes also in sonata form or a sonata-rondo

It should be noted, however, that even in the mid-18th century, variations on this layout were not uncommon - in particular, the middle two movements sometimes switched places, or a slow introduction was added to the beginning, sometimes resulting in a four-movement slow-quick-slow-quick form. The first symphony to introduce the minuet as the third movement appears to be a 1740 work in D major by Georg Matthias Monn. This is an isolated example, however, the first composer to consistently use the minuet as part of a four-movement form was Johann Stamitz.

Two major centres for early symphony writing were Vienna, where early exponents of the form included Georg Christoph Wagenseil, Wenzel Raimund Birck and Georg Matthias Monn; and Mannheim, home of the so-called Mannheim School. Symphonies were written throughout Europe, however, with Giovanni Battista Sammartini and Antonio Brioschi active in Italy, Carl Philipp Emanuel Bach in northern Germany, Leopold Mozart in Salzburg, François-Joseph Gossec in Paris, and Johann Christian Bach and Carl Friedrich Abel in London.

Later significant Viennese composers of symphonies include Johann Baptist Vanhal, Karl Ditters von Dittersdorf and Leopold Hoffmann. The most important symphonists of the latter part of the 18th century, however, are considered to be Joseph Haydn, who wrote 106 symphonies over the course of 40 years, and Wolfgang Amadeus Mozart. Their large number of widely performed and emmulated works are commonly considered the apotheosis of the Classical style.

In the late 18th century, vocal music, particularly cantatas and operas, were considered the major form of concert music, with concerti being next. With the rise of standing orchestras, the symphony assumed a larger and larger place in concert life. The period of transition can be seen in the 1790 to 1820 period. For Ludwig van Beethoven his first Academy Concert had "Christ on the Mount of Olives" as the major work, and not the two symphonies performed. Beethoven took the symphony into new territory by expanding, often dramatically, each of its parts. His nine symphonies set the standard for symphonic writing for generations afterwards. After two symphonies rather in the style of Haydn, his *Symphony No. 3* (the *Eroica*), has a scale and emotional range which sets it apart from earlier works. His *Symphony No. 9* takes the unprecedented step of including parts for vocal soloists and choir in the last movement. Beethoven, together with Franz Schubert, was also responsible for replacing the genteel minuet with the livelier scherzo as a third movement. The scherzo, with its greater scope for emotional expression, was more suited to the Romantic style.

The next generation of symphonists desired to combine the expanded harmonic vocabulary developed by chromatic composers such as John Field, Ludwig Spohr and Carl Maria von Weber, with the structural innovations of Beethoven. Robert Schumann and Felix Mendelssohn were two leading Germanic composers whose works attempted this fusion. At the same time a more experimental form of symphonic writing was coming into being, featuring a greater number of symphonies with textual meaning or specific programs. While "program symphonies" had been written as early as 1790, their place and role became expanded with Hector Berlioz' *Symphonie fantastique* and then Liszt's program symphonies, such as the Dante Symphony and the Faust Symphony.

This period corresponds with what is generally labelled the "Romantic" period, and ends around the middle of the 19th century, though the term "Romantic" is often used in music to correspond with the longer musical era from Beethoven all the way through Sergei Rachmaninoff.

In the second half of the 19th century, symphonies included movements using a much-expanded but often strict Sonata Form. Johannes Brahms, who took Schumann and Mendelssohn as his point of departure, set the standard for composing symphonies which very high levels of structural unity. At the same time symphonies grew in length, and became the centerpiece of the expanding number of symphony orchestras. Other important symphonists of the late 19th century include Anton Bruckner, Antonin Dvorak, Tchaikovsky and Saint Saens.

The twentieth century saw further diversification in the style and content of works which composers labelled "symphonies" - the idea that the "symphony" was a definite form which had certain standards was eroded, and the symphony instead came to be any major orchestral work which its composer saw fit to label such. While some composers - such as Sergei Rachmaninoff and Carl Nielsen, continued to write in the traditional four-movement form, other composers took different approaches.

Gustav Mahler, whose second symphony written at the end of the 19th century is in five movements, continued to write novel works in the form: his third symphony, like the second, has parts for soloists and choir and is in six movements, the fifth and seventh symphonies are in five movements, and the eighth symphony, which in another age would more likely have been called a cantata or oratorio, is in two large parts, with vocalists singing for virtually the duration of the work. Jean Sibelius' *Symphony No. 7*, his last, is in just one movement.

Despite this diversification, there remained certain tendencies - symphonies were still limited to being works for orchestra. Vocal parts were sometimes used alongside the orchestra, but remained rare, and the use of solo instruments was virtually unheard of. Designating a work a "symphony" still implied a degree of weightiness - very short or very frivolous works were rarely called symphonies. The label *sinfonietta* came into use to designate a work that was "lighter" than the term "symphony" implied.

Along with a widening of what could be considered a symphony, the 20th century saw an increase in the number of works which could reasonably be called symphonies but which were given some other name by their composer. The *Concerto for Orchestra* by Bela Bartok is just one such example (Bartók never wrote a work he called a symphony). Some present-day composers continue to write works which they call "symphonies", but the tendency in the 20th century has been for the symphony to be less a recognisable form with its own conventions and norms, and more a label which composers apply to orchestral works of a certain ambition.

Harmonic Orchestra

An orchestra is a musical ensemble used most often in classical music. A small orchestra is called a chamber orchestra.

Full size orchestras may sometimes be called "symphony orchestras" or "philharmonic orchestras"; these prefixes do not indicate any difference either to the instrumental content or role of the orchestra, but can be useful to distinguish different orchestras based in the same city (for instance, the London Symphony Orchestra and the London Philharmonic Orchestra).

The typical symphony orchestra consists of four groups of musical instruments:

— the strings (violins, violas, cellos, double basses),

— the woodwinds (flutes, clarinets, oboes, bassoons),

— the brass (trumpets, trombones, tuba, french horns), and

— the percussion (timpani, snare drum, bass drum, celesta, etc.).

Contemporaneously, the musicians are usually directed by a conductor, although early orchestras did not have one, using instead the principal violinist or the harpsichordist playing the continuo for this role. Some modern orchestras also do without conductors, particularly smaller orchestras and those specialising in historically accurate performances of baroque music and earlier.

The most frequently performed repertoire for a symphony orchestra is Western classical music or opera. They are also used in popular music, however.

At first the orchestra was an aristocratic luxury, performing privately at the courts of the princes and nobles of Italy; but in the 17th century performances were given in theatres, and Germany eagerly followed. Dresden, Munich and Hamburg successively built opera houses, while in England opera flourished under Henry Purcell, and in France under Lully, who with the collaboration of Moliere also greatly raised the status of the entertainments known as ballets, interspersed with instrumental and vocal music.

In the 17th Century and early 18th Century instrumental groups were taken from all of the available talent. A composer such as Johann Sebastian Bach had control over almost all of the musical resources of a town, where as Handel would hire the best musicians available. This placed a premium on being able to rewrite music for whichever singers or musicians were best suited for a performance - Handel produced different versions of the Messiah oratorio almost every year.

As nobility began to build retreats from towns, they began to hire standing bodies of musicians. Composers such as the young Franz Joseph Haydn would have, then, a fixed body of instrumentalists to work with. At the same time, travelling virtuoso performers would write concerti which featured their skills, and travel from town to town, arranging concerts from whoever was there.

This change - from civic music making where the composer had some degree of time or control, to smaller court music making and one off performance - placed a premium on music which was easy to learn, often with little or no rehearsal. The results were changes in musical style and emphasis on new techniques. Mannheim had one of the most famous orchestras of that time, where notated dynamics and phrasing, previously quite rare, became standard (see Mannheim school). It also attended a change in musical style from the complex counterpoint of the baroque period, to an emphasis on clear melody that would later give rise to the classical style.

Through out the late 18th century composers would continue to have to assemble musicians for a performance, often called an "Academy", which would, naturally, feature their own compositions. In 1781, however, the Leipzig Gewandhaus Orchestra was organized from the merchants concert society, and it began a trend towards the formation of civic orchetras which would accelerate into the 19th century. In 1818, Boston's Handel and Haydn Society was founded, in 1842 the New York Philharmonic was created, in 1848 the Vienna Philharmonic was formed, as was the Halla Orchestra in Manchester. There had long been standing bodies of musicians around operas, but not for concert music - this change ansion in composing symphonies and other purely instrumental forms. This was encouraged by composer critics such as ETA Hoffman who declared that instrumental music was the "purest form" of music.

In the 1830s conductor Habeneck, in order to perform the symphonies of Beethoven, which had not been heard in their entirety in Paris, began rehearsing a selected group of musicians. He developed techniques of rehearsing the strings separately, notating specifics of performance, and other techniques of cuing entrances which were spread across Europe. His rival and friend Hector Berlioz would adopt many of these innovations in his touring of Europe.

This was paralleled by a rapid standardization of instruments, the invention of the piston or valve by Stolzel and Blilmel, both Silesians, in 1815, was the first in a series of innovations, including the use of valves for the flute by Theobald Boehm and the innovations of Adolphe Sax in the woodwinds. These would lead Hector Berlioz to write his famous treatise on instrumentation, meaning the use of instrumental sound as an expressive element of music.

The effect of this invention was felt at once: instrument-makers in all countries helped with each other in making use of the contrivance and in bringing it to perfection; and the orchestra was before long enriched by a new family of valved instruments, variously known as tubas, or euphoniums and bombardons, having a chromatic scale and a full sonorous tone of great beauty and immense volume, forming a magnificent bass. This also made possible a more uniform playing of notes or intonation, which would lead to a more and more "smooth" orchestral sound which would peak in the 1950's with Eugene Ormandy and the Philadelphia Symphony Orchestra and the conducting of Herbert von Karajan.

During the transition to using these instruments, which made the performance of more difficult works easier, many composers, including Wagner and Berlioz, would demand the use of "natural" chromatic stops rather than the use of valves for their compositions. However, over time, the valved instruments became standard, and their use universal until the revival of older instruments in the contemporary movement towards authentic performance or "historically informed perfromance".

With the formation of standing orchestras, and the expansion of the winds and brass, as well as the ability of winds and brass instruments to be intune with each other, it created the ability of the wind and brass to be more easily massed. It also created a professional framework where musicians could rehearse and perform the same works over and over again, leading to the concept of a repertoire in instrumental music.

The next major expansion of symphonic practice came, ironically, from Wagner's Bayreuth orchestra, founded to play his musical dramas. Wagner needed to have a series of composers and notators for the complex scores which he wrote, and had a specific role for the conductor of an orchestra that he described in his influential work "On Conducting". This lead to a revolution in orchestral practice, and set the style for orchestral performance for the next eighty years. Wagner's theories changed tempi, dynamics, bowing of string instruments and the role of principals in the orchestra. Conductors who studied his methods would go on to be influential themselves.

As the early 20th Century dawned, symphony orchestras were larger, better funded and better trained than ever before, and consequently composers could compose larger and more ambitious works for them. With the recording era beginning, the standard of performance reached a pinnacle, with many older conductors and composers remembering a time when simply "getting through" the music as best as possible was the standard. Since recordings could "fix" small errors in a particular studio performance, and reach people who would never have been able to travel to distant cities - the ability of listeners to compare performances across decades lead to a renewed focus on particular conductors and on a high standard of orchestral execution.

In the 1920's and 1930's economic and artistic considerations lead to the formation of small concert societies, particularly those dedicated to the performance of music of the avant-garde, including Igor Stravinsky and Arnold Schoenberg. This tendency to start festival orchestras or dedicated groups would also be pursued in the creation of summer musical festivals, and orchestras for the performance of smaller works. Among the most influential of these was the Academy of St. Martin in the Fields under the baton of Sir Neville Marriner.

With the advent of the early music movement, orchestras were players worked on execution of works in styles derived from the study of older treatises on playing became common. These include the London Classical Players under the direction of Sir Roger Norrington and the

Academy of Ancient Music under Christopher Hogwood, among others.

The late 20th century saw a crisis of funding and support for orchestras in the United States and, to a lesser extent, in Europe. The size and cost of a symphony orchestra, compared to the size of the base of supporters, became an issue which struck at the core of the institution. Along with the drastic falling off of revenues from recording, tied to no small extent to changes in the recording industry itself, a period of change began which has yet to reach its conclusion. Critics such as Norman Lebrecht were vocal in their diagnosis of the problem as the "jet set conductor" and the problems of orchestral repertory and management, while other music administrators such as Michael Tilson Thomas and Esa-Pekka Salonen argued that new music, new means of presenting it, and a renewed relationship with the community could revitalize the symphony orchestra.

4

Rhythm Quantization

One important task in music transcription is rhythm quantization that refers to categorization of note durations. Although quantization of a pure mechanical performance is rather straightforward, the task becomes increasingly difficult in presence of musical expression, i.e. systematic variations in timing of notes and in tempo.

Expressive deviations are modelled by a probabilistic performance model from which the corresponding optimal quantizer is derived by Bayes theorem. There are different quantization schemata can be derived in this framework by proposing suitable prior and likelihood distributions. The derived quantizer operates on short groups of onsets and is thus flexible both in capturing the structure of timing deviations and in controlling the complexity of resulting notations.

One important task in music transcription is rhythm quantization that refers to categorization of note durations. Quantization of a "mechanical" performance is rather straightforward. On the other hand, the task becomes increasingly difficult in presence of expressive variations, that can be thought as systematic deviations from a pure mechanical performance. In such unconstrained performance conditions, mainly two types of systematic deviations from exact values do occur. At small time scale notes can be played accented or delayed. At large scale tempo can vary, for example the musician(s) can accelerate (or decelerate) during performance or slow down (ritard) at the end of the piece. In any case, these timing variations usually obey a certain structure since they are mostly intended by the performer. Moreover, they are linked to several attributes of the performance such as meter, phrase, form, style etc.

To devise a general computational model (i.e. a performance model) which takes all these factors into account, seems to be quite hard. Another observation important for quantization is that we can perceive a rhythmic pattern not as a sequence of isolated onsets but rather as a perceptual entity made of onsets. This also suggests that attributes of neighboring onsets such as duration, timing deviation etc. are correlated in some way.

This correlation structure is not fully exploited in commercial music packages, which do automated music transcription and score type setting. The usual approach taken is to assume a constant tempo throughout the piece, and to quantize each onset to the nearest grid point implied by the tempo and a suitable pre-specified minimum note duration (e.g. eight, sixteenth etc.).

Such a grid quantization schema implies that each onset is quantized to the nearest grid point independent of its neighbours and thus all of its attributes are assumed to be independent, hence the correlation structure is not employed. The consequence of this restriction is that users are required to play along with a fixed metronome and without any expression.

The quality of the resulting quantization is only satisfactory if the music is performed according to the assumptions made by the quantization algorithm. In the case of grid-quantization this is a mechanical performance with small and independent random deviations.

More elaborate models for rhythm quantization indirectly take the correlation structure of expressive deviations into account. In one of the first attempt to quantization, described a method in which he uses hierarchical structure of musical rhythms to do quantization use a relaxation network in which pairs of time intervals are attracted to simple integer ratios use several template grids and compare both onsets and inter-onset intervals (IOI's) to the grid and select the best quantization according to some distance criterion.

The Kant system developed at IRCAM uses more sophisticated heuristics but is in principle similar to. The common critic to all of these models is that the assumptions about the expressive deviations are implicit and are usually hidden in the model, thus it is not always clear how a particular design choice effects the overall performance for a full range of musical styles. Moreover it is not directly possible to use experimental data to tune model parameters to enhance the quantization performance.

Rhythm Quantization Problem

A *performed rhythm* is denoted by a sequence $[t_i]$[1] where each entry is the time of occurrence of an onset. For example, the performed rhythm in Figure 1 (a) is represented by $t_1 = 0$, $t_2 = 1.18$, $t_3 = 1.77$, $t_4 = 2.06$ etc. We can use the terms performance or rhythm interchangeably when we can refer to an onset sequence.

(a) Example: A performed onset sequence

(b) "Too" accurate quantization

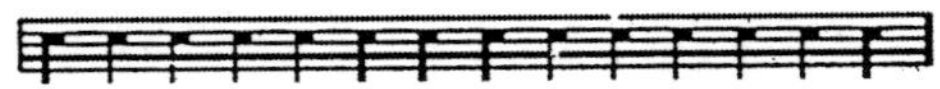

((c) "Too" simple notation.

(d) Desired quantization balances accuracy and simplicity.

Figure 1. The tradeoff between quantization and tempo tracking. Given any sequence of onset times, we can in principle easily find a notation (i.e. a sequence of rational numbers) to describe the timing information arbitrarily well. Consider the performed simple rhythm in 1 (a). A very fine grid quantizer produces a result similar to 1(b). Although this is a very accurate representation, the resulting notation is far too complex. Another extreme case is the notation in 1 (c), that contains notes of equal duration. Although this notation is very "simple", it is very unlikely that it is the intended score, since this would imply that the performer has introduced very unrealistic tempo changes (See 1. (e)).

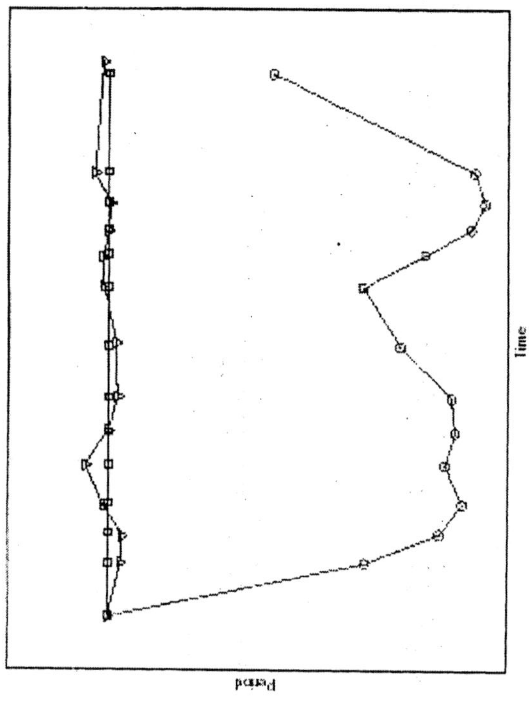

Figure 1. (e) Corresponding tempo-curves. Curves with square, oval and triangle dots correspond to the notation 1 (b), 1 (c) and 1 (d).

A very important subtask in transcription is tempo tracking, i.e. the induction of a sequence of points (i.e. beats) in time, which coincides with the human sense of rhythm (e.g. foot tapping) when listening to music. We can call such a sequence of beats a tempo track and denote it by

$$\vec{T} = [T_j]$$

where T_j is the time at which j'th beat occurs. We note that for automatic transcription, $\vec{T}$ is to be estimated from $[t_i]$.

Once a tempo track $\vec{T}$ is given, the rhythm can be segmented into a sequence of segments, each of duration $T_j - T_{j-1}$. The j'th segment will contain K_j onsets, which we enumerate by $k = 1 \ldots K_j$. The onsets in each segment are normalized and denoted by $t_j = [t^k_j]$, i.e. for all $T_{j-1} = t_i < T_j$ where

$$t_j^k = \frac{t_i - T_{j-1}}{T_j - T_{j-1}} \tag{1}$$

Note that this is merely a reindexing from single index i to double index $(k, j)^2$. In other words the onsets are scaled and translated such that an onset just at the end of the segment is mapped to one and another just at the beginning to zero. The segmentation of a performance is given in Figure 2.

Once a segmentation is given, quantization reduces to mapping onsets to locations, which can be described by simple rational numbers. Since in western music tradition, notations are generated by recursive subdivisions of a whole note, it is also convenient to generate possible onset quantization locations by regular subdivisions. We let $S = [s_i]$ denote a subdivision schema,where $[s_i]$ is a sequence of small prime numbers. Possible quantization locations are

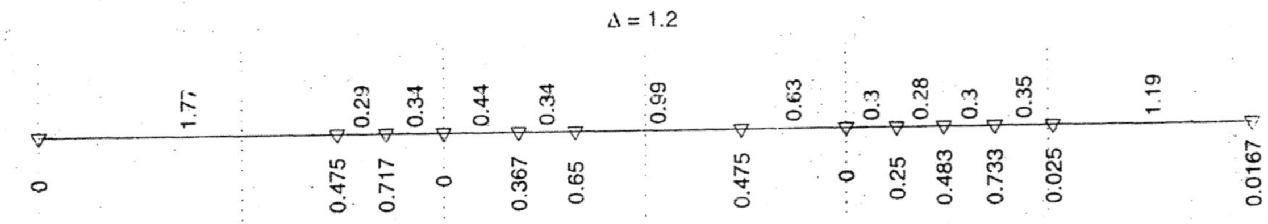

Figure 2. Segmentation of a performance by a tempo track (vertical dashed lines) $\bar{T} \sim t$ *=[0.0, 1.2, 2.4, 3.6, 4.8, 6.0, 7.2, 8.4]. The resulting segments are* t_0 *= [0],* t_1 *= [0.475, 0.717] etc.*

(a) Notation

Figure 4. A simplified schema of onset quantization. A notation (a) defines a score (b) which places onsets on simple rational points with respect to a tempo track (vertical dashed lines). The performer "maps" (b) to a performance (c).

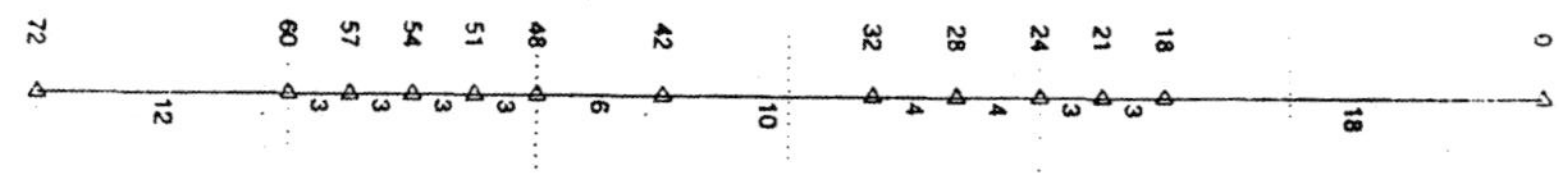

Figure 4. (b) Score

Figure 4. (c) Performance

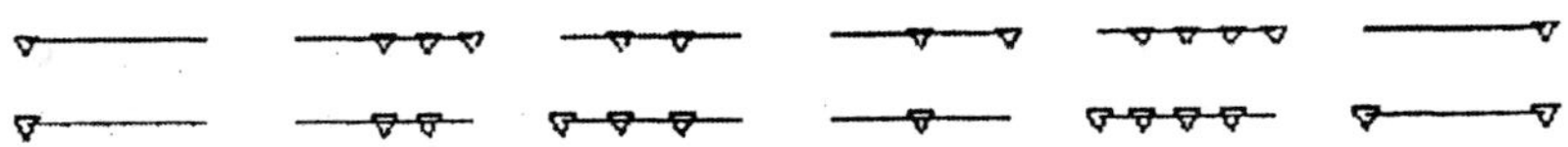

Figure 5. Two equivalent representations of the notation in Figure 4(a) by a code vector sequence. Here, each horizontal line segment represents one vector of length one beat. The endpoint of one vector is the samepoint in time as the beginning of the next vector. Note that the only difference between two equivalent representations is that some begin and endpoints are swapped.

generated by subdividing the unit interval [0, 1]. At each new iteration i, the intervals already generated are divided further into si equal parts and the resulting endpoints are added to a set C.

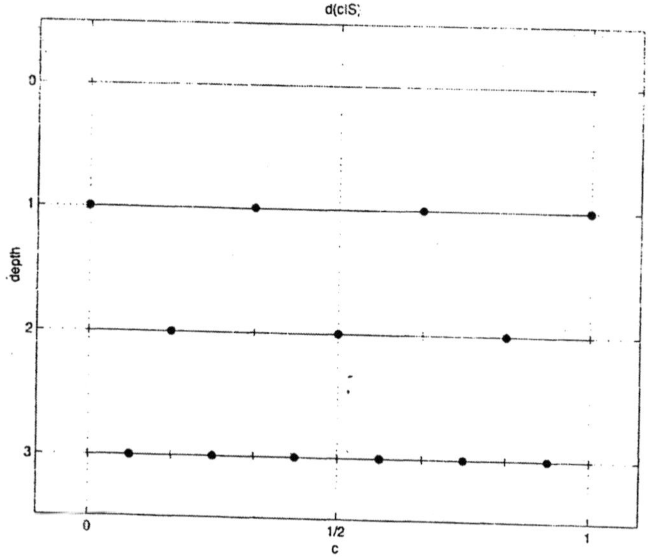

Figure 3. Depth of gridpoint c by subdivision schema $S = [3, 2, 2]$

Note that this procedure places the quantization locations on a grid of points c_n where two neighboring grid points have the distance $1/\Pi_i s_i$. We can denote the first iteration number at which the grid point c is added to C as the depth of c with respect to S. This number will be denoted as $d(c \mid S)$.

As an example consider the subdivision $S = [3, 2, 2]$. The unit interval is divided first into three equal pieces, then the resulting intervals into 2 and etc. At each iteration, generated endpoints are added to the list. In the first iteration, 0, 1/3, 2/3 and 1 are added to the list. In the second iteration, 1/6, 3/6 and 5/6 are added, etc. The resulting grid points (filled circles) are depicted in Figure 3. The vertical axis corresponds to $d(c \mid S)$.

If a segment t is quantized (with respect to S), the result is a K dimensional vector with all entries on some grid points. Such a vector we call a code vector and denote as c $= [c_k]$, i.e. $c \in C \times C \cdots \times C = C^K$. We call a set of code-vectors a codebook. Since all entries of a code vector coincide with some grid points, we can define the depth of a code vector as

$$d(\mathbf{c}|S) = \sum_{c_k \in \mathbf{c}} d(c_k|S) \quad (2)$$

A score can be viewed as a concatenation of code vectors c_j. For example, the notation in Figure 4 (a) can be represented by a code vector sequence as in Figure 5. Note that the representation is not unique, both code vector sequences represent the same notation.

Performance Model

Natural music performance is subject to several systematic deviations. In lack of such deviations, every score would have only one possible interpretation. Clearly, two natural performances of a piece of music are never the same, even performance of very short rhythms show deviations from a strict mechanical performance. In general terms, a performance model is a mathematical description of such deviations, i.e. it describes how likely it is that a score is mapped into a performance (Figure 4).

Bayes Theorem

The joint probability $p(A \mid B)$ of two random variables A and B defined over the respective state spaces S_A and S_B can be factorized in two ways:

$$p(A,B) = p(B \mid A)p(A) = p(A \mid B)p(B) \tag{3}$$

where $p(A \mid B)$ denotes the conditional probability of A given B: for each value of B, this is a probability distribution over A. Therefore $\Sigma_A\, p(A \mid B) = 1$ for any fixed B. The marginal distribution of a variable can be found from the joint distribution by summing over all states of the other variable, e.g.:

$$p(A) = \sum_{B \in S_B} p(A, B) = \sum_{B \in S_B} p(A|B)p(B) \tag{4}$$

It is understood that summation is to be replaced by integration if the state space is continuous. Bayes theorem results from Eq. 3 and Eq. 4 as:

$$\begin{aligned} p(B|A) &= \frac{p(A|B)p(B)}{\sum_{B \in S_B} p(A|B)p(B)} \\ &\propto p(A|B)p(B) \end{aligned} \tag{5}$$

$$\propto p(A \mid B)p(B) \tag{6}$$

The proportionality follows from the fact that the denominator does not depend on B, since B is already summed over. This rather simple looking "formula" has surprisingly far reaching consequences and can be directly applied to quantization. Consider the case that B is a score and S_B is the set of all possible scores. Let A be the observed performance. Then Eq 5 can be written as

$$p(\text{Score} \mid \text{Performance}) \propto p(\text{Performance} \mid \text{Score}) \times p(\text{Score}) \tag{7}$$

$$\text{posterior} \propto \text{likelihood} \times \text{prior} \tag{8}$$

The intuitive meaning of this equation can be better understood, if we think of quantization as a score selection problem. Since there is usually not a single true notation for a given performance, there will be several possibilities. The most reasonable choice is selecting the score c which has the highest probability given the performance t. Technically, we can name this probability distribution as the posterior $p(\mathrm{c} \mid \mathrm{t})$. The name posterior comes from the fact that this quantity appears after we observe the performance t. Note that the posterior is a function over c, and assigns a number to each notation after we fix t. We look for the notation c that maximizes this function. Bayes theorem tells us that the posterior is proportional to the product of two quantities, the likelihood $\mathrm{p}(\mathrm{t} \mid \mathrm{c})$ and the prior $p(\mathrm{c})$. Before we explain the interpretation of the likelihood and the prior in this context, we first summerize the ideas in compact notation as

$$p(\mathrm{c} \mid \mathrm{t}) \propto p(\mathrm{t} \mid \mathrm{c})\mathrm{p}(\mathrm{c}). \tag{9}$$

The best code vector c* is given by

$$\mathrm{c}^* = \operatorname*{argmax}_{\mathrm{c} \in C^K} p(\mathrm{c} \mid \mathrm{t}) \tag{10}$$

In technical terms. this problem is called a maximum a-posteriori (MAP) estimation problem and c* is called the MAP solution of this problem. We can also define a related quantity L (minus logposterior) and try to minimize this quantity rather then maximizing Eq. 9 directly. This simplifies the form of the objective function without changing the locations of local extrema since log(x) is a monotonically increasing function.

$$\mathcal{L} \;=\; -\log p(\mathbf{c}|\mathbf{t}) \propto -\log p(\mathbf{t}|\mathbf{c}) + \log \frac{1}{p(\mathbf{c})} \qquad (11)$$

The –log p(t | c) term in Equation 11, which is the minus logarithm of the likelihood, can be interpreted as a distance measuring how far the rhythm t is played from the perfect mechanical performance c. For example, if $p(t \mid c)$ would be of form $\exp(-(t-c)^2)$, then –log(t | c) would be $(t-c)^2$, the square of the distance from t to c. This quantity can be made arbitrary small if we use a very fine grid, however, as mentioned in the introduction section, this eventually would result in a complex notation. A suitable prior distribution prevents this undesired result. The log $\frac{1}{p(c)}$ term, which is large when the prior probability $p(c)$ of the codevector is small, can be interpreted as a complexity term, which penalizes complex notations. The best quantization balances the likelihood and the prior in an optimal way. The form of a performance model, i.e. the likelihood, can be in general very complicated. We can consider a subclass of performance models where the expressive timing is assumed to be an additive noise component which depends on c. The model is given by

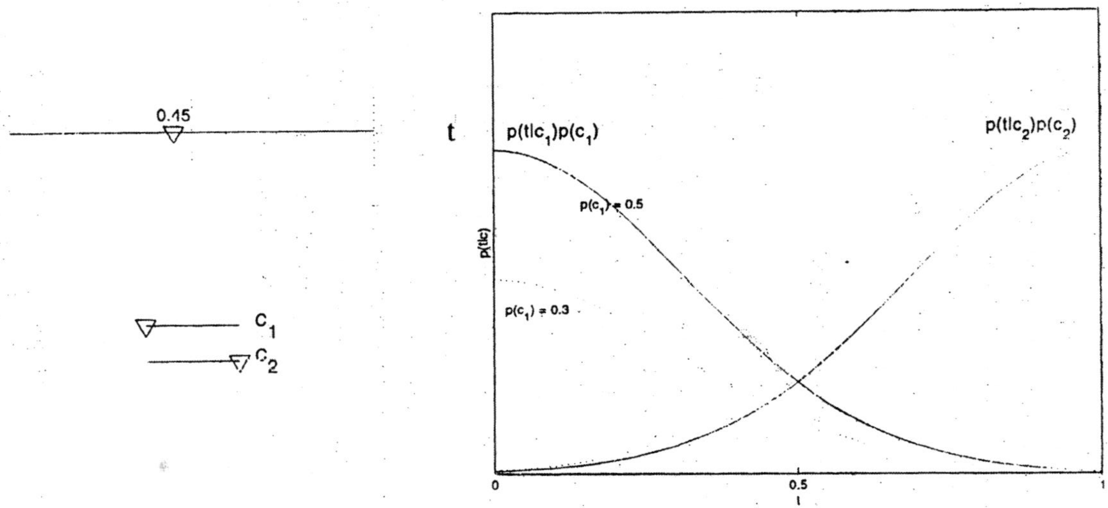

Figure 6. Quantization of an onset as Bayesian Inference. When $p(c) = [1/2, ½]$, at each t, the posterior $p(c \mid t)$ is proportional to the solid lines, and the decision boundary is at $t = 0.5$. When the prior is changed to $p(c) = [0.3, 0.7]$ (dashed), the decision boundary moves towards 0.

$$t_j = c_j + \varepsilon_j \tag{12}$$

where ε_j is a vector which denotes the expressive timing deviation. We can assume that ε is normal distributed with zero mean and covariance matrix $\Sigma\varepsilon(c)$, i.e. the correlation structure depends upon the code vector. We denote this distribution as $\varepsilon \sim N(0,\Sigma_\varepsilon(c))$. Note that when ε is the zero vector, $(\Sigma_\varepsilon(c).\ 0)$, the model reduces to a so-called "mechanical" performance.

Scalar Quantizer (Grid Quantizer)

We will now demonstrate on a simple example how these ideas are applied to quantization. Consider a one-onset segment t = [0.45]. Suppose we wish to quantize the onset to one of the endpoints, i.e. we are using effectively the codebook C = {[0], [1]}. The obvious strategy is to quantize the onset to the nearest grid point (e.g. a grid quantizer) and so the code-vector c = [0] is chosen as the winner.

The Bayesian interpretation of this decision can be demonstrated by computing the corresponding likelihood $p(t \mid c)$ and the prior $p(c)$. It is reasonable to assume that the probability of observing a performance t given a particular c decreases with the distance $|c - t|$. A probability distribution having this property is the normal distribution. Since there is only one onset, the dimension $K = 1$ and the likelihood is given by

$$p(t|c) = \frac{1}{\sqrt{2\pi}\sigma}\exp\left(-\frac{(t-c)^2}{2\sigma^2}\right)$$

If both codevectors are equally probable, a flat prior can be choosen, i.e. $p(c) = [1/2, ½]$. The resulting posterior $p(c \mid t)$

Figure 7. Two Onsets

(a) In lack of any other context, both onset sequences will sound the same. However the first notation is more complex

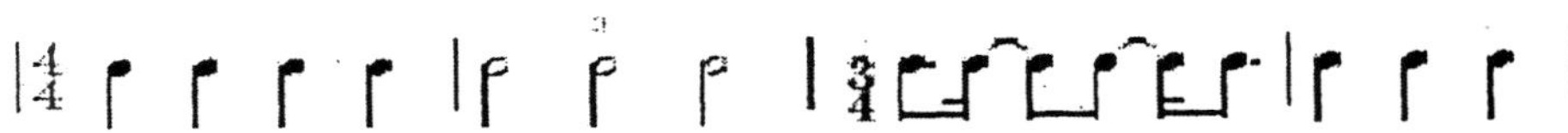

(b) Assumed time signature determines the complexity of a notation

Figure 9. Complexity of a notation

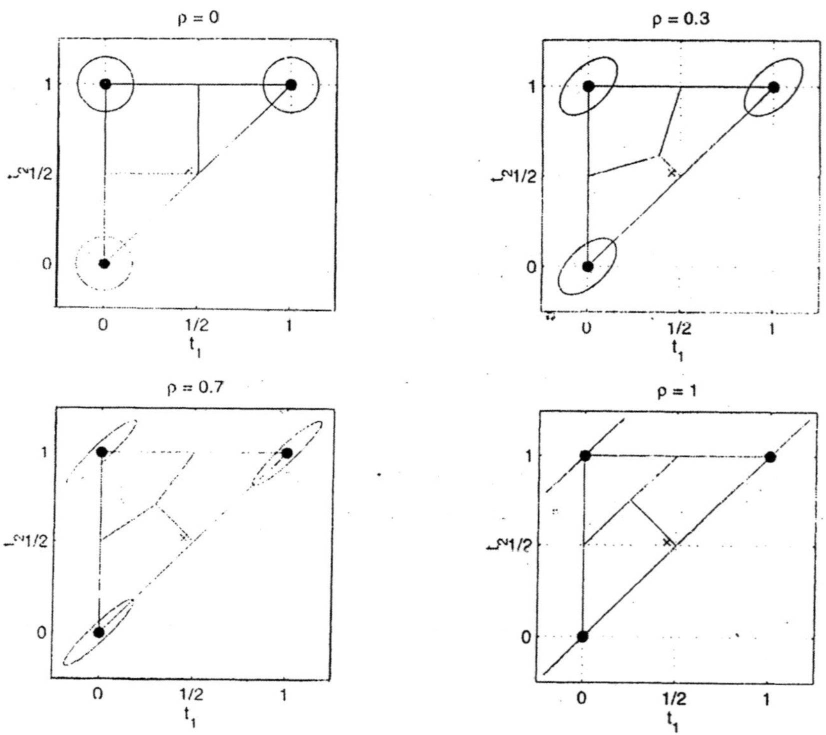

Figure 8. Tiling for choices of ρ and constant $p(c)$. Onset quantization (i.e. grid quantization) used by many commercial notation packages corresponds to the case where $\rho = 0$. IOI quantization appears when $\rho \to 1$. Note that different correlation structures imply different quantization decisions, not necessarily onset- or IOI-quantization. The cross

is plotted in 5. The decision boundary is at $t = 0.5$, where $p(c_1 | t) = p(c_2 | t)$. The winner is given as in Eq. 10

$$c^* = \underset{c}{\operatorname{argmax}}\ p(c | t)$$

Different quantization strategies can be implemented by changing the prior. For example if c = [0] is assumed to be less probable, we can choose another prior, e.g. $p(c)$= [0.3, 0.7]. In this case the decision boundary shifts from 0.5 towards 0 as expected.

Vector Quantizer

Assigning different prior probabilities to notations is only one way of implementing different quantization strategies. Further decision regions can be implemented by varying the conditional probability distribution $p(t | c)$. In this section we will demonstrate the flexibility of this approach for quantization of groups of onsets.

Consider the segment t = [0.45, 0.52] depicted in Figure 7. Suppose we wish to quantize the onsets again only to one of the endpoints, i.e. we are using effectively the codebook C ={[0, 0], [0, 1], [1, 1]}. The simplest strategy is to quantize every onset to the nearest grid point (e.g. a grid quantizer) and so the code-vector c = [0, 1] is the winner. However, this result might be not very desirable, since the inter-onset interval (IOI) has increased more than 14 times, (from 0.07 to 1). It is less likely that a human transcriber would make this choice since it is perceptually not very realistic. We could try to solve this problem by employing another strategy: If $\delta = t_2 - t_1 > 0.5$, we use the code-vector [0, 1]. If $\delta = 0.5$, we quantize to one of the code-vectors [0, 0] or [1, 1] depending upon the average of the onsets. In this strategy the quantization of [0.45, 0.52] is [0, 0].

Although considered to be different in the literature, both strategies are just special cases which can be derived from Eq. 11 bymaking specific choices about the correlation structure (covariance matrix Σ_ε) of expressive deviations. The first strategy assumes that the expressive deviations of both onsets are independent of each other. This is apparently not a very realistic model for timing deviations in music. The latter corresponds to the case where onsets are linearly dependent; it was assumed that $t_2 = t_1 + \delta$ and only δ and t_1 were considered in quantization. This latter operation is merely a linear transformation of onset times and is implied by the implicit assumption about the correlation structure. Indeed some quantization models in the literature focus directly on IOI's rather then on onset times.

More general strategies, which can be quite difficult to state verbally, can be specified by different choices of Σ_ε and $p(c)$. Some examples for the choice $\Sigma_\varepsilon = \begin{pmatrix} 1 & \rho \\ \rho & 1 \end{pmatrix}$ and constant $p(c)$ are depicted in Figure 8. The ellipses denote the set of points which are equidistant from the center and the covariance matrix Σ_ε determines their orientation. The lines denote the decision boundaries. The interested reader is referred to for a discussion of the underlying theory.

Likelihood for the Vector Quantizer

For modeling the expressive timing ε in a segment containing K onsets, we propose the following parametric form for the covariance matrix

$$\Sigma_\varepsilon(c) = \sigma^2 \begin{pmatrix} 1 & \rho_{1,2} & \cdots & \rho_{1,K} \\ \rho_{1,2} & 1 & \rho_{n,m} & \vdots \\ \vdots & \rho_{n,m} & \ddots & \vdots \\ \rho_{1,K} & \cdots & \cdots & 1 \end{pmatrix} \qquad (13)$$

where

$$p_{n,m} = \eta \exp(-\frac{\lambda^2}{2}(c_m - c_n)^2) \tag{14}$$

Here, c_m and c_n are two distinct entries (grid points) of the code vector c. In Eq. 14, η, is a parameter between -1 and 1, which adjust the amount of correlation strength between two onsets. The other parameter λ adjusts the correlation as a function of the distance between entries in the code vector. When λ is zero, all entries are correlated by the equal amount, namely η. When λ is large, the correlation approaches rapidly to zero with increasing distance.

This particular choice for $p(\varepsilon)$ reflects the observation that onsets, which are close to each other, tend to be highly correlated. This can be interpreted as follows: if the onsets are close to each other, it is easier to quantify the IOI and then select an appropriate translation for the onsets by keeping the IOI constant. If the grid points are far away from each other, the correlation tends to be weak (or sometimes negative), which suggests that onsets are quantized independently of each other.

Prior for the Vector Quantizer

The choice of the prior $p(c)$ reflects the complexity of codevector c=[c_i]. A complexity measure from a probabilistic point of view. In this measure, the complexity of a codevector c = [c_i] is determined by the depth of c_i with respect to the beat (See Eq. 2) and the time signature of the piece. See Figure 9. The prior probability of a code-vector with respect to S is chosen as

$$p(c \mid S) \propto e^{-\gamma d(c \mid S)} \tag{15}$$

(a) In lack of any other context, both onset sequences will sound the same. However the first notation is more complex

(b) Assumed time signature determines the complexity of a notation

Note that if $\gamma = 0$, then the depth of the codevector has no influence upon its complexity. If it is large, (e.g. $\gamma \approx 1$) only very simple rhythms get reasonable probability mass. practice, we choose $\gamma \approx 0.02$. This choice is also in accordance with the intuition and experimental evidence: simplerrhythms are more frequently used then complex ones. The marginal prior of a codevector is found by summing out all possible subdivision schemes.

$$p(c) = \sum_{S} p(c|S)p(S) \tag{16}$$

where $p(S)$ is the prior distribution of subdivision schemas. For example, one can select possible subdivision schemas as $S_1 = [2, 2, 2]$, $S_2 = [3, 2, 2]$, $S_3 = [2, 3, 2]$. If we have a preference towards the time signature (4/4), the prior can be taken as $p(S) = [1/2, ¼, ¼]$. In general, this choice should reflect the relative frequency of time signatures. We propose the following form for the prior of $S = [s_i]$

Table 1: $w(s_i)$

s_i	2	3	5	7	11	13	17	o/w
$w(s_i)$	0	1	2	3	4	5	6	8

(a) *Stimulus*

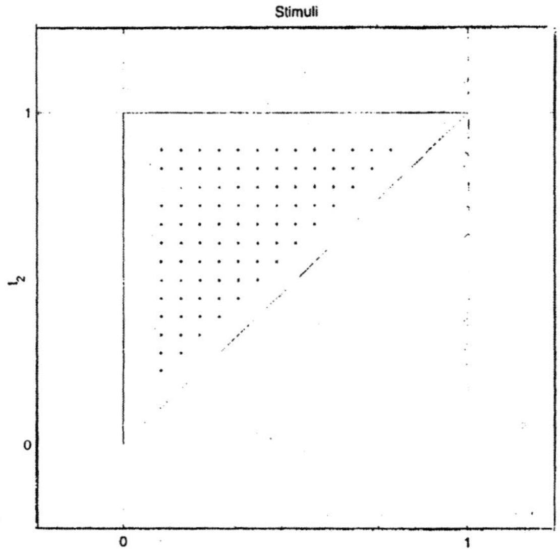

(b) Stimuli for the perception experiment. The dots denote the rhythms t_k, where k = 1 . . . 91. Grid spacing is 56ms.

Figure 10. Stimulus of the Perception Task

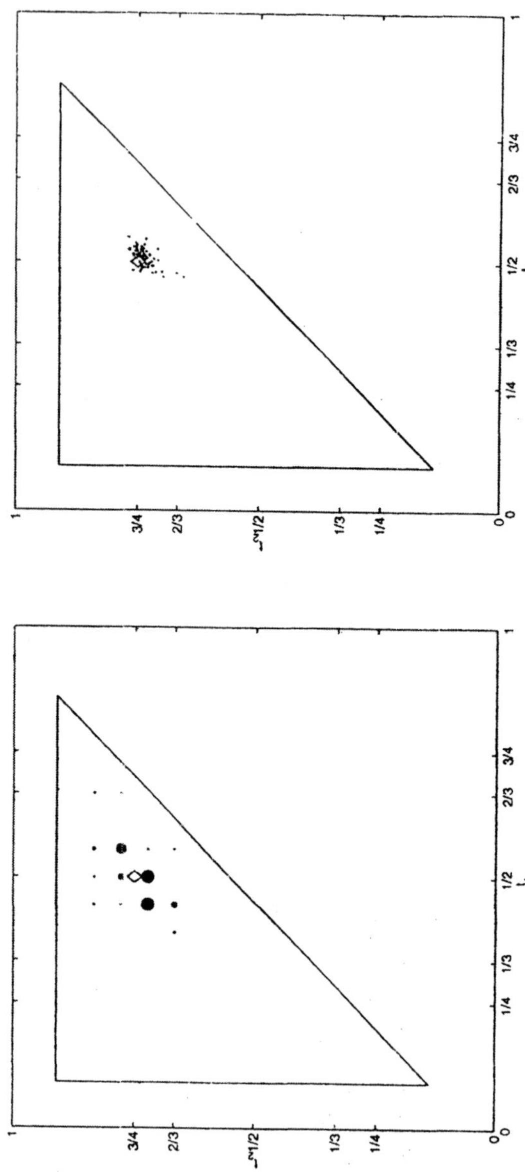

(a) Perception

(b) Production

*Figure 11. Perception and Production of the rhythm [2 1 1] (c = [0.5 0.75]). The **diamond** corresponds to the mechanical performance. In 11(a), the size of the circles is proportional to the **estimated** posterior $q(c_j \mid t_k)$. In 11(b), the dots correspond to performances of the rhythm.*

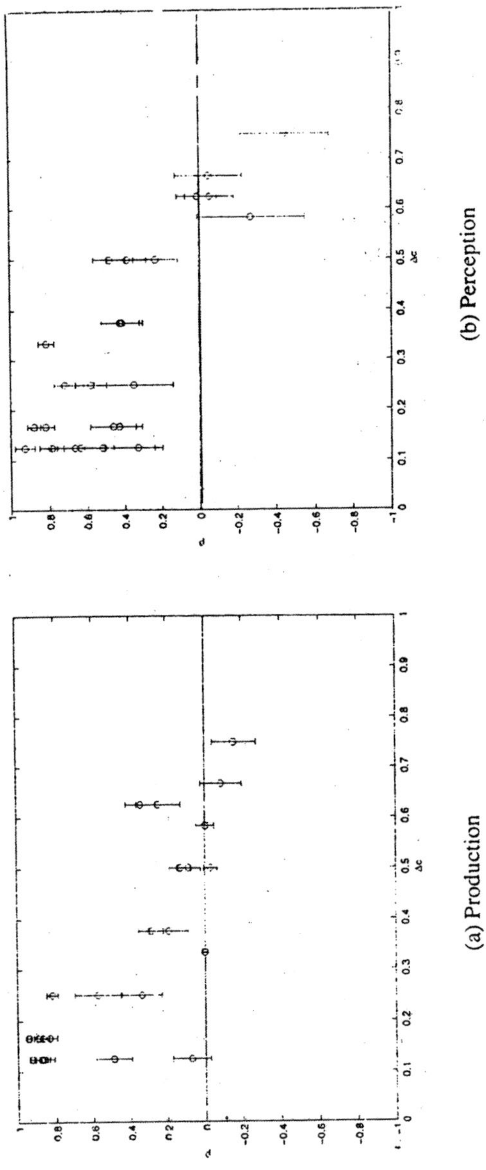

Figure 12. Estimated correlation coefficient as a function of $\Delta c = (c_2 - c_1)$ on all subject responses.

$$p(S) \propto e^{-\xi \sum_i w(s_i)} \tag{17}$$

where $w(s_i)$ is a simple weighting function given in Table 1. This form prefers subdivisions by small prime numbers, which reflects the intuition that rhythmic subdivisions by prime numbers such as 7 or 11 are far less common then subdivisions such as 2 or 3. The parameter ? distributes probability mass over the primes. When $\xi = 0$, all subdivision schemata are equally probable. As $\xi \to \infty$, only subdivisions with $s_i = 2$ have non-zero probability.

Verification of the Model

To choose the likelihood $p(t \mid c)$ and the prior $p(c)$ in a way which is perceptually meaningful, we analyzed data obtained from an psychoacoustical experiment where ten well trained subjects (nine conservatory students and a conservatory professor) have participated. The experiment consisted of a perception task and a production task.

Perception Task

In the perception task the subjects were asked to transcribe 91 different *stimuli*. These rhythms consisted of four onsets $t_0 \ldots t_3$ where t_0 and t_3 were fixed and occur exactly on the beat (Figure 10). First a beat is provided to subjects (count in), and then the stimulus is repeated 3 times with an empty bar between each repetition. Subjects were allowed to use any notation as a response and listen to the stimulus as much as they wanted. In total, subjects used 125 different notations, from which 57 were used only once and 42 are used more than three times. An example is depicted in Figure 11(a). From this data, we can estimate the posterior as

$$q(\mathbf{c}_j|\mathbf{t}_k) = n_k(\mathbf{c}_j) / \sum_j n_k(\mathbf{c}_j)$$

where $n_k(c_j)$ denotes the number of times the stimulus t_k is associated with the notation c_j.

Production Task

In the production task the subjects are asked to perform the rhythms that they have notated in the perception task. An example is shown in Figure 11(a). For each notation c_j we assume a gaussian distribution where

$$\hat{q}(\mathbf{t}|\mathbf{c}_j) = \mathcal{N}(\mu_j, \Sigma_j) \tag{18}$$

The mean and the covariance matrix are estimated from production data by

$$\mu_j = \frac{1}{N_j} \sum_k \mathbf{t}_{k,j} \tag{19}$$

$$\Sigma_j = \frac{1}{N_j - 1} \sum_{k,l} (\mathbf{t}_{k,j} - \mu_j)(\mathbf{t}_{l,j} - \mu_j)^T \tag{20}$$

where $t_{k,j}$ is the k'th performance of c_j and N_j is the total count of these performances in the data set. The correlation coefficient and the estimated error bars are depicted in Figure 12, where we observe that the correlation decreases with increasing distance between onsets.

Estimation of model parameters

The probabilistic model $p(\mathrm{c} \mid \mathrm{t})$ can be fitted by minimizing the "distance" to the estimated target $q(\mathrm{c} \mid \mathrm{t})$. A well known distance measure between two probability distributions is the Kullback-Leiber divergence which is given as

$$\mathrm{KL}(q||p) = \int d\mathrm{x} q(\mathrm{x}) \log \frac{q(\mathrm{x})}{p(\mathrm{x})} \tag{21}$$

The integration is replaced by summation for discrete probability distributions. It can be shown that $\mathrm{KL}(q \mid \mid p) = 0$ for any q, p and vanishes if and only if $q = p$.

KL divergence can be interpreted as a "weighted average" of the function $\log \frac{q(x)}{p(x)}$ with respect to weighting function $q(x)$. If $q(x)$ and $p(x)$ are significantly different for some x (for which $q(x)$ is sufficently large), the KL divergence would be also large and would indicate that the distributions are different. On the other if the distributions have almost the same shape, $\frac{q(x)}{p(x)} \approx 1$ for all x, and KL would be close to zero since $\log(1) = 0$.

The KL divergence is an appropriate measure for the rhythm quantization problem. Many stimuli, subjects give different responses and consequently it is difficult to choose just one "correct" notation for a particular stimulus. In other words, the target distribution $q(c \mid t)$ has its mass distributed among several codevectors. By minimizing the KL divergence one can approximate the posterior distribution by preserving this intrinsic uncertainty.

The optimization problem for the perception task can be set as

$$\min . \ KL(q(c \mid t)s(t) \,||\, p(c \mid t)s(t)) \tag{22}$$

$$\text{s.t. } \sigma > 0$$

$$-1 < \eta < 1$$

$$\lambda, \xi, \gamma \text{ unconstrained}$$

where $s(t) \propto \sum_k \delta(t - t_k)$ is the distribution of the stimuli. This is a distribution, which has positive mass only on the stimuli points tk. This measure forces the model to fit the estimated posterior at each stimulus point t_k. We note that

$$p(c|t) = \frac{p(t|c;\sigma,\lambda,\eta)p(c:\xi,\gamma)}{\sum_c p(t|c;\sigma,\lambda,\eta)p(c;\xi,\gamma)} \tag{23}$$

This is in general a rather difficult optimization problem due to the presence of the denominator. Nevertheless, since the model has only five free parameters, we were able to minimize Eq. 22 by a standard BFGS Quasi-Newton algorithm (MATLAB function fminu).

Results of Experiments

The model is trained on a subset of the perception data by minimizing Eq. 22. In the training, 112 different notations (out of 125 that the subjects used in total), are used which could be generated by one of the subdivision schemas in Table 2. To identify the relative importance of model parameters, we optimized Eq. 22 by clamping some parameters. In the experiment there are different labeling are used as follows:

Model-I is the "complete" model, where all parameters are unclamped.

Model- II is an onset quantizer ($\Sigma = \sigma^2 I$), where only prior parameters are active.

Model-III is (almost) an IOI quantizer where the correlation between onsets is taken to be ? = 0.98.

Model-IV is similar to Model I with the simplification that the covariance matrix is constant for all codevectors. Since $\lambda = 0$, $\rho = \eta$.

Model-V is an onset quantizer with a flat prior, similar to the quantizers used in commercial notation packages and Model-VI has only the performance model parameters active.

In Model-VII, the parameters of the performance model $p(t \mid c)$ are estimated from the production data. The model is fitted to the production data $\hat{q}$ by minimizing

$$\mathrm{KL}(\hat{q}(t|c)q(c)||p(t|c)q(c)) \tag{24}$$

where $q(c_j) = \Sigma_k n_k(c_j) / \Sigma_{k,j} n_k(c_j)$, i.e. a histogram obtained by counting the subject responses in the perception experiment. Although approximating the posterior at stimuli points is our objective in the optimization, for automatic transcription we are also interested into the classification performance. At each stimuli t_k, if we select the response which the subjects have chosen the most, i.e. $c^{*}_{k} = \arg\max_{c} q(c \mid t_k)$, we can achieve maximum possible classification rate on this dataset, which is given as

$$\mathrm{CR}_{\mathrm{Target}} = \frac{n_k(c^{*}_{k})}{Z} \times 100 \qquad (25)$$

Here, $Z = \sum_{k,c} n_k(c^{*}_{k})$, the total number of measurements. Similarly, if we select the codevector with the highest predicted posterior $c^{*}_{k} = \arg\max_{c} p(c \mid t_k)$ at each stimulus, we achieve the classification rate of the Model denoted as CRModel. The results are shown in Table 3. The clamped parameters are tagged with an '=' sign. The results are for a codebook consisting of 112 codevectors, which the subjects have used in their responses and could have been generated by one of the subdivisions in Table 2.

Model-I performs the best in terms of the KL divergence, however the marginal benefit obtained by choosing a correlation structure, which decreases with increasing onset distances (obtained by varying λ) is rather small. One can achieve almost the same performance by having a constant correlation between onsets (Model-IV). By comparing Model-IV to Models II and III, we can say that under the given prior distribution the subjects are employing a quantization strategy, which is somehow between a pure onset quantization and IOI-quantization.

Table 2. Subdivisions

i	S_i
1	[2, 2, 2, 2]
2	[3, 2, 2]
3	[3, 3, 2]

4	[5, 2]
5	[7, 2]
6	[11]
7	[13]
8	[5, 3]
9	[17]
10	[7, 3]

Table 3. Optimization Results. CRTarget = 48.0. Values tagged with a '=' are fixed during optimization. Values estimated from the production experiment are tagged with a '!'.

Model		Prior		Likelihood			Results
Label	ξ	γ	σ	λ	η	KL	CR_{Model}/CR_{Target}
I	1.35	0.75	0.083	2.57	0.66	1.30	77.1
II	1.34	0.75	0.086	= 0	= 0	1.41	71.3
III	1.33	0.77	0.409	= 0	= 0.98	1.96	51.4
IV	1.34	0.74	0.084	= 0	0.39	1.34	75.3
V	= 0	= 0	0.085	= 0	= 0	1.92	29.7
VI	= 0	= 0	0.083	2.54	0.66	1.89	32.7
VII	1.43	0.79	! 0.053	! 3.07	! 0.83	1.89	84.3

The choice of the prior is very important which can be seen from the results of Model-V and Model-VI, which perform poor due to the flat prior assumption. Model-VII suggests that for this data set the perception and production processes are different. This is mainly due to the spread parameter s, which is smaller for the production data. The interpretation of this behavior is that subjects deviate less from the mechanical mean in a performance situation.

However, this might be due to the fact that performances were carried out in lack of any context, which forces the subjects to concentrate on exact timing. It is interesting to note that almost the same correlation structure is reserved in both experiments. This suggests that there is some relation between the production and perception process. The classification performance of Model-VII is surprisingly high; it predicts the winner accurately. However the prediction of the posterior is poor, which can be seen by the high KL divergence score.

For visualization of the results we employ an interpolation procedure to estimate the target posterior at other points than the stimuli. The rhythm space can be tiled into regions of rhythms, which are quantized to the same codevector. Estimated tiles from experimental data are depicted in Figure 13(a).

In practice, it is not feasible to identify explicitly a subset of all possible codevectors, which have non-zero prior probability. For example, the number of notations which can be generated by subdivisions in Table 2 is 886 whereas the subjects used only 112 of these as a response. This subset must be predicted by the model as well. A simple grid quantizer tries to approximate this subset by assigning a constant prior probability to codevectors only up to a certain threshold depth.

The proposed prior model can be contrasted to this schema in that it distributes the probabilitymass in a perceptually more realistic manner. To visualize this, we generated a codebook consisting of all 886 codevectors. The tilings generated by Model-I and Model-V are depicted in Figure 13(b) and 13(c). To compare the tilings, we estimate the ratio

$$\text{Match} = \frac{A_{match}}{A_{total}} \times 100 \tag{26}$$

where A_{match} is the area where the model matches with the target and A_{total} is the total area of the triangle. Note that this is just a crude approximation to the classification performance under the assumption that all rhythms are equally probable. The results are shown in Table. 4.

Table 4: Amount of match between tilings generated by the target and models

	I	II	III	IV	V	VI	VII
Match	58.8	53.5	36.1	59.0	3.8	3.1	56.7

5

Rhythmic Rock Music

In the 1980s and 1990s, after two and a half decades of resistance, American colleges and universities at last moved toward accepting rock as a legitimate subject of study. As late as 1976, Robert Pielke, author of *You Say You Want* a Revolution, requested permission from George Mason University to teach amultidisciplinary course in rock and was turned down. In just a few years, however, Pielke began seeing attitudes and policies change. Of rock's eventual recognition, he explains: "The significance of rock music as a cultural phenomenon has long been recognized even by its most ardent detractors. Thus the scholarly community has been unable to avoid its impact." Yet the significance of rock, not just as a generic cultural phenomenon but as music, has not been universally recognized; Pielke's proposed class was to have emphasized only its history, social impact, and meaning. Academic music circles have been much slower to acknowledge rock. As Andrew Chester wrote:

> "The acceptance of a cultural definition of the object of criticism [rock] leads inevitably to a cultural as opposed to an aesthetic criticism. Musical form and musical practice are studied as an aspect of social relations, and significance is determined by social, not musical, criteria."

This exclusion of rock from music curriculums is changing, albeit slowly.

Many college music educators, however, assume that its inclusion is merely to provide accessible examples of traditional structures, a result of a second assumption: that rock stubbornly adheres in the most unsophisticated way to the simplest principles of the common practice. Christopher Gordon's Form and Content in Commercial Music, for instance, teaches standard common-practice chord progressions and claims that they are valid for popular music, his list of which explicitly includes rock. Stefan Kostka expresses the belief clearly:

> "Perhaps the healthiest and most vital continuation of traditional harmony was in the 'popular' music of the twentieth century, which includes everything from Broadway musicals to folk music to jazz to rock music."

The assumption that rock is simply a crude extension of common-practice music is false. Rock, in fact, exhibits melodic, rhythmic, and harmonic characteristics that are not found in any other musical style. This is not to say that rock was created in a musical vacuum; no musical style ever is. The stylistic norms of rock depend on ideas from the common practice, but differ from common-practice norms in crucial ways. An understanding of the typical patterns peculiar to rock is essential to the analysis of individual rock pieces, and vital to the explanation of this music's power as a vehicle of expression for the culture that claims it as its own.

Few have attempted to establish the stylistic norms of rock. As mentioned before, most of the academics interested in rock have taken a sociological approach, whereas music scholars have, in general, not been forced until recently to accept its legitimacy. Even within the circle of scholars who deal with the musical aspects of the genre, however, a further factor has limited work on defining normal structures: the rise of the notion that traditional theoretical models, because of inherent biases, cannot accommodate or are inappropriate for dealing with the music.

For instance, Robert Walser, in his *Running with the Devil,* states the deconstructionist view that traditional, formalist analysis of any music, including heavy metal, the subject of the book, is worthless unless it is used to reveal the political message inherent in the act of composition. In his words, structural analysis is "useful only if it is grounded culturally and historically and if it acknowledges its interests forthrightly." Charles Keil, speaking of unnotated music in general, gives a nodding acknowledgment to the value of musical analysis but says that it "will not go far in accounting for expression." Approaches like Walser's arbitrarily deny the possibility of value in purely musical analysis, while those like Keil's simply bypass aspects of form, harmony, and the like in their concentration on other, less formal aspects.

As Richard Middleton, author of *Studying Popular Music,* puts it: "There is in fact a common tendency for the 'critique of musicology' to go too far. . . . By associating musicology as such with classical music and completely separating that sphere from the sphere of popular music, [the critic of traditional musicology] throws away any chance for musical analysis. Chester's lament that the prevailingly "patronizing" attitude that 'precludes the possibility of an aesthetic based on the specificity of rock as a musical genre" leaves us with little in the way of musical analysis of rock is as true today as it was in 1970, when he expressed it. Perhaps the clearest summary of the arguments against a musicological approach to the analysis of rock is offered by Roy Shuker, in his *Understanding*

Popular Music. Shuker points out that few musicological, structural analyses of rock have been published; he lists only three works. Although he acknowledges the need for more research in this area, he feels that it should be subject to severe limitations because of certain flaws in such an approach:

1) The musicological approach excludes the sociological approach.
2) No one but musicologists would understand these analyses.
3) Structural analyses of rock pieces do not align with the way listeners and composers of rock talk about the music. Each of these criticisms deserves a response.

As to the first, Shuker says, "The obvious difficulty with the musicological approach is that the preoccupation with the [musical] text in and of itself omits any consideration of music as a social phenomenon." Using that kind of argument, we could simply turn the tables and say that the obvious difficulty with the sociological approach is that its preoccupation with the social context omits any consideration of music as music.

As to the second, the "pretentious" language of the musicologist's analyses, Shuker contends that the overspecialized terminology "erects barriers to the musically nonliterate" and that "there is much to be said for utilizing musicology, provided that such analysis is kept easily accessible to those who have never encountered music theory." Such a limitation is unacceptable if knowledge and discourse are to advance. If medical research, for instance, were limited to works easily accessible to those unfamiliar with chemistry and biology, we would see fewer advances in that field. And if sociological analyses of rock were limited to works easily accessible to those who have never studied sociology, academic treatments of rock would be scarce indeed. The reader must bear some of the burden for the resolution of the disparity between the sophistication of the written argument and the ability of the reader to understand it. If the author must always descend to the reader's level, the reader's level, and the state of public knowledge, will never rise.

As to the third, the disparity between the concerns theorists have about this music and the way players and listeners think about it, Shuker says, "Traditional musicology neglects the social context, emphasises the transcription of the music (the score), and elevates harmonic and rhythmic structure to pride of place as an evaluative criterion. Rock, on the other hand, emphasises interpretation through performance, and is received primarily in terms of the body and emotions rather than as pure text." The reasons for raising this critique, which is not unique to Shuker, are puzzling. In other fields, this disparity seems to be taken for granted as normal. In fact, this disparity might be said to define what most research is all about. Five-year-olds cannot express a set of grammatical rules consistently, but this does not stop Noam Chomsky from seeking the rules that children as well as adults seem to follow. That the producers and receivers of language do not normally think in terms of grammar does not invalidate the research. Most people do not know why eggs are nutritious, and chickens know even less about the matter, but the ignorance of producer and consumer does not invalidate research in biochemistry.

Research means attempting to discover new knowledge, and if the object of some particular research project is an aspect of human activity, then by definition a disparity will arise between the way the average human agent understands her activity and the way the researcher understands it. Whether the subjects of the research adopt the researcher's mode of understanding is irrelevant because although that mode may not benefit some people (e.g., some pitchers think about physiology whereas others think only about focus or the batter), improvement of skills is usually not the purpose of research.

But in fact harmonies and scales are not as irrelevant to rock composers as Shuker assumes. Listening to many of the songs by such composers as Buddy Holly, Brian Wilson, George Harrison, Carly Simon, Billy Joel, and Sting makes it clear that they are indeed interested in harmony. As for casual listeners, most may not think of such things as important; but anyone who can hum the tune of a favourite song or detect a wrong note in a dance band's rendition of a rock standard (even without being able to explain that ability) merely lacks terminology and trained discernment.

Most of this literature concentrates on analyses of individual works; Middleton and Steussy contribute toward establishing stylistic norms, but in each case the treatment is sporadic and forms only part of a work with a broader or different overall topic. What is needed then is a foundation of ideas about stylistic norms, something akin to what the typical undergraduate textbook does for earlier tonal music.

Stylistic analysis simplifies complexities and ignores exceptions; it is the nature of generalizations to do so. But generalizations are nonetheless useful. Without an established understanding of the stylistic norms of rock, we run the risk of two weightier errors: first, of underappreciating the genre because of a mistaken belief in its adherence to centuries-old standards; the second, of being surprised by structures common in the genre and of reading too much into their local significance (under the mistaken assumption that these standard structures are moments of creative transcendence), while missing other, truly significant structures or events. A note on the source of examples: in the case of practically every piece of rock music, if a composer's score exists (and in many cases no scores ever existed), it is unavailable to the general public.

The commercial piano-vocal arrangements available through publishing houses are usually derived from attempted transcriptions of recordings. Such arrangements therefore have no direct connection to any score or instructions given by the composer to the performers. And in fact, because such arrangements are targeted to consumers of a particular level of ability and because of the difficulties of notating the often intricate melodies of the music, published versions often differ substantially from the recorded song. Abstraction and generalization are facts of life; to avoid them entirely would necessitate the end of communication.

Prase Rhythm

Because musical pitches function in time, it is difficult to discuss the function of tones or harmonies without an understanding of the temporal framework of a style. Rock borrows standard structures from earlier song styles, although it often alters and combines them in new ways. Defining normal lengths in terms of measures can be problematic in either of these bodies of music. Because performers and listeners of both rock and earlier folk music depend so much more on aural tradition than on scores, in many pieces it is impossible to determine objectively how long a measure is or how many beats a measure contains. One listener might count "1-2-1-2" where another would

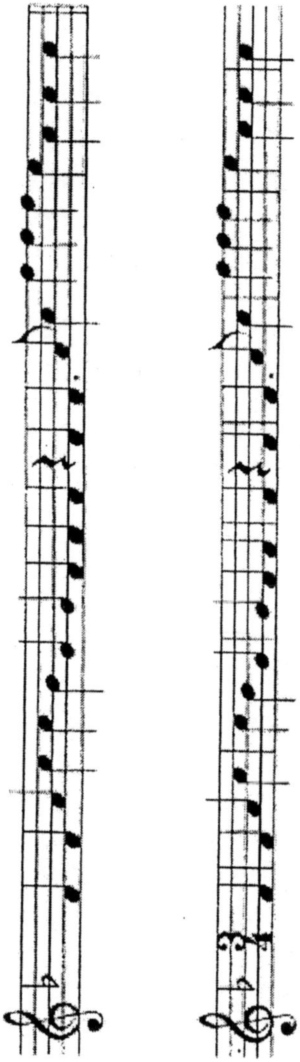

1. Determination of the length of a measure in primarily nonnotated music by examination of cadence.

2. Different metrical interpretations of "Daisy." The ratio of melodic motion to melodic rest remains constant: 3:1.

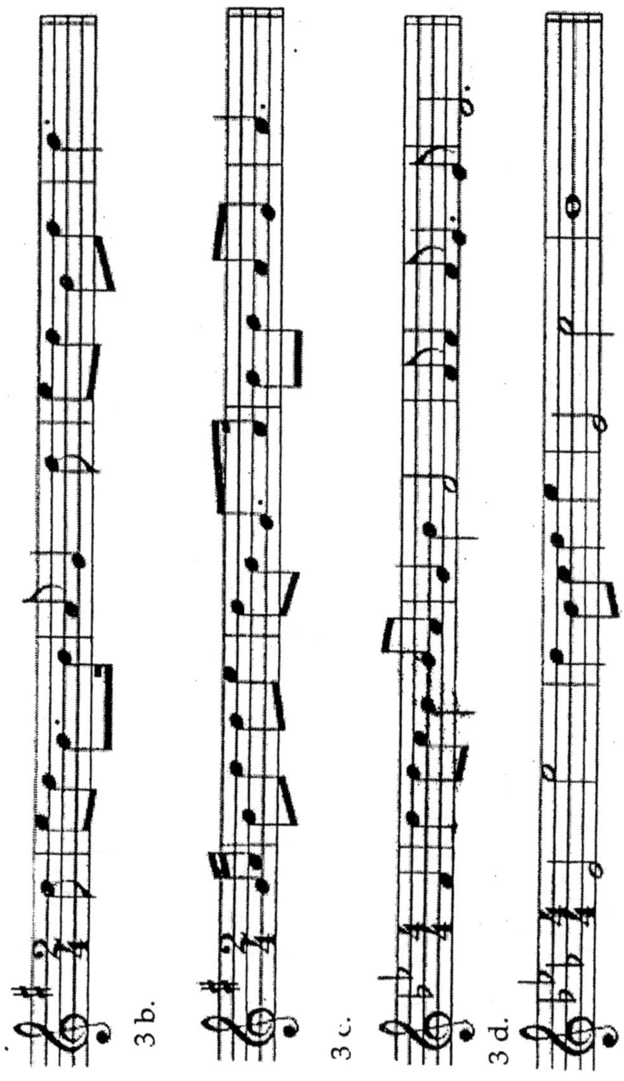

3. Elements of standard phrase rhythm in folk and popular song before the rock era: (a) "Cindy," (b) "Oh, Susanna!" (c) "Tenting To-night," and (d) "Over The Rainbow."

count "1-2-3-4." Or one might count 1-and-2-and" where another counts "1-2-1-2." This problem is not insurmountable, however. In much traditional music, for instance, we could simply stipulate that a measure is the amount of time between the last strong beat of one phrase and the first strong beat of the next. Therefore, in "Betsy From Pike," while a transcriber might use either a moderately paced compound meter or a fast triple meter, the stipulated method would favour the triple meter. In rock, steady backbeats (beats 2 and 4) on the snare drum usually help make the length of a measure clear.

Determination of the length of a measure in primarily nonnotated music by examination of cadence. Sometimes, however, we may find it more useful to avoid the term measure altogether and simply talk in terms of relative length of time, referring to the ratio of the lengths of the spans of melodic motion and of melodic rest. The term melodic motion refers to the period of rhythmic activity within a given phrase; it lasts from the beginning of a phrase to the attack time of its last (metrically accented) note. The term melodic rest refers to the period of rhythmic inactivity normally associated with cadences; it lasts from the attack time of the last note of one phrase to the beginning of the next phrase.

Therefore, the melodic rest at the end of a phrase normally incorporates a long note as well as a literal rest. According to these definitions, in the case of a four-measure unit with the melodic cadence on the fourth downbeat, such as in "Betsy From Pike" or "Daisy," the span of melodic motion is three times as long as the span of melodic rest. When speaking of ratios in this way, listeners may disagree on what span of time to call a beat or on how many beats make up a measure while still agreeing on the basic temporal recipe of the phrase, which in each of the examples above is three parts melodic motion followed by one part melodic rest.

Folk songs, nursery songs, nineteenth- and early twentieth-century popular songs, and the like normally exhibit a regular unit length of four measures. The division of these units is normally marked by a cadence-in the literal sense of that word: a falling off of melodic motion or of rhythmic energy, or in simpler terms, a long last note. This clear delineation of phrases by means of a melodic rest comes as no surprise; this kind of music is primarily vocal, and the tunes simply need to provide the singer with some breathing time at regular intervals.

In a four-measure phrase, the cadence, or long note, normally comes on the downbeat of the fourth measure. Placement of the cadential note on the fourth downbeat creates a motion-to-rest ratio of 3:1. Again, quite naturally, the pattern perfectly suits the nature of the music: because the music is primarily vocal music, to preserve continuity the melody needs to be active as long as possible, given the singer's need to breathe.

When music moves in a regular series of four-bar units, many listeners perceive a phenomenon known as hypermeter-that is, the a regular pattern of accents in the downbeats of successive measures. Theorists have long debated how downbeat accents are arranged in these typical four-measure groups: do they alternate strong-weak-strong-weak as the accents do in a four-beat measure, or does the importance of the cadence result in a weak-strong-weakstrong pattern-or even a more subtle pattern such as strong-weak-weakstrong?

4. Length of morphological unit as defined by regular repetition of (a) the harmonic pattern in the Bee Gees' "I Started A Joke" and (b) the instrumental hook in Chicago's "25 Or 6 To 4."

4 a.

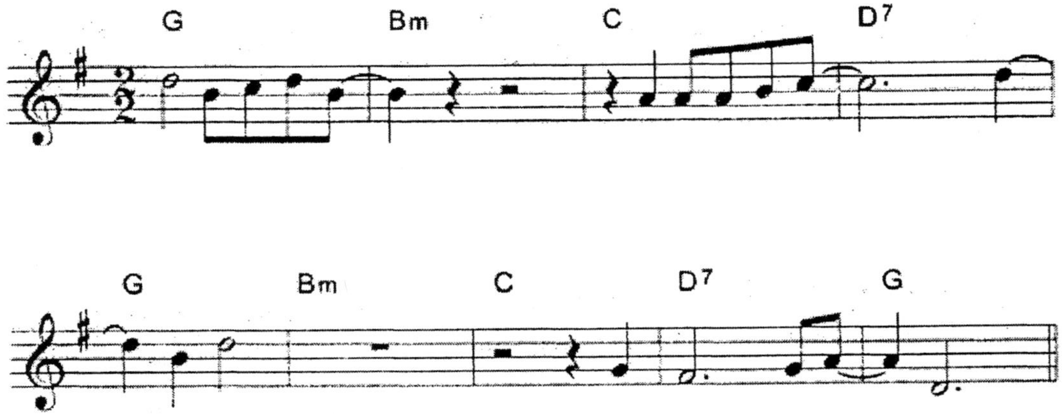

4 b.

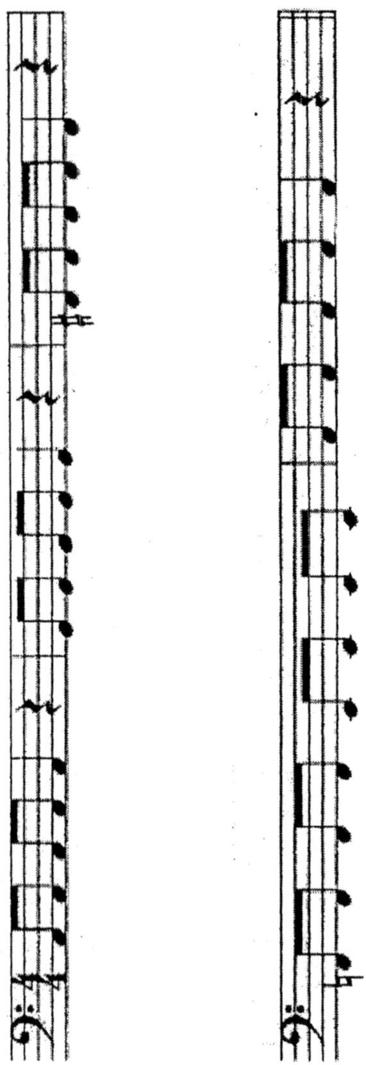

5. Motion-to-rest ratio of 1:1 in .rst hypermeasure of Chuck Berry's "Roll Over, Beethoven," as indicated in (a) transcription and (b) a metrical chart.

5 a.

5 b.

1 2 3 4 | 2 2 3 4 | 3 2 3 4 | 4 2 3 4 | 1 2 3 4 | 2 2 3 4 | 3 2 3 4 | 4 2 3 4 |

William Rothstein agrees:

> Because of the difference between phrase structure and hypermeter, phrases-especially the simpler ones-can end very comfortably in relatively weak metrical positions, for example in the last bar of a four-bar hypermeasure. When a phrase ends in this way, there is no contradiction between the weak metrical position and the arrival of an important tonal goal (presumably a cadence). This is because the experience of "accent" - of heightened importance-that is involved in reaching a tonal goal is not the same as the experience of a metrical accent-the impulse felt upon reaching a metrical downbeat. . . . Rhythmic theorists of our time have often found themselves unable to follow hypermeter even in simple instances because they have been paralyzed by their confusion of categories.

When a piece consists mostly of four-bar groups, then, each of those forms a hypermeasure. The downbeats of the four measures relate to one another in the same way the four beats in a regular measure do: strong-weak-strongweak. As a result, the odd-numbered measures in a four-bar hypermeasure can be called strong measures, and the downbeats of these measures strong downbeats. In the same way, the even-numbered measures are weak measures, and their downbeats weak downbeats.

Rock normally proceeds in four-bar units just as traditional songs do. In most rock songs, the rigid adherence to this standard encourages the perception of hypermeter and contributes to the widely acknowledged perception of a natural, steady-even driving-beat.

Rock and traditional song, therefore, share the prevalence of the four-bar unit. But the similarity ends there. Melodic cadences in rock do not contribute as regularly to the delineation of these units as they do in traditional music. Instead, the perception of these units normally arises as a

6. 2 + 2 model in Sting's "If I Ever Lose My Faith In You."

result of repetitive patterns in the instrumental accompaniment, for instance, the regular recurrence of tonic harmony or of an instrumental hook every four (or two or eight) measures. (See example 4.) Because rock depends less on the vocal phrase than on harmony for continuity and formal delineation, the vocal phrase is free to line up within these units in a variety of ways. Generally speaking, where a melodic cadence in traditional music normally occurs on a weak downbeat, namely the downbeat of the fourth measure, a melodic cadence in rock normally occurs on a strong downbeat.

This norm is not as prevalent in rock as the traditional norm is in traditional music; in rock traditional cadence placement often exists side-by-side with the newer pattern (the contrast sometimes contributing to the delineation of form;

In addition, the rhythmic models involving a cadence on a strong downbeat are numerous enough that no particular one can be called a new standard. But much rock employs hypermetrically strong cadences exclusively-or almost so-and most of the rest of the repertoire makes frequent use of the newer pattern. Even in pieces where the newer pattern is infrequent, it lends, because of its lack of association with any other style, a distinctive quality to the phrase structure.

Because vocal phrases do not normally line up with hypermeasures in a single, traditional way, the term phrase cannot be used as it commonly is in theoretical literature to refer indiscriminately to both the melodic line and the morphological unit. We need to distinguish between the word phrase, which refers only to a vocal phrase and the terms unit and hypermeasure, which refer to the smallest morphological (i.e., formal) division larger than a measure.

7. A period of melodic rest in a vocal line .lled by an instrumental line in the Beach Boys' "Help Me, Rhonda."

HELP ME RHONDA, by Brian Wilson and Mike Love.

Although any given beat is part of a morphological unit, not every beat is part of a phrase. Where phrase lengths are measured, pickups and syncopations are treated as rhythmic embellishments; lengths are calculated by counting downbeats. Now let's define some of these standard phrase rhythms and look at some examples.

2 + 2 MODEL

Within the general category of cadences on hypermetrically strong downbeats, several patterns are found. The most common we will call the 2 + 2 model. In this most frequent pattern, the vocal cadence comes on the third downbeat of the four; two measures of melodic activity are followed by two measures of melodic rest, creating a motion-to-rest ratio of 1:1, as in Chuck Berry's "Roll Over Beethoven."

The 2 + 2 model is a salient characteristic of much blues music and, therefore, pervades the early blues-based rock repertoire, which played an important role in the further development of the style. Among other features, the 2 + 2 model plays a part in many later rock pieces that otherwise bear few resemblances to the blues. Thirtyseven years after "Roll Over Beethoven," for instance, one finds it in Sting's "If I Ever Lose My Faith In You." (example 6.) Many songs not employing the 2 + 2 model throughout use it as the basic phrase structure of one section. The multitude of songs featuring the 2 + 2 model and its resulting 1:1 motion-to-rest ratio only in the chorus or the refrain includes Aretha Franklin's "Do Right Woman," the Eagles' "Heartache Tonight," and Emerson, Lake & Palmer's "Still . . . You Turn Me On."

As noted above, traditional music such as folk song is primarily vocal, and the 3:1 ratio found in most phrases of that music suits the partially conflicting needs of having the voice carry the continuity of the piece and allowing the singer to breathe.

Rock, however, is widely acknowledged as primarily rhythmic; the voice need not carry the burden of establishing continuity as it does in earlier popular styles. Instead, the hypermeter (frequently strengthened, after all, by the melody's agogic accents on the strong downbeats, as indicated above) keeps the piece moving, especially between vocal phrases; nothing but a continuation of the beat by instrumentalists is required in the period of melodic rest between phrases of the 2 + 2 model.

However, unwilling to settle for the bare minimum required to preserve continuity, musicians sometimes. The primary melody's period of rest with background-vocal motives or instrumental hooks, thereby creating a call-and-response pattern, as in the verse to the Beach Boys' "Help Me, Rhonda," the Beatles' "The Night Before," the first verses in Emerson, Lake & Palmer's "Karn Evil 9," and the first line of James Taylor's "Your Smiling Face."

Extension-Overlap Model

In the most usual scenario, the 2 + 2 model, the melodic phrase in rock comes to a cadence sooner than its traditional counterpart, on the third downbeat rather than the fourth. In many other instances, the melodic phrase lasts longer than the traditional norm; it is not uncommon in rock for a melodic phrase beginning near the first downbeat of a four-measure unit to delay coming to a cadence until the fifth downbeat-that is, the first downbeat of a new four-measure (sometimes two-measure) unit. In this way, the closure of one gesture, a melodic phrase, happens at the same time as the beginning of another gesture, a hypermeasure, but with no disruption of the regular four-bar.

8. *Vocal phrases with cadences on a fifth downbeat, i.e., the first downbeat of a subsequent hypermeter, in (a) a generic metrical chart, (b) the Beatles' "If I Fell," and (c) Bruce Springsteen's "Born To Run."*

8 a.

| 1 2 3 4 | 2 2 3 4 | 3 2 3 4 | 4 2 3 4 || 1 2 3 4 | etc.

8 b.

If I Fell. from A HARD DAY'S NIGHT. Words and Music by John Lennon and Paul McCartney.

8 c.

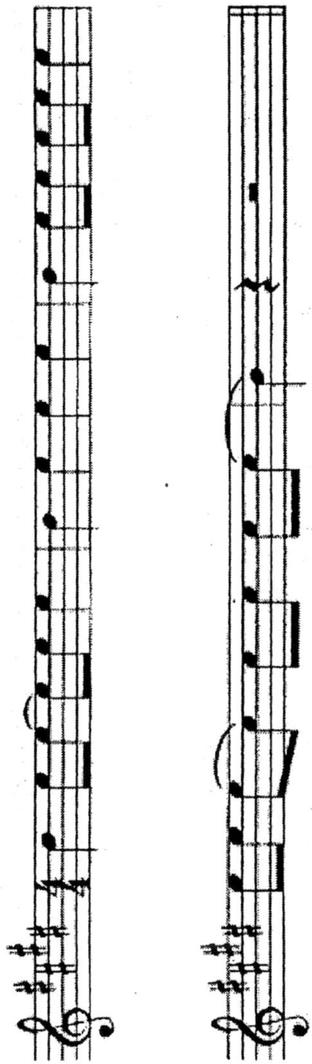

"Born to Run" by Bruce Springsteen. Copyright 1984 by Bruce Springsteen (ASCAP).

9. A delayed beginning in the first phrase of Chicago's "(I've Been) Searchin' So Long," as shown in (a) transcription and (b) a metrical chart.

9 a.

"(I've Been) Searchin' So Long". Written by James Pankow. © 1974 Make Me Smile Music/Big Elk Music (ASCAP).

9 b.

As my life . . . **Somehow . . .**

1 2 3 4 | 2 2 3 4 | 3 2 3 4 | 4 2 3 4 | 1 2 3 4 | etc.

10. The repetition of sections involving a combination of extension-overlap and delayed start in (a) Billy Joel's "A Matter Of Trust," and (b) James Taylor's "B.S.U.R. (S.U.C.S.I.M.I.M.)."

10 a.

10 b. *"A Matter Of Trust," written by Billy Joel. Copyright © 1986 JoelSongs.*

BSUR, by James Taylor. © 1979 Country Road Music, Inc. All Rights Reserved.

Following William Rothstein's lead, we shall call this combination an overlap. The extension-overlap model is rarely used as the consistent phrase structure for an entire song, or even an entire section, because of the logistical problems inherent in the use of melodic overlap: if one phrase ends on the first downbeat of a hypermeasure, how can the singer perform the beginning of the following phrase? One solution would be simply to wait another four measures before the beginning of the second phrase; the resulting combination of four measures of melodic motion and four measures of melodic rest creates a 1:1 ratio one morphological level higher than that of the common 2 + 2 model.

Through this method, Neil Young's "Harvest Moon" proceeds exclusively by extended, five-measure phrases while maintaining a consistent four-measure hypermeter. A listener counting in double-length measures, however, would say the song simply uses the 2 + 2 model. It is clear, then, that consistent use of the extension-overlap model is hard to distinguish and need not be looked for as a common occurrence.

More often the extension-overlap model is used at one or two key points in a song's form. The verse of the Eagles' "Take It To The Limit," for instance, consists of two 2 + 2 units and one extended phrase whose cadence overlaps with the inception of four bars of melodic rest. Example 8 includes several rock songs that demonstrate overlap, that is, vocal phrases that come to rest on (or very near) the first downbeat of a new four-bar hypermeasure. Some instances precede four measures of melodic rest; in others the hypermeasure after the extended phrase contains its own short vocal phrase.

11. OVERLAP BY MEANS OF AN ISOLATED FIRST NOTE IN STEPHEN BISHOP'S Tootsie). How is this listed on the music? "It Might Be You" (theme from Tootsie).

IT MIGHT BE YOU, by Alan Bergman, Marilyn Bergman, and Dave Grusin. © *1982 EMI Golden Torch Music and EMI Gold Horizon Music.*

12. Melodic overlap achieved through overdubbing in (a) the Bee Gees' "Run To Me" and (b) Chicago's "Look Away."

12 a.

Run To Me. Words and Music by Barry Gibb, Maurice Gibb and Robin Gibb. © 1972 GIBB BROTHERS MUSIC.

12 b.

LOOK AWAY, by Diane Warren. © 1988 Realsongs.

13. The short first phrases in (a) the Everly Brothers' "Lucille," (b) Foreigner's "Luanne," (c) the Beatles' "Girl," and (d) John Lennon's "Woman."

13 a.

Lucille. Words and Music by B.B. King. Copyright © 1968 by Careers-BMG Music Publishing, Inc. and Universal—Duchess Music. Corporation.

13 b.

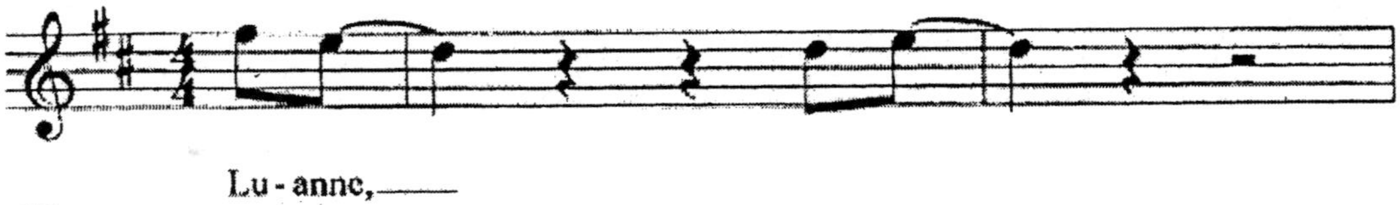

13 c.

"LUANNE" (GRAMM/JONES). © 1981 Somerset Songs Publishing, Inc.

13 d.

Girl. Words and Music by John Lennon and Paul McCartney. Copyright © 1965 Sony/ATV Songs LLC.

Woman. Words and Music by John Lennon. © 1980 LENONO.MUSIC.

14. Elision involving two melodic ideas in Elton John's "Goodbye Yellow Brick Road" as shown in (a) transcription and (b) a metrical chart.

14 a.

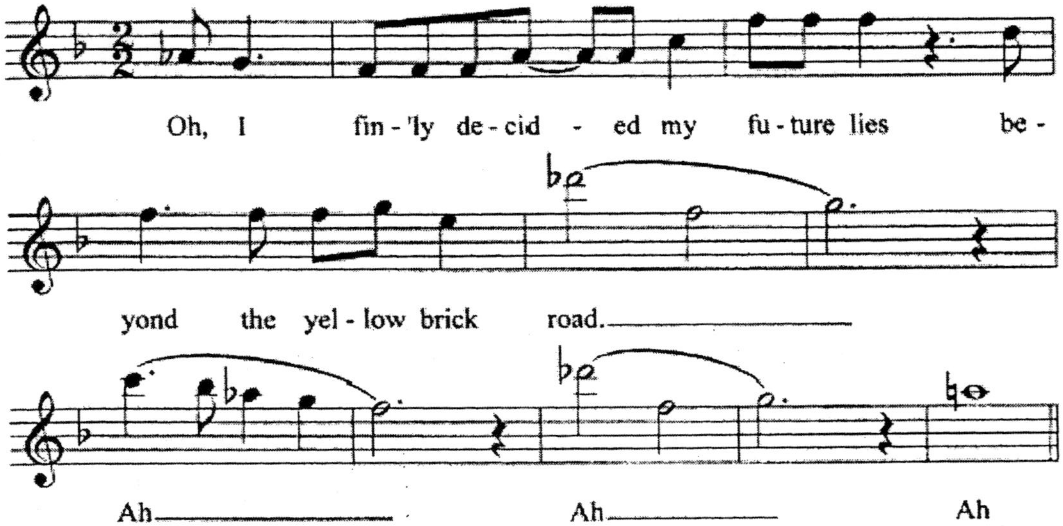

GOODBYE YELLOW BRICK ROAD, by Elton John and Bernie Taupin.

14 b.

```
                         road.        Ah . . .
Oh, I . . .
 | 1  2 | 2  2 | 3  2 | 4  2 |
                      | 1  2 | 2  2 | 3  2 | 4  2 | etc.
```

15. Elision involving an extra measure of melodic rest in the Doobie Brothers' "China Grove," measures 9–16 of verse.

```
| 1 2 3 4 | 2 2 3 4 | 3 2 3 4 | 4 2 3 4 |
                              | 1 2 3 4 | 2 2 3 4 | 1 2 3 4 | 2 2 3 4 | 3 2  etc.
```

Additional examples are found in Michael Jackson's "Billie Jean," Simon and Garfunkel's "Mrs. Robinson," the chorus of Heart's "Magic Man," the chorus of Don Henley's "The Heart Of The Matter," "Up On The Roof" (recorded by the Drifters in 1963 and James Taylor in 1979), Paul McCartney's "Jet," the chorus of Billy Joel's "Rosalinda's Eyes," and the chorus of "Because Of You" by 98. The overlap, as noted above, normally forces the delay of the ensuing verse, and a repetition of the introductory material provides a natural way of leading back into the verse. Even when an overlap is involved, however, many songs are able to have one chorus (or verse) immediately follow another by having one of two configurations at the beginning of the section, or through electronic techniques. Both of the compositional configurations are found frequently even when no overlap is involved.

In the first of these patterns, the first vocal phrase of the section begins on the second or third beat of the first measure of the four-measure unit. (example 9.) When combined with a last phrase extended to a cadence on the fifth downbeat in the manner described above, the delayed beginning allows the immediate repetition of the section in that the vocal line never has to overlap itself. Instead, the vocal line of the first statement ends on the first beat of the measure, and the second statement begins a beat or two later. The nearly breathless quality of the overlap in each of the instances shown in example 10 contributes to the impression in these particular cases of the singer's earnestness.

The second compositional means of allowing immediate repetition of a section ending in overlap finds the section (usually a verse in this case) beginning with an isolated first note. In the second statement of the section, this long first note also serves as the cadential note of the first statement. Example 11 shows portions of Stephen Bishop's "It Might Be You" (the theme from Tootsie).

A similar example is provided by the Beatles' "Here, There, And Everywhere", by Lennon and McCartney. The first verse begins with the single word "here," the second verse with the word "there." After a bridge, the third verse starts, as expected, with the word "everywhere." But while the pattern established by the title and the beginning of each of the first two verses (in conjunction with the harmonic structure, of course) makes it clear that the word "everywhere" marks the beginning of a verse, grammatically the word belongs to the last line of the bridge: "But to love her is to need her everywhere."

Because of overdubbing, a studio technique in which two or more recordings by a singer are combined and heard simultaneously, the purely physical, logistical problems of melodic overlap become moot.

We have noted examples of vocal phrases ending on the third downbeat of four (2 + 2 model) and of vocal phrases extending to the fifth downbeat, or the first downbeat of a succeeding hypermeasure (extension-overlap model). It is also common to find pieces in which a short vocal phrase ends on the first downbeat of a hypermeasure. Such melodic phrases can be a measure or more long but often consist of no more than a single word of perhaps two syllables,

Elision Model

Although vocal phrases in rock do not exhibit a common length as consistently as do phrases of traditional songs, many are similar in that they incorporate a cadence on a hypermetrically strong downbeat. But, as noted above, the standard of cadences on strong downbeats accounts for a mere majority-not an overwhelming majority-of cases; traditional cadence placement, on the fourth downbeat, appears side-by-side with the newer model in many songs. But even in the case of the cadence on a weak downbeat, rock normally maintains its distinctiveness from traditional song styles. We'll now examine two of the idiomatic ways rock uses the fourth-downbeat cadence: the elision model and the 1 + 1 model.

The pattern of strong-downbeat cadences is so much a norm that even in many cases involving a traditional cadence placement-that is, on a fourth downbeat-an elision occurs: what is considered a weak downbeat in relation to the previous material proves upon further listening to have become a strong downbeat. As in an overlap, this elision involves a melodic phrase coming to a close at the same time as the beginning of a new four-bar hypermeasure. But in the case of an elision, the fourth measure of the first unit is the same as the first measure of the second; the end result is as if a measure has been left out, that is, elided.

The elision model is easiest to hear when the downbeat in question coincides with the beginning of a new melodic idea, as in Elton John's "Goodbye Yellow Brick Road." (example 14.) Most often, however, the point of elision simply marks the beginning of either two or four measures of melodic rest, as in the Doobie Brothers' "China Grove."

1 + 1 MODEL

Even when a melodic cadence arrives on the downbeat of the fourth measure of a unit and no elision occurs, a phrase structure different from traditional models is often present, a structure termed here the "1 + 1 model." In traditional

16. Durational lengthening of anticipatory V in songs dealing with anticipation and longing: (a) Carly Simon's "Anticipation" (the chorus and beginning of verse) and (b) Foreigner's "I Want To Know What Love Is."

16 a.

```
        Anticipation,                      Anticipation . . .

|1  2  3  4  |2  2  3  4  |3  2  3  4  |4  2  3  4  |
|IV          |IV          |I           |I           |

|1  2  3  4  |2  2  3  4  |3  2  3  4  |4  2  3  4  |5  2  |
|ii    V     | (drum fill)|ii    V     |(V)         |(V)   |

|1  2  3  4  | etc.
|I           |
```

16 b.

```
I      vi  |V        | ii     vi  |V        |
I      vi  |V        | ii     vi  |V        |V        |
```

song, a musical phrase often corresponds to two textual phrases:

Rock also commonly pairs textual phrases but often separates the pair by melodic rest equal in duration to that following the second textual phrase: the first textual phrase comes to a close on the second downbeat of a four-bar unit, and the second phrase (usually starting near the beginning of the third measure) comes to rest on the fourth downbeat. With regard to the two textual phrases and the cadence on a fourth downbeat, the structure appears to be traditional. The structure differs from that of a traditional phrase, however, in the lack of continuity caused by the melodic rest in the second measure. In addition, the harmonic pattern in such cases is often two measures long and, as a result, supports the perception of two two-measure units.

Little reason other than the expectation of a four-measure standard remains for calling such a four-measure passage a phrase in the traditional sense of the word with a traditionally located cadence in the fourth measure. The 1 + 1 model pervades Bob Dylan's "All Along the Watchtower," the Doors' "Light My Fire," Credence Clearwater Revival's "Up Around The Bend," and the chorus of Tom Petty's "Into The Great Wide Open." (By counting half as many beats in a measure, a listener can interpret such examples, of course, as being based on the 2 + 2 model. Such an interpretation, however, does not alter the judgment that the phrase structure is nontraditional.) Pieces consisting mostly of 1 + 1 models frequently deny the traditional standard further through placement of the final cadence of the chorus or refrain on an odd-numbered downbeat. Such is the case, for instance, in Elton John's "Goodbye Yellow Brick Road" and Eric Clapton's "Tears In Heaven."

V-I Motion Between Units

Dominant-to-tonic motion is, of course, traditional and would seem to require no special notice here. But in the type of piece under consideration here, this V-I motion always happens at the juncture of units rather than at the end of one. The tonal resolution provided by the harmonic formula, therefore, does not line up with the metrical resolution traditionally associated with the end of a phrase. Joel Lester, in his argument against excessive recognition of the notion of hypermeter, points out as one difference between a phrase and measure that the last measure of a phrase functions as an ending while the last beat of a measure acts as an anticipation of the next measure. In the many rock pieces like "Sherry" and "Hotel California," however, this distinction does not exist. The harmony of the last measure of every unit in these cases always, because of the lack of tonal resolution, invites anticipation of the following morphological unit, acting as the last beat of a measure in this respect and thus suggesting the virtual equation of hypermeasure and formal unit in these pieces.

Composers occasionally make affective (and effective) use of the anticipatory nature of the cadence on V by extending its length, increasing the sense of anticipation even more than usual. Example 16 presents two instances. In each case, the idea of waiting for a resolution or answer that may or may not come is a central theme of the lyrics. The first is, of course, Carly Simon's "Anticipation." In the chorus of this song, the second phrase comes to a cadence one and a half beats into the fifth measure of the chorus, that is, one and a half beats later than the normal time for a cadence in an overlapped phrase.

The singer and most of the instrumentalists are then kept waiting for a measure and a half by a syncopated drum fill. In the next phrase ("Is keeping me waiting"), after a false restart by the band, it is the vocalists who keep the instrumentalists waiting with a long melisma on the syllable "wait." Then two extra beats are added before the tonic harmony arrives with the beginning of the subsequent verse.

The second case shown in example 16 is Foreigner's "I Want To Know What Love Is." At the end of this song, the singer, joined gradually by more and more voices, each voice desperately lonely in the midst of the crowd, repeats several times his desire to learn about love. Every plea, each covering two measures, ends on the V chord; every fourth melodic cadence is extended by one extra measure of the dominant harmony, expressing more clearly the sense of yearning for an answer.

Two traditional signals of closure, then-the rhythmic closure associated with melodic cadences and the tonal closure prompted by dominant-to-tonic harmonic motion-are in rock dissociated from traditional gestures of formal closure. That is, they are often relocated in rock from their traditional position at the end of a formal unit to a point of inception, the beginning of a hypermeasure. As a result, many rock songs proceed through a long series of overlapping propelling gestures. During the last measure of a four-measure unit, the standard time for closure in traditional music, harmonic forces, and sometimes melodic forces (e.g., in an extension-overlap model), carry the music into the next measure. This next measure, however, does not represent a point of metrical repose: the hypermetrical downbeat in its turn implies the succession of three more measures. Then, at the end of this new hypermeasure, the cycle begins again. In this way, the normal language of rock makes no provision for final resolution, has no way to end. For this reason, the fade-out, far from being the studio musician's easy solution to not being able to think of an ending, is actually the only way to end most rock while respecting the integrity of the style's phrase structure.

Having noted the common occurrence of V-I motion at the juncture of two units as well as the standards represented by the five models of phrase structure described above, let us now examine a rather complex example, appreciating the truly idiosyncratic without being distracted by structures that, though they may look unusual with regard to traditional practice, are actually standard in the rock style. The verse of Billy Joel's "She's Always A Woman" is represented by a chart of the harmonic scheme, with phrasing marked in brackets above. The piece was charted in a quick triple time in order to avoid the problems involved in talking about half measures.

As mentioned above, formal units are normally defined in rock by harmonic patterns; in this piece, the harmonic pattern of the opening measures conforms to a four-measure standard. As a result, the first phrase seems to start with pickups to the fourth measure of a unit. The tonic harmony in the ninth measure of the song (the second measure of the vocal phrase) marks the beginning

Everything about the first phrase, then, seems normal according to rock standards, except perhaps the long anacrusis. This is an important exception, however, because the anacrusis spans enough time to make the vocal phrase four measures long, one measure longer than the typical phrase having a cadence on the third downbeat; this feature causes some ambiguity in subsequent phrases. The expectation of regular continuation of the four-measure unit assumes that measure 13 marks the beginning of the next formal unit. This measure also bears the beginning of a new vocal phrase, a phrase coming to a cadence on the fourth downbeat of the unit and followed by two measures of melodic rest. The structure could be seen simply as an instance of the elision model.

But the equivalence of the rhythmic structure of the first two vocal phrases-three measures of motion followed by two measures of melodic rest-raises questions. If the first downbeat of the previous unit coincides with the second downbeat of the vocal phrase, should not the same be true of the second? Could we not consider the third formal unit to be five measures long, the fourth unit then beginning in measure 14 rather than measure 13? The delay of harmonic motion until the second measure of the vocal phrase strengthens the case. On the other hand, the oddity of such a long anacrusis weakens the case.

The next five measures, present a similar dilemma. If measures 13-17 are viewed as an instance of the elision model, 18-22 will likely be also. But if measure 13 is viewed as a formal pickup to measure 14, measure 18 (the first full measure of the third vocal phrase) will likely be heard as a pickup also, the strong downbeat arriving in measure 19 (the second measure of the vocal phrase) with the tonic harmony. After two measures of V/vi, the arrival of the vi chord indicates the beginning of the next formal unit in measure 23. The simultaneous inception of a new vocal phrase, an instance of the extension-overlap model common at the end of sections, con.rms that interpretation.

The start of a unit in m. 23 leaves twenty-two measures preceding, and twenty-two measures cannot be divided evenly into four. If they are to be divided into units, it seems two five-measure units must be recognized somewhere. The question of where need not be settled definitively. The passage can be interpreted validly in two ways (at least); the features normally associated with strong measures just do not line up neatly enough to suggest strongly a single interpretation. Consequently, an individual's parsing of the passage may change with the conditions of each hearing; the listener might even voluntarily change the parsing. In fact, the noncoordination of clues might even suggest a reading that denies division at de.nite points and accepts a more gradual, fluid transition from one unit to the next.

In the bridge of the song, the phrase rhythm becomes less ambiguous as the harmonies become more interesting . The bridge does, however, exemplify the rock standard by its exclusive use of fourmeasure units and by means of phrases of the extension-overlap and first downbeat models, vocal cadences on a first downbeat. Also of note later in the song is the overlapped, seven-measure phrase found in the coda; its origins can easily be seen easily in the standard five-measure, extension-overlap phrase starting in measure.

Phrase Structure and Postmodernism

The history of Western civilization is often divided into three periods: antiquity, the Middle Ages, and the modern era. It is in this broadly conceived modern era that, as J. B. Bury and others have pointed out, the idea of progress came about.In his work on Chaucer, G. K. Chesterton notes that in the medieval age "life was conceived as a Dance," or motion around a central object, whereas "after that time [i.e., in the modern era] life was conceived as a Race," or as progress toward an object. Now, writers such as Jean-François Lyotard, Charles Jencks, and Umberto Eco in a sense suggest expanding the classical scheme in order to recognize a new era, the postmodern. One unifying feature in their approaches to the meaning of postmodernism is the acknowledgment of the end of progress as the result of the loss, for various reasons, of historically accepted goals.

Lyotard, in his essay "Defining the Postmodern," points to a loss of faith; for instance, after Auschwitz, the goal of the emancipation of humankind seems to have been a mirage. On a related subject, he says, "The development of techno-sciences has become a means of increasing disease, not of fighting it. We can no longer call this development by the old name of progress." Anthony Giddens explains that the term postmodernity refers, in part, to the idea that "'history' is devoid of teleology and consequently no version of 'progress' can plausibly be defended." Suzi Gablik argues, in her Has Modernism Failed?, that the goal of modern art, namely, constant innovation, has become impossible. As she says,

Neither science nor art in our era has been content with what has been believed before, associating traditional beliefs with backwardness and a lack of momentum. . . . Beliefs had to be continually changed, replaced, discarded -always in favour of newer and better ones, which would only be rejected in turn. . . . The reflex of negation, in the effort to perpetuate itself as a mode of thought, has ended up destroying not only tradition, but also the art of the previous avant-garde. At this point, the possibilities for stylistic innovation seem, paradoxically, to have reached a limit. . . . All this has led, in the last few years, to a disaffection with the terms and conditions of modernism-a repudiation of the ideology of progress and originality.

Traditional phrase structure, which by the way is only about four hundred years old, mirrors the typical modern belief in progress: the last event in a chain of events-the final measure of a phrase, for instance-should conclude a pattern, satisfy a need, solve a problem. In rock, however, what sound to the traditional ear like endings (melodic rest and V-I harmonic motion) often occur at points of beginning; a chain of events leads not to resolution but simply to the inception of another chain of events. The musical situation, in other words, shares postmodernism's rejection of progress toward a goal. The correspondence may not be accidental; many rock lyrics reveal a common philosopher's postmodernism, reflecting a lack of faith in the idea of progress or exhibiting a belief in eternity or in a never-ending cycle of life.

6

Musical Tuning

Musical tuning is the system used to define which tones, or pitches, to use when playing music. In other words, it is the choice of level and spacing of frequency values which are used. The tuning systems are usually defined in such a way that a listener perceives it as "nice".

Pythagorean tuning, in which the ratios of the frequencies between all notes are all multiples of 3:2. Just intonation, in which the ratios of the frequencies between all notes are based on relatively low whole numbers, such as 3:2, 5:4 or 7:4; or in which all pitches are based on the harmonic series, which are all whole number multiples of a single tone. Such a system may use two different ratios for what is the same interval in equal temperament depending on context; for instance, a major second may be either in the ratio 9:8 or 10:9. For this reason, just intonation may be less a suitable system for use on keyboard instruments or other instruments where the pitch of individual notes is not flexible. On fretted instruments like guitars and lutes, multiple frets for one interval is practical.

Meantone temperament, a system of tuning which averages out pairs of ratios used for the same interval (such as 9:8 and 10:9), thus making it possible to tune keyboard instruments. Next to the twelve-equal temperament, which some would not regard as a form of meantone, the best known form of this temperament is quarter comma meantone, which tunes major thirds justly in the ratio of 5:4 and divides them into two whole tones of equal size. To do this, eleven perfect fifths in each octave are flattened by a quarter of a syntonic comma, with the remaining fifth being left very sharp (such an unacceptably out-of-tune fifth is known as a wolf interval).

However, the fifth may be flattened to a greater or lesser degree than this and the tuning system will retain the essential qualities of meantone temperament; examples include the 31-equal fifth and Lucy tuning. Both just intonation and meantone temperament can be regarded as forms of regular temperament. Well temperament, any one of a number of systems where the ratios between intervals are unequal, but approximate to ratios used in just intonation.

Unlike meantone temperament, the amount of divergence from just ratios varies according to the exact notes being tuned, so that C-G will probably be tuned closer to a 3:2 ratio than, say, F#-C#. Because of this, well temperaments have no wolf intervals. A well temperament system is usually named after whoever first came up with it. Equal temperament, in which adjacent notes of the scale are all separated by logarithmically equal distances.

All musical tuning have advantages and disadvantages. Twelve tone equal temperament is the standard and most usual tuning system used in western music today because it gives the advantage of modulation to any key without dramatically going out of tune, as all keys are equally and slightly out of tune. However, just intonation provides the advantage of being entirely in tune, with at least some, and possible a great deal, loss in ease of modulation. Referring to 12-tet the composer Terry Riley, who has written music for both tuning systems, has been quoted as saying "Western music is fast because it's not in tune".

Twelve tone equal temperament also, currently, has an advantage over just intonation in that most musicians will have instruments that can only play in equal temperament, since these are readily available. Other tuning systems have other advantages and disadvantages and are chosen for these qualities. It must be realized however, that just as many people who play music today in equal temperament without having heard of it, many musicians throughout the world and the past used just intonation without "knowing" it.

The octave (or even other intervals, such as the so-called tritave, or twelfth) can advantageously be divided into a number of equal steps different than twelve. Popular choices for such an equal temperament include 19, 22, 31, 53 and 72 parts to an octave, each of these and the many other choices possible have their own distinct characteristics. Non-equal and non-just tunings also provide advantages. For instance, William Sethares shows that the tunings of Balinese gamelans are related to the inharmonic spectra or timbre of their metallophones and the harmonic spectra of stringed instruments such as the rebab, just as just intonation and twelve tone equal temperament are related to the spectra or timbre of harmonic instruments alone.

Some instruments, such as the violin, don't limit the musician to particular pitches, allowing to choose the tuning system "on the fly". Many performers on such instruments adjust the notes to be more in tune than the equal temperament system allows, perhaps even without realizing it.

MUSICAL SCALES

A musical scale is a discrete set of pitches used in making or describing music. Typically a scale has an interval of repetition, which is normally the octave. This means that for any pitch in the scale, we have also an equivalent pitch an octave above and an octave below it. While the limits of human hearing are finite, matters are somewhat simplified if we ignore that fact, as is usually done in discussions of theory though of course never in practice. Because we are often interested in the relations or ratios between the pitches rather than the precise pitches themselves in describing a scale, it is usual to refer all the scale pitches in terms of their ratio from a particular pitch, which is given the value of one. This note can be, but is not necessarily, a note which functions as the tonic of the scale.

For comparison with the current standard tuning cents are often used. The most important scale in the Western tradition is the diatonic scale, but the scales used and proposed in various historical eras and parts of the world have been many and varied. Scales may broadly be classed as scales of just intonation, tempered scales, and practice-based scales. A scale is in just intonation if the ratios between the frequencies for all degrees of the scale are either ratios of small integers, or obtained by a succession of such ratios. It is tempered if it represents an adjustment, or tempering, of just intonation. It is practice-based if it simply reflects musical practice, as for instance various measurements of the tuning of a gamelan might do.

0	1:1	unison
1	135:128	major chroma
2	9:8	major second
3	6:5	minor third
4	5:4	major third

5	4:3	perfect fourth
6	45:32	diatonic tritone
7	3:2	perfect fifth
8	8:5	minor sixth
9	27:16	Pythagorean major sixth
10	9:5	minor seventh
11	15:8	major seventh
12	2:1	octave

(In theory unisons and octaves and their multiples are also "perfect" but this terminology is rarely used.) To calculate the frequency of a note in a scale given in terms of ratios, the frequency ratio is multiplied by the frequency we associate to the unison, which will often be the tonic frequency. For instance, with a tonic of A4 (A natural above middle C), the frequency is 440 Hz, and a justly tuned fifth above it (E5) is simply

$$440*(3/2) = 660 \text{ Hz.}$$

TEMPERAMENT

Western common practice music usually cannot be played in just intonation, even when it is confined to a single key. This is because the supertonic chord, or ii-chord, which is the most important of the minor triads in a major key, serves to bridge between the dominant and subdominant, having a root at once a minor third below the root of the subdominant triad, and hence sharing two of its notes, and a fifth above the root of the dominant triad or dominant seventh chord.

The problem becomes still worse when modulation, the key changes so important to common practice music, comes into play. The scale of the Western tradition is by its very nature neither one of just intonation nor one defined only in practice, but is a systematically tempered scale. The tempering can involve either the irregularities of well temperament or be constructed as a regular temperament, either some form of equal temperament or some other regular meantone, but in all cases will involve the fundamental features of meantone temperament.

Meantone, however, is not the only worthwhile temperament nor is the equal division of the octave into twelve parts the only reasonable way to so divide it. Many other systems of temperament are possible, leading to a variety of harmonic relationships characteristic to them. These characteristics depend on what just intervals, called commas, which differ slightly from the unison become a unison when tempered. In meantone, for example, the root of a ii-chord regarded as being a fifth above the dominant would be a major whole tone of 9/8 if the fifths were tuned justly, but would be a minor whole tone of 10/9 if it is taken to be a just minor third of 6/5 below a just subdominant degree of 4/3.

These are being equated, so meantone temperament is tempering out the difference between 9/8 and 10/9. This means their ratio, (9/8)/(10/9) = 81/80, is tempered to a unison. The interval 81/80, called the syntonic comma or comma of Didymus, is the key comma of meantone temperament, and the fact that it becomes a unison in meantone temperament is a key fact of Western music.

Equal Temperament

Equal temperament is a scheme of musical tuning in which the octave is divided into a series of equal steps (equal frequency ratios). The best known example of such a system is twelve-tone equal temperament, sometimes abbreviated to 12-TET, which is nowadays used in most Western music. Other equal temperaments do exist (some music has been written in 31-TET for example), but they are so rare that when people use the term equal temperament it is usually understood that they are talking about the twelve tone variety.

The distance between each step and the next is aurally the same for any two adjacent steps, though, because steps form a geometric sequence, the difference in frequency increases from one to the next. A linear sequence of one frequency difference would create ever smaller intervals (ratios), such as the harmonic series.

Twelve-tone equal temperament

The ratio between two adjacent semitones can be found with a few steps:

— Let an be the frequency of a semitone n, with a_{12} an octave above a_0. This creates twelve tones for each octave.

— Since the frequency ratio of a tone from one octave to the next is 2:1, the ratio of the frequency of one tone (a_{12}) to the frequency of a tone an octave lower (a_0) is 2:1 as well, so

$$\frac{a_{12}}{a_0} = 2$$

— Since the tones are in a geometric sequence, the frequency for a tone k (relative to the tone designated zero) will be equal to ska0 where s is the constant ratio between adjacent frequencies. This gives for k = 12,

$$a_{12} = s^{12} a_0$$

Table 1

Name	Exact value 12-TET	Decimal value	Just intonation interval	Percent in difference
Unison	1	1.000000	1 = 1.000000	0.00%
Minor second	$\sqrt[12]{2^1} = \sqrt[12]{2}$	1.059463	16/15 = 1.066667	-0.68%
Major second	$\sqrt[12]{2^2} = \sqrt[12]{4}$	1.122462	9/8 = 1.125000	-0.23%
Minor third	$\sqrt[12]{2^3} = \sqrt[12]{8}$	1.189207	6/5 = 1.200000	-0.91%
Major third	$\sqrt[12]{2^4} = \sqrt[12]{16}$	1.259921	5/4 = 1.250000	+0.79%
Perfect fourth	$\sqrt[12]{2^5} = \sqrt[12]{32}$	1.334840	4/3 = 1.333333	+0.11%
Diminished fifth	$\sqrt[12]{2^6} = \sqrt[12]{64}$	1.414214	7/5 = 1.400000	+1.02%
Perfect fifth	$\sqrt[12]{2^7} = \sqrt[12]{128}$ $\sqrt[12]{2^7} = \sqrt[12]{128}$	1.498307	3/2 = 1.500000	-0.11%
Minor sixth	$\sqrt[12]{2^8} = \sqrt[12]{256}$	1.587401	8/5 = 1.600000	-0.79%
Major sixth	$\sqrt[12]{2^9} = \sqrt[12]{512}$	1.681793	5/3 = 1.666667	+0.90%
Minor seventh	$\sqrt[12]{2^{10}} = \sqrt[12]{1024}$	1.781797	16/9 = 1.777778	+0.23%
Major seventh	$\sqrt[12]{2^{11}} = \sqrt[12]{2048}$	1.887749	15/8 = 1.875000	+0.68%
Octave		2.000000	2/1 = 2.000000	0.00%

$$\frac{a_{12}}{a_0} = s^{12}$$

— Since a_{12} / a_0 was found to be two, the formula with constant ratio s is

$$2 = s^{12}$$

$$s = \sqrt[12]{2}$$

Therefore, the ratio between two adjacent frequencies is equal to the twelfth root of two or approximately 1.05946309 to one.

The half tone interval:

$$1:2^{1\,/\,1200}$$

is also known as 100 cent. 1 cent is therefore the ratio between two tone frequencies with an interval of one hundredth of an equal-tempered semitone.

Cent values of equal temperament

Tone	Cents
c^1	0
c#	100
d	200
d#	300
e	400
f	500
f#	600
g	700
g#	800
a	900
a#	1000
b	1100
c^2	1200

Twelve tone equal temperament was designed to permit the playing of music in all keys with an equal amount of mis-tuning in each, while still approximating just intonation.

This allows much more facile harmonic motion, while losing some subtlety of intonation. True equal temperament was not available to musicians before about 1870 because scientific tuning and measurement was not available. And in fact, from about 1450 to about 1800 musicians tolerated even less mistuning in the most common keys, like C major. Instead, they used approximations that emphasized the tuning of thirds or fifths in these keys, such as Meantone temperament.

J. S. Bach wrote The Well-Tempered Clavier to demonstrate the musical possibilities of well temperament. There is some reason to believe that when composers and theoreticians of this era wrote of the "colors" of the keys, they described the subtly different dissonances of particular tuning methods, though it is difficult to determine with any exactness the actual tunings used in different places at different times by any composer.

12-TET also allows the use of integer notation and modulo 12, and this allows for proofs concerning pitch. This may be used for atonal music, such as that written with the twelve tone technique or serialism, or tonal music. The table inthe above page (Table 1) shows the values of the intervals of 12 TET, along with one interval from just intonation that each approximates, and the percentage by which they differ:

These mappings from equal temperament to just intonation are by no means unique. The minor seventh, for example, can be meaningfully said to approximate both 16/9 and 9/5, depending on context or simultaneously in a chord - and probably even 7/4.

Non-12 TET

Five and seven tone equal temperament, 240 and 171 cent steps relatively, seem the most common outside of 12-tET.

A Thai xylophone measured by Morton "varied only plus or minus 5 cents," from 7-tET. A Ugandan Chop xylophone measured by Haddon also tuned to 171 cent steps. Gamelans are tuned to 5-tET according to Kunst, but according to Hood and McPhee their tuning varies widely and according to Tenzer contain stretched octaves. It is now well-accepted that of the two primary tuning systems in Gamelan music, Slendro and Pelog, only Slendro somewhat resembles 5-tone equal temperament while Pelog, highly unequal, can be roughly approximated by a subset of 9-, 16-, or 23-tone equal temperament.

However, a Ugandan harp and women singing unaccompanied, measured with a Stroboconn and variations of 15 and 5 cents relatively by Wachsmann. (<— that looks like an unintelligible sentence fragment — the author should fix it.) A South American Indian scale from a preinstrumental culture measured by Boiles featured 175 cent equal temperament which stretches the octave slightly as with instrumental gamelan music. The quarter tone scale or 24-tET is, similarly, based on powers of.

Other equal divisions of the octave, though, can be better considered temperaments. 19-tET and especially 31-tET are extended varieties of Meantone temperament and approximate most just intonation intervals considerably better than 12-tET. They have been used sporadically since the 16th century, with 31-tET particularly popular in Holland, there advocated by Christiaan Huygens and Adriaan Fokker. 53-tET is much better still at approximating the traditional just intonation consonances, but has had very little use. It doesn't fit the Meantone mold that shaped the development of Western harmony and tonality.

In 53-tET, most traditional compositions would necessitate subtle microtonal pitch shifts or a drifting pitch level in order to make use of the tuning's excellent just intonation triads. 55-tET, not as close to just intonation, was a bit closer to common practice. As an excellent representative of the variety of meantone temperament popular in the 18th century, 55-tET it was considered ideal by Georg Philipp Telemann and other prominent musicians. Wolfgang Amadeus Mozart's surviving violin lessons conform closely to such a model.

In the 20th century, standardized Western pitch and notation practices having been placed on a 12-tET foundation made the quarter tone scale a much more popular microtonal tuning. A further extension of 12-tET is 72-tET, which though not a Meantone tuning, approximates most just intonation intervals, including non-traditional ones like 7/4, 9/7, 11/5, 11/6 and 11/7, better. 72-tET has been taught, written and performed in practice, for example by Joe Maneri and his students -- whose atonal inclinations typically avoid any reference to just intonation intervals whatsoever.

Still other equal temperaments occupying more than a few musicians include 5-tET, 7-tET, 15-tET, 22-tET, and 48-tET. More generally, every step in n tone equal temperament is 1200/n cents. However, if one wishes to create an equal tempered scale that does not repeat at the octave, a scale with n equal steps in a pseudo-octave p is based on the ratio r

$$r = \sqrt[nth]{p}$$

This still may be easier to calculate in cents, for instance the pseudo-octave of ratio 2.1:1 is an interval of 1284 cents. Equal tempered scales can also be generated simply by picking the number of cents that each step will consist of.

Wendy Carlos created two equal tempered scales for the title track of her album Beauty In The Beast, the Alpha and Beta scales. Beta splits a perfect fourth into two equal parts, which creates a scale where each step is almost 64 cents. Alpha does the same to a minor third to create a scale of 78 cent steps. The equal tempered version of the Bohlen-Pierce scale consists of the ratio 3:1, 1902 cents, conventionally an octave and a just fifth, used as a tritave, and split into a thirteen tone equal temperament where each step is

$$\sqrt[13]{3}$$

or 146.3 cents. This provides a very close match to justly tuned ratios consisting only of odd numbers. Australian aboriginal music extensively measured by Ellis was based on arithmetic scales (the harmonic series is an arithmetic scale, though presumably the Australian scales began an interval smaller than an octave) with an equal separation in hertz.

Meantone Temperament

Meantone temperament is a system of musical tuning. In it, the major third is tuned to a particular ratio (5:4), and then divided in half to make two whole tones of equal size. Since two fifths up and an octave down make up a whole tone,

$$\frac{(3/2)^2}{2} = \frac{9/4}{2} = \frac{9}{8}$$

four fifths up and two octaves down make a major third in meantone temperament,

$$\frac{(3/2)^4}{4} = \frac{81/16}{4} = \frac{81}{64} \approx \frac{5}{4} = \frac{5\times 16}{4\times 16} = \frac{80}{40}$$

and hence four fifths in meantone temperament make an interval of a seventeenth (5+(5-1)+(5-1)+(5-1)=20-3=17), which is two octaves (4:1) above the major third (5:4), and so has a ratio at or about 5:1, i.e.

$$4:1\times5:4=5:1$$

Meantone tuning involves flattening the fifth so as to bring the seventeenth more nearly, or exactly, equal to this ratio. Letting x be the ratio of the flattened fifth, it is desired that four fifth have a ratio of 5:1,

$$x^4=5$$

therefore

$$x=\sqrt[4]{5}$$

so that

$$\frac{x^2}{2}=\frac{\sqrt{5}}{2}=whole-tone$$

The most common form of meantone temperament tunes all the major thirds to the just ratio of 5:4 (so, for instance, if A is tuned to 440 Hz, C#' is tuned to 550 Hz). This is achieved by tuning the perfect fifth a quarter of a syntonic comma flatter than the just ratio of 3:2. It is this that gives the system its name of quarter comma meantone or 1/4-comma meantone.

$$5^{1/4}=1.495348=696.578428 \text{ cents},$$
$$3/2=1.5=701.955001 \text{ cents},$$
$$696.578428-701.955001=-5.376572 \text{ cents}$$
$$5.376572\times4=21.506290=1200\lg(81/80),$$

Since

$$4\left(1200\lg\frac{3}{2}-1200\lg 5^{1/4}\right)$$

$$=1200\left(\lg\left(\frac{3}{2}\right)^{4}-\lg 5\right)$$

$$=1200\lg\left(\frac{81/16}{5}\right)=1200\lg\frac{81}{80}.$$

This system gives whole tones in the ratio. diatonic semitones in the ratio. and perfect fifths in the ratio of. which is 1.495349.., compared with a justly tuned fifth of 3:2, which is 1.5. (A semitone is equal to three octaves up and five fifths down, since the octave equals 12 semitones and the fifth equals 7 semitones, so that 3x12 – 5x7 = 36 – 35 = 1 semitone . Then, in terms of ratios, 23/x5 = 23:(51/4)5 = 8 : 55/4.) One of the fifths will be a wolf interval, which means it will be so sharp it will not sound at all the same as a perfect fifth, and will not normally be used in music of the common practice period. This is because twelve perfect fifths, each flattened by a quarter of a syntonic comma, do not add up to an exact number of octaves.

The term meantone temperament is sometimes used to refer specifically to 1/4-comma meantone. However, systems which flatten the fifth by differing amounts but which still equate the major whole tone, which in just intonation is 9/8, with the minor whole tone, tuned justly to 10/9, are also called meantone systems. Since (9/8) / (10/9) = (81/80), the syntonic comma, the fundamental character of a meantone tuning is that all intervals are generated from fifths, and the syntonic comma is tempered to a unison.

Meantones can be specified in various ways. We can, as above, specify what fraction (logarithmically) of a syntonic comma the fifth is being flattened by, what equal temperament has the meantone fifth in question, or what the ratio of the whole tone to the diatonic semitone is. This ratio was termed "R" by American composer, pianist and theoretician Easley Blackwood, but in effect has been in use for much longer than that.

It is useful because it gives us an idea of the melodic qualities of the tuning, and because if R is a rational number, so is (3R+1)/(5R+2), which is the size of fifth in terms of logarithms base 2, and which immediately tells us what division of the octave we will have. If we multiply by 1200, we have the size of fifth in cents. In these terms, some historically important meantone tunings are listed below. The relationship between the first two columns is exact, while that between them and the third is closely approximate.

Table 2.Meantone tunings

R	Equal temperament	Fraction of a comma
2	7/12	1/11
9/5	32/55	1/6
7/4	25/43	1/5
5/3	18/31	7/29
33/20	119/205	1/4
8/5	29/50	2/7
3/2	11/19	1/3

Because of the wolf interval which arises when twelve notes to the octave are tuned to a meantone with fifths significantly flatter than the 1/11-comma of equal temperament, well temperaments and eventually equal temperament became more popular.

Quarter-comma Meantone Diatonic Scale

As discussed above, in the 1/4-comma meantone temperament, the ratio of a tone is. the ratio of a semitone is 8:55 / 4, and the ratio of a fifth is 51 / 4. Let these ratios be represented by letters: T for the tone, S for the semitone and P for the fifth.

It can be verified through calculation that three tones and one semitone equals a fifth:

$$T^3 \cdot S = \frac{5^{3/2}}{2^3} \cdot \frac{8}{5^{5/4}}$$

$$= 5^{6/4-5/4} = 5^{1/4} = P.$$

A diatonic scale can be constructed by starting from the fundamental note and multiplying it either by T to move up by a tone or by S to move up by a semitone. The result is shown in the following table:

Table 3

Note	Formula	Ratio	Cents
C	1	1	0
D	T	1.118033	193.156856
E	T^2	1.25	386.313713
F	T^2S	1.337480	503.421571
G	P	1.495348	696.578428
A	PT	1.671850	889.735285
B	PT^2	1.869185	1082.892142
C'	PT^2S	2	1200

Construction

Construction of a 1/4-comma meantone chromatic scale can

proceed by taking the 1/4-comma meantone diatonic scale as its foundation. The tones in the diatonic scale can be divided into pairs of semitones. However, S2 is not equal to T. Instead, let

$$\bar{S} = \frac{T}{S} = \frac{\sqrt{5}/2}{8/5^{5/4}} = \frac{5^{1/2}\cdot 5^{5/4}}{8\cdot 2} = \frac{5^{7/4}}{16}$$

Thus, each tone can be divided into a pair of unequal semitones, the major one being S, and the minor one being. Notice that S is equal to 117.107 cents, and that is equal to 76.048 cents. These can be compared to the just intonated ratio 18/17 which equals 98.954 cents. S deviates from it by +18.153 cents, and deviates from it by -22.906 cents. These two deviations, in cents, may be considered acceptable: they are comparable to the syntonic comma.

The following quarter-meantone chromatic scale was constructed by Pietro Aaron in 1523:

```
C    C#    D     D#    E     F     F#    G     G#    A     A#    B     C'
|-----|-----|-----|-----|-----|-----|-----|-----|-----|-----|-----|-----|
   S     S     S     S     S     S     S     S̄     S     S     S̄     S
  nov   dec   jan   feb   mar   apr   may   jun   jul   aug   sep   oct
```

The scale is a series of 12 semitones, each of which may either by major — S — or minor —. The diagram compares the semitones to months of a year: months with 31 days correspond to major semitones, and months with 30 days or less correspond to minor semitones. The chromatic scale is also presented in the following table, which has been constructed by starting from the fundamental note and multiplying it either by $\bar{S}$ to move up by a major semitone or by to move up by a minor semitone.

Table 4. The chromatic scale

Note	Formula	Ratio	Cents
C	1	1	0
C#	$\bar{S}$	1.04490672653	76.0489992634
D	T	1.11803398875	193.156856932
D#	T S	1.19627902498	310.264714601
E	T^2	1.25	386.313713865
F	T2 S	1.33748060995	503.421571534
F#	T^3	1.39754248594	579.470570797
G	P	1.49534878122	696.578428466
G#	P $\bar{S}$	1.5625	772.62742773
A	P T	1.67185076244	889.735285399
A#	P T S	1.788854382	1006.84314307
B	P T^2	1.86918597653	1082.89214233
C'	P T^2 S	2	1200

Notice that this scale is an extension of the diatonic scale shown in the previous table. Only five notes have been added: C#, D#, F#, G# and A#. These five pitches form a pentatonic scale: the difference between a chromatic scale and a diatonic scale is a pentatonic scale.

Triads in the quarter-meantone chromatic scale

The major triad can be defined by a pair of intervals from the root note: a major third and a fifth. The minor triad can likewise be defined by a pair of intervals: a minor third and a fifth. A chromatic scale has twelve different major thirds, twelve minor thirds, and twelve fifths. In an equally tempered chromatic scale, all major thirds have the same size, all minor thirds have the same size, and all fifths have the same size. In the meantone temperament, intervals of the same type may have different sizes. Thus it is necessary to examine each of the possible intervals, to examine their sizes, and to see how much each of these intervals deviates from their justly intoned ideal ratios. If the deviation is too large, then the given interval is not usable, either by itself or in a chord.

Regular Temperament

Regular temperament is a system of musical tuning such that each frequency ratio is obtainable as a product of powers of a finite number of generators, or generating frequency ratios. The classic example of a regular temperament is meantone temperament, where the generating intervals are usually given in terms of a flat fifth and the octave. If the generators are all of the prime numbers up to a given prime p, we have what is called p-limit just intonation. However, normally we aspire to adjust the tuning of one or more of these primes, to produce an actual "tempering" of the justly tuned ratios, as in meantone.

In mathematical terminology, the products of these generators defines a free abelian group. The number of independent generators is the rank of an abelian group, but for historical reasons one less than this number is called the dimension of the temperament. A "0-dimensional" tuning system with a single generator is normally regarded as having approximated an octave after a certain number of steps, and therefore of constituting an equal temperament. A linear or one-dimensional temperament has two generators, one of which is usually taken to be an octave or some equal subdivision of an octave. By far the best-known example of a linear temperament is meantone, but others include the schismic temperament of Hermann von Helmholtz and miracle temperament.

An example of a temperament which is neither equal nor linear is the tempering of the septimal kleisma of 225/224 to a unison with no other tempering, something which is often advantageous if we wish to introduce 7-limit harmony without detuning 5-limit just intonation very greatly. In studying regular temperaments, it is generally advantageous to regard the temperament as having both a map from p-limit just intonation for some prime p, and a tuning map to particular values for the generators. From that point of view, it is no longer required that the generators of the temperament be independent, which is demoted to a mere matter of tuning. Hence, for instance, an equal division into 31 parts is still to be regarded as a means of tuning a linear temperament. The first map can now be studied by the methods of linear and multilinear algebra. The kernel of the map, consisting of p-limit intervals called the commas of the temperament, can be used to gain insight into the properties of the temperament.

Well Temperament

Well temperaments are a form of musical tuning, also known as circular temperaments, or irregular temperaments. Any tuning system which is not equal temperament but which tunes the chromatic scale in a way suitable for a keyboard instrument and in such a way that music in any key can be played in tune is a well temperament. In regular temperaments like Pythagorean tuning and meantone temperament all the fifths are the same size, except one (typically Eb-G#) which is badly out of tune (a "wolf fifth"). This means that as long as you stay with keys that don't involve the wolf fifth, eveything is fine, but the remote keys are unusable.

Well temperaments have fifths of different sizes (hence the name "irregular temperament"), usually smaller ones round the home keys to get sweet thirds, and bigger ones in the distant keys to make it all add up. In a well temperament you can modulate through all the keys (hence the name circulating temperament), but all the keys have slightly different tuning, hence distinct characters. Well temperaments evolved in the baroque period, were current in the classical period, and survived into the late nineteenth centuary. Bach's Well Tempered Clavier was written for a well tempered instrument.

Musical Set Theory

Although musical set theory is often assumed to be the application of mathematical set theory to music, there is little coincidence between the terminology and even less between the methods of the two. In fact musical set theory is better characterized as the application of group theory and combinatorics to certain aspects of music theory. In musical set theory what is called a set is often in fact a tuple, an ordered collection of things (such as the term set form for tone row).

Musical set theory also uses the terms linear and nonlinear for ordered and unordered sets, which has nothing to do with what these terms mean in mathematics. Allen Forte's book, *The Structure of Atonal Music,* one of the primary developments in musical set theory, is sometimes criticised for its supposedly faulty calculations and terminology. Musical set theory is best regarded however as an unrelated field from mathematical set theory, with its own vocabulary; whose only connection to mathematical set theory is in sometimes using the language of naive set theory to talk about finite sets.

Assumptions of Atonal Theory

In addition to octave and enharmonic equivalency assumed in twelve tone theory and equal tempered tonal theory, set theory also makes use of inversional and transpositional equivalency. Though the degree of equivalency varies among theorists. Set theory does not, however, use diatonic functionality that is assumed in tonal theory, and this is the reason for the use of integer notation and modulo 12. Since the structures of tonal theory may then be constructed rather than assumed, tonal theory can be regarded as specific area of atonal theory.

The fundamental concept of musical set theory is, of course, the set. A set is a collection of any musical materials or qualities, ordered or unordered, most often though sets of pitch classes are considered. Sets may be simultaneities or successions. A set is indicated by being enclosed in brackets: {}, an ordered set is indicated by <>, and an unordered set by (). Thus the set of pitch classes 0, 1, and 2 is {0,1,2}, the ordered set <0,1,2>, and the unordered set (0,1,2). The domain of all pitch class sets may be partitioned into types or equivalence classes based on cardinality or number of pitch classes, or other criteria. There are thirteen cardinalities from 0-12: the null set, monad, dyad, trichord, tetrachord, pentachord, hexachord, septachord, octachord, nonachord, decachord, undecachord, and aggregate or dodecachord.

The basic operations that may be performed on a set are transposition and inversion and multiplication. Order operations include retrograde and rotation. Compound operations, the result of two basic operations, may be performed and the product of operations X and Y on z is written "Y(X(z))" with X performed on z, and then Y performed on that result. These operations may also be called transformations, mappings, morphisms, or permutations; and in music theory, but not in mathematics, derivations.

Taking all combinations of a certain number of basic operations (for example taking all combinations of transposition, inversion, and multiplication by 7) produces permutation groups. Transposition is moving a set up or down in pitch by a constant interval. If x is the original pitch transposed n semitones, Tn=x+n (mod12). Inversion is turning a set upside-down reversing the order of the intervals between pitch classes. More specifically the compound operation transpositional inversion is TnI(x)=-x+n (mod12).

Multiplication is multiplying the pitch class numbers of a set, the most useful multipliers are 1, 5, 7, 11, as multiplication by 1 is the same, multiplication by 11 is inversion, multiplication of the chromatic scale by 5 produces the circle of fourths and multiplication by 7 produces the circle of fifths. Retrograde is reversing the order of the set so the first member is last and the last is first. Rotation is placing the last member of the set first.

Another useful concept used in musical set theory is that of normal form. Since sets may be listed in any order without changing their identity, normal form is used as a way to compare sets. Normal order is that which is stacked to the left, rises from left to right, within one octave and fits within the smallest interval. In the event of any ties for what produces the smallest outside interval, one compares the next most outside interval until the tie is broken, or the ordering that starts on the smallest pitch class integer is chosen. Normal order can be used to quickly compare if two sets may be transposed onto each other. For example, it is harder to compare {4,8,1} and {7,0,3} as quickly as {0,3,7} and {1,4,8}.

Transpositional and Inversional Types

Each of the cardinality types listed above may be further partitioned into transpositional type (Tn type) and/or inversional type (Tn/TnI type). A list of all sets which are in the same transpositional type as a given set may be found by transposing the original set by all intervals. Thus the trichord {8,4,1}, {1,4,8} in normal form, is in the same transpositional type as {1,4,8}+1={2,5,9}, {1,4,8}+2={3,6,10}, {4,7,11}, {5,8,0}, {6,9,1}, {7,10,2}, {8,11,3}, {9,0,4}, {10,1,5}, {11,2,6}, and {0,3,7}. All of the above are in the transpositional type {0,3,7}Tn, as the representative set is that which is in the most normal form. {0,3,7} is equivalent under transposition and/or inversion with twenty four rather than twelve sets, the twelve above and their inversions. It happens to be the representative set for its class: {0,3,7}Tn/TnI, as it is the most normal ordered form between the most normal ordered form uninverted, {0,3,7}, and the most normal ordered transposition of its inversion, {0,4,7} (T7I{0,3,7}={0,4,7}).Thus, to find the type of a set:

List the set in normal form.

— Transpose the set so that the first pitch class is zero.

— This is the representative form of the Tn type.

— Perform TnI and repeat the steps above.

— This is the representative form of the inversions Tn type.

— Compare the Tn type representative forms.

The most normal form of the two representative types above is the representative form of the set's TnI type. Given any set of numbers from zero to eleven, there is a corresponding indexing integer ranging from 0 to 4095, defined as the sum of the numbers 2i for each number i in the set. Transpositions, or transpositions with inversion, are examples of permutation groups. Given any such group on the numbers from 0 to 11, we can find a corresponding representative form by finding the smallest index in the orbit of the set under the transformations of the group.

Symmetry

The number of times which a set may be mapped onto itself through different operations is its degree of symmetry. Every set has at least one degree of symmetry, as it maps onto itself under the identity operation T0. Transpositional symmetry is the property of set which maps onto itself for Tn where n does not equal 0. Inversional symmetry is the property of a set which maps into itself under TnI. For any given Tn/TnI type all sets will have the same degree of symmetry. The number of distinct sets in a type is 24 (the total number of operations, transposition and inversion, for n = 0 through 11) divided by the degree of symmetry of Tn/TnI type. Inversionally symmetrical set have a canonical ordering. The canonical ordering is the ordered such that the interval series of the set is its own retrograde or rather is retrograde symmetrical. For each of these canonical orderings a set will map onto itself under TxI, x being the inversional index which is the sum of the first and last members of each canonical ordering.

The first and last members, and each pair of members farther in, of sets of even cardinality will all equal the inverional index. For odd cardinality sets the middle number is a 1/2 index and the center of inversional symmetry. Transpositional symmetrical sets in normal form may be partitioned into segments which under transposition map onto each other cyclically, so that the last segment maps onto the first.

BASICS OF TWELVE-TONE ATONALITY

Two Equivalence Assumptions (Pitch Class Equivalence):

1. Octave equivalence
2. Enharmonic equivalence

Octave equivalence has been an assumption in tonal music, and it does not require extra attention here except to mention that the terminology used in "atonal" theory is much more specific. The term "pitch" refers to a specific tone with a specific frequency. The term "pitch class" (abbreviated "pc") employs the notion of octave equivalence and refers to any member of the set of pitches of the same "name" (i.e. C-sharp). When looking at the non-diatonic relationships among the twelve chromatic pitches, it can be useful to look at the chromatic scale as a mathematical group (the Z-12 additive group).

For reasons of convenience, integers are assigned to the chromatic scale members. One reason for this is that it simplifies the naming of pitch classes which have historically been named according to their tonal function. A-sharp was seen as a theoretically different entity from B-flat. Music that does not use this fundamentally tonal distinction between chromatic scale members that are enharmonically the same is easier to analyze without the confusion of this system. This integer system of note naming employs the notion of enharmonic equivalence (i.e. B, C-flat, and A double-sharp are all pc 11), and is organized thus:

PC	# Names
0	C,B#,Dbb
1	C#,Db,B##

2	D,C##,Ebb
3	D#,Eb,Fbb
4	E,Fb,D##
5	F,E#,Gbb
6	F#,Gb,E##
7	G,F##,Abb
8	G#,Ab
9	A,G##,Bbb
10*	A#,Bb,Cbb
11*	B,Cb,A##

*The numbers 10 and 11 are often represented with letters so that they are not confused with a "1" followed by a "0", or two "1"s in a row. The letters traditionally used for 10 and 11 in base-12 arithmetic are "A" and "B", but some theorists object to these because they are already symbols in common use for designating musical pitch classes (pc 9 and pc 11, or, in the German system, pc 9 and pc 10). Some theorists have used "T" for 10 and "E" for 11, but, once again, "E" is already a note name.

The numbering is arbitrary in that 0 could just as easily be assigned to A-flat as it is to C. However, the use of integers 0 - 11 is not arbitrary, as it makes the mod-12 arithmetic that is characteristic of the mod-12 group possible and applicable to the musical scale.

Pitch-class set equivalence

Collections of pcs (harmonic or melodic) can be analyzed according to "Set Theory" as proposed by Allen Forte. Forte assumed two additional types of equivalence related to collections:

1. Transpositional equivalence
2. Inversional equivalence

Transpositional equivalence has also been in place in tonal theory. Any sonority (collection of pcs, or "pc set") can be transposed to another pitch level and retain its character (though the function may change in tonal music). In other words, an F-major triad and an A-major triad are highly related in sound, and thus equivalent at some level. The operation of addition mod-12 on the pitch classes in the set corresponds to transposition of the chord or melody represented by the set. Inversional equivalence is the most problematic of all of the equivalence assumptions made so far.

If the collection is flipped upside down, it retains the same interval content as before, however the chord also can sound somewhat different. For example, if a major triad is inverted, it becomes a minor triad. There is equivalence because they both contain one perfect fifth (fourth), one major third (minor sixth), and one minor third (major sixth). However, in most musical contexts they are distinguished because of their difference in sound rather than their equivalence. So in the case of inversional equivalence, the equivalence will be assumed for the purposes of identifying pc sets by their equivalence classes, but it may often be more useful to distinguish between a sonority and its inversion.

Prime form, an expression of sets' equivalence

According to these rules of equivalent intervallic content, Forte devised a list of all possible collections of chromatic pitches. The number of possible combinations without equivalence classes is astronomical. However, Forte devised a "lowest ordering" that is considered the standard form for all members of an equivalence class (set class). All members of any equivalence class can be reduced to this prime form by a single method. This results in an ascending version of the collection's members within the span of an octave that is transposed to 0 (the first pc in the collection is 0) and is rotated and inverted to be "left-packed".

One can determine the set class of any collection of pitch classes using the Set Analyzer Applet. The technique for determining the equivalence class of a pc set (without the use of the Set Analyzer) is to follow the technique given below, and then look up the result in the table.

Procecure for finding normal form:

— Excluding doublings, write the pitch classes ascending within an octave. There will be as many different ways of doing this as there are pitch classes in the set, since an ordering can begin on any of the pitch classes in the set.

— Choose the ordering that has the smallest interval from first to last (from the lowest to highest).

— If there is a tie under Rule 2, choose the ordering that is most packed to the left. To determine which is most packed to the left, compare the intervals between the first and second-to-last notes. If there is still a tie, compare the intervals between the first and third-to-last notes, and so on.

— If the application of Rule 3 still results in a tie, then choose the ordering beginning with the pitch class represented by the smallest integer. For example, (A, C#, F), (C#, F, A), and (F, A, C#) are in a three-way tie according to Rule 3. So we select [C#, F, A] as the normal form since its first pitch class is 1, which is lower than 5 or 9.

Procedure for finding Prime Form:

— Put the set into normal form.

— Transpose the set so that the first element is 0.

— Invert the set and repeat steps 1 and 2.

— Compare the results of step 2 and step 3; whichever is more packed to the left is the prime form. (Use the procedure for determining "left-packedness" given above in Rules 3 and 4 of finding Normal Form.)

Some important terms and concepts in atonal theory that are not explicitly mentioned above are briefly defined in the Post-Functional Theory Terminology glossary. The analysis of music based on parsing melodies and chords into these small collections of pitch classes is useful in non-functional music where no serial process is involved, and also it can be useful in analyzing the construction of a particular tone row and the atonal results of its use in a complex work.

The twelve-tone method

One of the most dominating ideas in twentieth century music has been the development of techniques for systematic ordering of musical events. The first significant advance in this trend toward serialism in music was the twelve-tone atonal composition system devised by the German experimental composer Arnold Schönberg in the late 1910s. In order to promote consistency and order in atonal composition Schoenberg adopted specific precepts for his "method of composing with twelve notes only related to each other":

— The row, or series, must contain all twelve pitch-classes of the chromatic scale in a specific and predetermined order with no repetitions of any one pitch-class.

— The permissible row forms include a row's original or prime form, inversion, retrograde, and retrograde-inversion and the twelve transpositions of each. The total number of row forms, or permutations, is forty-eight and can be represented concisely in a form of chart called a matrix.

— Consistently atonal treatment of the row requires that no notes be doubled at the octave, tonal melodic or harmonic elements (intervals) are to be avoided, and no note should be sustained to the point where it becomes a focal pitch.

— In order to maintain uniformity of musical material one must make exclusive use of one series per composition.

To Schoenberg and his students, the purpose of twelve-tone technique was primarily avoidance of tonality through the systematic creation of a "democracy of tones." Experimental music without tonality prior to the development of the twelve-tone process seldom succeeded in offering enough musical cohesion to allow for movements of considerable length. Schoenberg's method solved this problem by offering the opportunity for the creation of musically significant and orderly structures that offer a piece both unity and variety. Finally, Schoenberg's twelve-tone procedure could even help the composer to avoid the traditional notions of 'theme' and 'development' that were inextricably linked with tonal composition, while offering twelve-tone music's own unique brand of both.

The matrix

The matrix is a concise representation of all 48 possible row permutations in a 12x12 grid. The four possible row forms are given by the four directions in which one can read the row notes off of the matrix for a given row. It is important to remember that a tone row is an ordered set of pcs, while a pitch class set is unordered.

Prime form

First, the prime form of the row (not to be confused with

prime form of a pc set) is read from the matrix from left to right. As there are 12 possible transpositions of the row, there are twelve left-to-right rows (as opposed to columns) in the matrix. The transpositions of the prime form of the row are labeled with the letter P and the pc number of the first pc in the row form (P0, P3, etc.).

Inversion

Inversion is the operation of turning the melody contour upside down, as if across a horizontal line of symmetry. Whereas the prime form of a series is always given in left-to-right rows on the series' matrix, the inversion row form is the top-to-bottom reading of a column of the matrix. The inversion forms are called by the letter I followed by the number of the first pitch class (I3, I8, etc.).

Retrograde

The retrograde, or backward form of the row, is the third possible manipulation that can be used in serial composition. Since it is simply the reverse of the prime form, it is most conveniently found in a matrix by reading the desired transposition of the prime form backwards (from right to left). Because there is a one-to-one correspondence between the prime forms and the retrograde forms that are their backwards-renditions, the retrograde forms are labeled with an R and the number of the pc that ends the row form (R3, etc.). This is so that R0 is always the retrograde of P0 and not some other row form. Although a composer's main concern with using retrograde material is the question of whether the listener will recognize that two melodies are from the same source when one is presented backwards, this concern seems not to have bothered composers who work with series.

Retrograde-inversion

The final operation that can be performed on a tone row is retrograde inversion. As this upside down and backwards presentation of a tone row is simply the inversion form in reverse, it is found on the matrix by reading the desired transposition of the inversion form backwards (from bottom to top). Once again the retrograde-inversion transpositions will be labeled with RI plus the pc number that ends the row form (RI3, etc.). Thus RI0 is always the reverse of I0.

Advanced Twelve-tone Techniques

The twelve-tone technique quickly gave rise to several further developments of the system that help to promote consistency in atonal music.

Combinatoriality

The first of these advanced techniques of twelve-tone composition, hexachordal combinatoriality, was first used by Schoenberg, although the specific terminology and the full extent of its possible uses were only adopted later by serial composer Milton Babbitt. A combinatorial series is constructed in such a way that when it is simultaneously stated with another of its permutations, each half (hexachord, six notes) of the prime form combines with the corresponding half of the other row form to create an aggregate, which is a new twelve-tone series that is not a form of the piece's primary series.

Row Inbreeding (Invariance)

Another development upon twelve-tone technique that was developed primarily by Anton Webern is a sort of "row inbreeding" or the use of a series with fewer than 48 possible permutations. This is accomplished by using intervallic similarity within the row with the intention of making two or more of the row forms identical. The resulting "inbred" series is called a "derived row". To see this in action, try entering the chromatic scale (0, 1, 2, 3, 4, 5, 6, 7, 8, 9, T, E) into the Matrix Generator, and see how this reduces the number of unique row forms. An ancillary side-effect of this technique is that invariant rows are also combinatorial.

Series with fewer than twelve tones

Many who tried twelve-tone composition also experimented with applying the technique to sets of fewer than twelve tones. When Russian composer Igor Stravinsky began to compose using the twelve-tone technique in the early 1950s, some of his pieces successfully displayed serialism with fewer than twelve pitch-classes. The easiest analytic technique with this type of row is to "complete the aggregate" (i.e. fill out the rest of the chromatic scale when generating a matrix). This technique allows all 12 transpositions of the row forms to be seen, even if analytically extraneous pitch classes appear in the matrix.

Tonal implications within the row

Another manipulation of the twelve-tone method is found in many composers' return to tonal materials and structures within the twelve-tone system. This seems to represent a regression in technique rather than an advance because it undermines Schoenberg's most basic precept that he had developed his method in order to create orderly atonal structures that could replace tonality entirely (without reference to the tonal system).

The most notable early examples of this trend in twelve-tone composition can be found in many of Schoenberg's own late compositions and in much of his student Alban Berg's twelve-tone music. Many other more recent composers have experimented with serial technique within an extended (not always harmonically functional) tonal language.

Integral Serialism

Serialism, as defined as a musical trend encompassing more organizing principles than the twelve-tone system alone, came into full force around 1950 in association with the Darmstadt International Summer Course for New Music in Germany. The main idea developed by composers such as Olivier Messiaen, Karlheinz Stockhausen, and Pierre Boulez (and also by Milton Babbitt in America, though not associated with Darmstadt) is that Schoenberg's serial ordering process should be applied to all of the other musical perameters including rhythm, dynamics, timbre, the types of attacks and articulations used, etc. This so-called "Total Serialism" became the dominating force in music composition for much of the second half of the twentieth century.

The process of serializing musical elements other than pitch involves the selection of twelve (or however many elements are in the series used in the piece) rhythmic values, dynamic levels, types of attacks, etc. The row orderings are then followed in adding all of these parameters to the music. The complexity and algorithmic precision of such composition techniques led composers to try allowing computers to carry out the compositional process once the series has been selected.

Contour Analysis

Post-tonal music that eschews tonal functionality certainly demands more of its audience because of the relative difficulty in perceiving harmonic relations without tonal function. Often listeners are forced (at least before intensively studying a work) to attend to more primitive meaning-creating structures that exist in music, based on perameters independent of harmony, diatonicism, intervallic size, and tonal content. These features of the music, including rhythm, motive, shape, and gesture, are often associated with the relative height of pitches regardless of pitch class or intervallic content. The techniques of contour analysis are designed to offer insights into the non-pitch-specific aspects of all music, both tonal and post-functional.

CSEGs and Contour Class Equivalence

Contour analysis thus ignores the exact notes and intervals of the musical material, instead attending to which notes are higher and lower. A contour segment (CSEG), is a numeric representation of the relative heights the notes in any melody or melodic fragment. It is an ordered collection, with as many elements as there are notes (n), each numbered from lowest to highest (beginning with 0) according to the height of the note within the segment.

For instance, a motive that appears as (D4, C4, B4, F6) in one presentation, and as (F#5, F5, B5, D6) in a later presentation will be described using the CSEG <1,0,2,3>. This shows the motivic unity between these two melodic fragments, while ignoring their differences. (The two pc sets ((0136) and (0147)) have different (but similar) interval vectors.)

Like twelve-tone rows, these ordered collections can be inverted, retrograded, and retrograde-inverted and still retain their motivic identity. For this reason, CSEGs can be organized into CSEG-classes, and a method for finding the "prime form" of contours has been determined as follows:

(n = the number of notes in the segment, or the cardinality of the CSEG)

— If necessary, translate the CSEG so that it consists of integers from 0 to (n - 1).

— If (n - 1) minus the last number in the CSEG is less than the first number in the CSEG, invert the CSEG.

— If the last number in the CSEG is less than the first number in the CSEG, retrograde the CSEG.

Contour Reduction Technique

The Contour Analyzer returns the prime form of the CSEG given. However, it also abstracts the general shape of longer melodic segments before determining the prime form. The process by which longer melodies can be reduced to simpler contours was introduced by Robert Morris. In a method loosely modeled upon Schenkerian analysis, the inner members of "melodically fluent" (Schenker's term, not Morris') lines between structurally important contour events can be removed from the analysis without detriment to the perception of contour. For example, a CSEG <2,0,1,3,5,6,4>, after removing the passing tones between 0 and 6, would reduce to <1,0,3,2>. Morris' criterion for deciding the structural importance of certain c-pitches is their status as "minima" and "maxima", or c-pitches at local low and high points in a melody.

The first and last c-pitches are never reduced out, and the process is recursive, repruning the CSEG until it can be reduced no further (all c-pitches are maxima or minima). A useful example of the application of contour analysis is given by Joseph Straus. He takes two excerpts from Ruth Crawford (Seeger)'s String Quartet, 1st mvt:

F#5	G4	Db5	C6	B5	G#5	C#5	F#5	E6	F5	G4	Db5	C6
<2013>					<2013>				<2013>			

F#4	G3	B3	A#4	C5	G#4	C#4	E4	D#5	D4	A4	F#4	G3	B3	A#4
<2013>					<2013>						<2013>			
									<1320>					
	<0231>					<0231>								

The CSEGs that Straus selects from the melody are all instances of CSEG class 4-4, <0,2,3,1>. Using Morris' technique on each melodic excerpt (using the Contour Analyzer) reveals another unifying feature: Both melodies exhibit the same general contour (CSEG class 4-7, <1032>). Further, within the process by which each is reduced one can find a similar "middleground" contour exhibited by both melodies (<3,0,4,2,5,1,4> in the first case, and <3,0,5,2,6,1,4> in the second).

PC set comparison among CSEGs that are members of the same CSEG class or exhibit similarity relations may also provide useful insights into a piece's construction. Morris suggests that contour analysis may also be applicable to other perameters of the music other than relative pitch height, such as relative note duration and relative dynamic levels or accents. Contour analysis is thus a valuable analytical tool for extracting meaningful structures from both tonal and atonal pieces of music.

Diatonic Functionality

Diatonic functionality, in music, is the assumption used in tonal music theory that a pitch or pitch class and its enharmonic equivalents can not be used in the same way. For example a C# cannot be used as a Db, however this is not to say that they are not enharmonic equivalents, for they are in equal temperament, but rather that a Bb minor chord does not have a C# as its third, but a Db, and an F# major scale does not have a Db as its fifth degree, but a C#.

Thus a pitch may or may not fulfill one or more functions. Functional tonality refers to tonality which uses diatonic functions, non-functi[onal tonality being when the diatonic elements are present (for instance the major scale) but do not use or fulfill their possible function as in, for instance, pandiatonicism.

In theory as commonly taught in the US, there are seven different functions, while in Germany, from the theories of Hugo Riemann, there are only three, and functions besides the tonic, subdominant and dominant are named as "parallels" (US: relatives) to those functions. For instance in C major an a minor is the Tonic parallel or Tp. German musicians use only upper case note letter and roman numeral abbreviations, while in the US often upper and lower-case are used to designate major and augmented, and minor and diminised, respectively.

In the United States, Germany, and other places the diatonic functions are:

Function	Roman Numeral	German	German abbreviation
Tonic	I	Tonic	T
Supertonic	II	Subdominant] parallel	Sp

Mediant	III	Dominant parallel	Dp
Sub-Dominant	IV	Subdominant	S
Dominant	V	Dominant	D
Sub-Mediant	VI	Tonic parallel	Tp
Leading/Subtonic	VII	incomplete Dominant seventh	diagonally slashed D7

The degrees listed according to function, in hierarchical order according to importance or centeredness (related to the tonic): I, V, IV, vi, iii, ii, vii°.

First three chords are major, the next minor, and the last diminished. Tonic, subdominant, and dominant chords, in root position, each followed by its parallel. Parallel is formed by rasing the fifth a whole tone, the root position of the parallel chords is indicated by small noteheads.

In the US the minor mode or scale is considered a variant of the major, while in German theory it is often considered, per Riemann, the inversion of the major. In the late eighteenth-early nineteenth centuries a large amount of symmetrical chords and relations known as "dualistic" harmony. The root of a major chord is its bass note in first inversion or normal form at the bottom of a third and fifth, but, symmetrically, the root of a major chord is the US fifth of a first inversion minor chord, and the US root is the "fifth". The plus and degree symbols, + and o are used to denote that the lower tone of the fifth is the root, as in major, +d, or the higher, as in minor, od. Thus, if the major tonic parallel is the tonic, with the fifth raised a whole tone, then the minor tonic is the tonic with the US root/German fifth lowered a whole tone.

Major			Minor		
Parallel	Note letter in C	US name	Parallel	Note letter in C	US name
Tp	A minor	Submediant	tP	Eb major	Mediant
Sp	D minor	Supertonic	sP	Ab major	Submediant
Dp	E minor	Mediant	dP	Bb major	Subtonic

The minor tonic, subdominant, dominant, and their parallels, created by lowering the fifth (German)/root (US) a whole tone.

If chords may be formed by raising (major) or lowering (minor) the fifth a whole step, they may also be formed by lowering (major) or raising (minor) the root a half-step to wechsel, the leading tone or leitton. These chords are Leittonwechselklänge, sometimes called gegenklang or "contrast chord".

Leittonwechselklänge					
Major			Minor		
Tl	Sl	Dl	tL	sL	dL
E minor	A minor	B minor	Ab major	Db major	Eb major

Major Leittonwechselklänge, formed by lowering the root a half step.

Minor Leittonwechselklänge, formed by raising the root (US)/fifth (German) a half step.

"Three categories can appear in any one of three chordal guises in either of two modes, eighteen positions in all: T, Tp, Tl, t, tP, tL, S, Sp, Sl, s, sP, sL, D, Dp, Dl, d, dP, dL. Why all this complexity? Perhaps the central reason is that this ingenious, occasionally convoluted system enabled Riemann to achieve a grand and masterful synthesis of both the old and the new in late 19-century music. Ostensibly remote triads could be interpreted through the traditional terms of the I-IV-V-I, or now T-S-D-T, cadential schema.

A sequence of Ab-major, Bb-major, and C-major chords, for example, could be neatly interpreted as a subdominant (sP) to dominant (dP) to tonic (T) progression in C-major, a reading of these chords not without support in certain late-Romantic cadences. And a chord that often perplexes harmony students, the Neapolitan chord Db major in a C-major context, could be shown to be nothing more than a minor-mode subdominant Liettonwechselklang (sL). Some may at first be put off by the overt theorizing apparent in German harmony, wishing perhaps that a choice be made once and for all between Reichmann's Functionstheorie and the older Stufentheorie, or possibly believing that so-called linear theories have settled all earlier disputes. Yet this ongoing conflict between antdithetical theories, with its attendent uncertainties and complexities, has special merits. In particuler, whereas an English-speaking student may falsely believe that he or she is learning harmony as it really is, the German student encounters what are obviously theoretical constructs and must deal with them accordingly.

Tonicization and Modulation

Functions during or after modulations and especiallyl tonicizations are often notated in relation to the function, in the original key, which the tonicization was to. Sometimes called "function of function", for example, in C major, a D major chord root, is notated as II, but during a tonicization on G major, it would be notated, as in G major, V, as it is the dominant of (in C major) the dominant, it is notated V/V (five of five). For example, the twelve bar blues turnaround, I-V-IV-I, considered tonally inadmissable, may be interpreted as a doubled plagal cadence, IV/V-V-IV-I (IV/V-I/V, IV/I-I/I).

7

Tempo Tracking

An important and interesting subtask in automatic music transcription is tempo tracking: how to follow the tempo in a performance that contains expressive timing and tempo variations. When these tempo fluctuations are correctly identified it becomes much easier to separate the continuous expressive timing from the discrete note categories (i.e. quantization). The sense of tempo seems to be carried by the beats and thus tempo tracking is related to the study of beat induction, the perception of beats or pulse while listening to music. However, it is still unclear what precisely constitutes tempo and how it relates to the perception of rhythmical structure.

Tempo is a perceptual construct and cannot directly be measured in a performance. In the context of tempo tracking, wavelet analysis and related techniques are already investigated by various researchers. The tempogram is also related to the periodicity transform proposed by Sethares & Staley in 1999, but uses a time localized basis. Kalman filters are already applied in the music domain such as polyphonic pitch tracking and audio restoration. Tempogram representation extract beats from performances and discuss the probabilistic interpretation.

Dynamical Systems

Mathematically, a dynamical system is characterized by a set of state variables and a set of state transition equations that describe how state variables evolve with time. For example, a perfect metronome can be described as a dynamical system with two state variables: a beat $\hat{\tau}$ and a period. Given the values of state variables at j - 1'th step as $\hat{\Delta}_{j-1}$ and $\hat{\Delta}_{j-1}$, the next beat occurs at $\hat{\tau}_j = \hat{\tau}_{j-1} + {}_{j-1}$. The period of a perfect metronome is constant so $\hat{\Delta}_j = \hat{\Delta}_{j-1}$. By using vector notation and by letting $s_j = [\hat{\tau}_j, {}_j]^T$ we can write a linear state transition model as

$$\mathrm{s}_j = \begin{pmatrix} 1 & 1 \\ 0 & 1 \end{pmatrix} \mathrm{s}_{j-1} = \mathrm{As}_{j-1} \qquad (1)$$

When the initial state $\mathrm{s}_0 = [\hat{\tau}_0, \hat{\Delta}_0]^T$ is given, the system is fully specified. For example if the metronom clicks at a tempo 60 beats per minute ($\hat{\Delta}_0 = 1$ sec.) and first click occurs at time $\hat{\tau}_0 = 0$ sec., next beats occur at $\hat{\tau}_1 = 1$, $\hat{\tau}_2 = 2$ e.t.c. Since the metronom is perfect the period stays constant.

Such a deterministic model is not realistic for natural music performance and can not be used for tracking the tempo in presence of tempo fluctuations and expressive timing deviations. Tempo fluctuations may be modeled by introducing a noise term that "corrupts" the state vector

$$\mathrm{s}_j = \mathrm{As}_{j-1} + \mathrm{v}_j \qquad (2)$$

where v is a Gaussian random vector with mean 0 and diagonal covariance matrix Q, i.e. v ~ $N(0,Q)$. The tempo will drift from the initial tempo quickly if the variance of v is large. On the other hand when Q → 0, we have the constant tempo case.

In a music performance, the actual beat $\hat{\tau}$ and the period $\hat{\Delta}$ can not be observed directly. By actual beat iterpretation that coincides with human perception when listening to music. For example, suppose, an expert drummer is tapping along a performance at the beat level and we assume her beats as the correct tempo track. If the task would be repeated on the same piece, we would observe each time a slightly different tempo track. As an alternative, suppose we would know the score of the performance and identify onsets that coincide with the beat. However, due to small scale expressive timing deviations, these onsets will be also noisy, i.e. we can at best observe "noisy" versions of actual beats. We can denote this noisy beat by τ in contrast to the actual but unobservable beat $\hat{\tau}$. Mathematically we have

$$\tau_j = \hat{\tau}_j + w_j \tag{3}$$

where $w_j \sim N(0,R)$. Here, tj is the beat at step j that we get from a (noisy) observation process. In this formulation, tempo tracking corresponds to the estimation of hidden variables $\hat{\tau}_j$ given observations upto j'th step. In a "blind" tempo tracking task, i.e. when the score is not known, the (noisy) beat τ_j can not be directly observed since there is no expert drummer who is tapping along, neither a score to guide us. The noisy-beat itself has to be induced from events in the music.

Equations 2 and 3 define a linear dynamical system, because all noises are assumed to be Gaussian and all relationships between variables are linear. Hence, all state vectors s_j have Gaussian distributions. A Gaussian distribution is fully characterized by its mean and covariance matrix and in the context of linear dynamical systems, these quantities can be estimated very efficiently by a Kalman filter. The operation of the filter is illustrated in Figure 1.

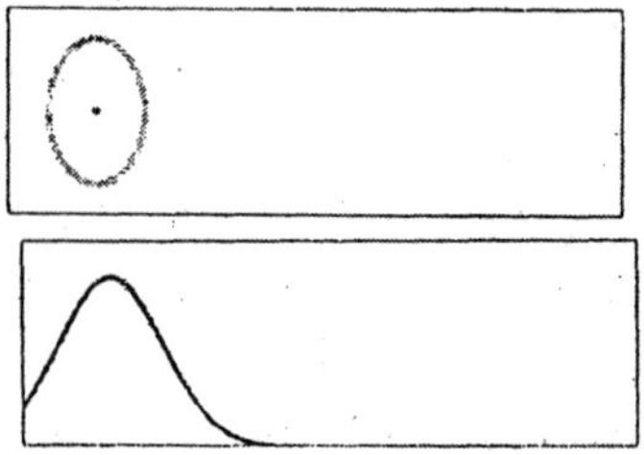

(a) The algorithm starts with the initial state estimate $N(\mu_{1|0}, P_{1|0})$.

The system is given by Equations 2 and 3. In each subfigure, the above coordinate system represents the hidden state space $[\hat{\tau}, \hat{\Delta}]^T$ and the below coordinate system represent the observable space τ. In the hidden space, the x and y axes represent the phase $\hat{\tau}$ period $\hat{\Delta}$ of the tracker. The ellipse and its center correspond to the covariance and the mean of the hidden state estimate $p(s_j \mid \tau_1 \ldots \tau_k) = N(\mu_{j|k}, P_{j|k})$ where $\mu_{j|k}$ and $P_{j|k}$ denote the estimated mean and covariance given observations $\tau_1 \ldots \tau_k$. In the observable space, the vertical axis represents the predictive probability distribution $p(\tau_j \mid \tau_j\text{-}1 \ldots \tau_1)$.

The basic model can be extended in several directions. First, the linearity constraint on the Kalman filter can be relaxed. Indeed, in tempo tracking such an extension is necessary to ensure that the period $\hat{\Delta}$ is always positive. Therefore the state transition model in a warped space defined by the mapping $\omega = \log_2 \Delta$. This warping also ensures the perceptually more plausible assumption that tempo changes are relative rather than absolute.

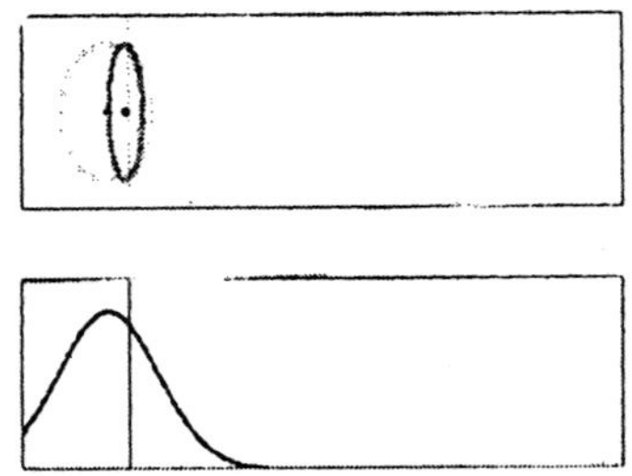

(b) The beat is observed at τ_1, The state is updated to $N(\mu_{1|1}, P_{1|1})$ according to the new evidence. Note that the uncertainty "shrinks",

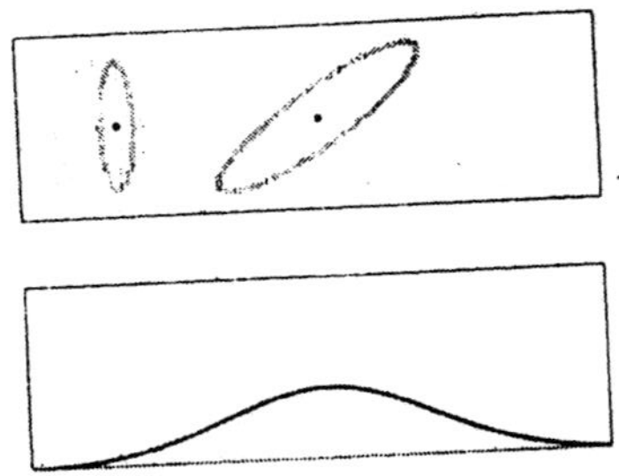

(c) On the basis of current state a new prediction $N(\mu_{2|1}, P_{2|1})$ is made,

Figure 1. Operation of the Kalman Filter and Smoother.

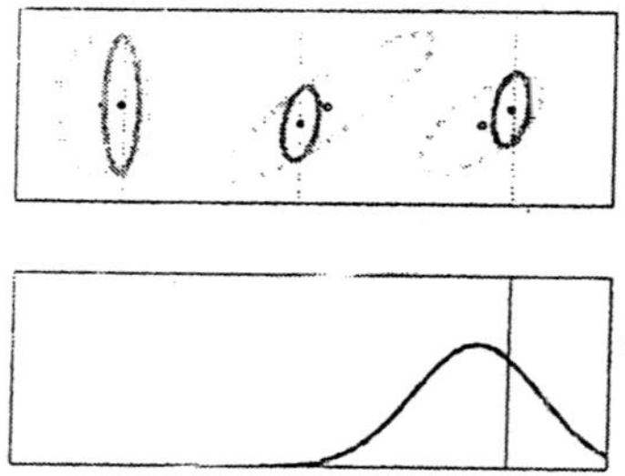

(d) Steps are repeated until all evidence is processed to obtain filtered estimates $N(\mu_{j|j}, P_{j|j})$, $j = 1 \ldots N$. In this case $N = 3$.

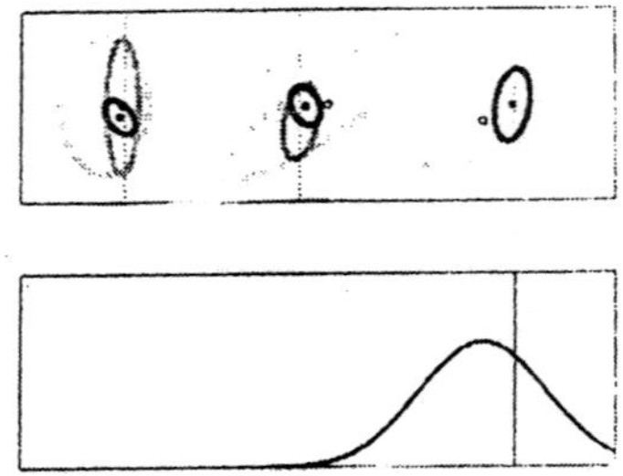

(e) **Filtered estimates are updated by backtracking to obtain smoothed estimates** $N(\mu_{i|N}, P_{i|N})$.

For example, under this warping, a deceleration from $\Delta \rightarrow 2\Delta$ has the same likelihood as an acceleration from $\Delta \rightarrow \Delta/2$. The state space s_j can be extended with additional dynamic variables $\hat{\tau} j$. Such additional variables store information about the past states (e.g. in terms of acceleration e.t.c.) and introduce inertia to the system. Inertia reduces the random walk behavior in the state space and renders smooth state trajectories more likely. Moreover, this can result in more accurate predictions.

The observation noise w_j can be modeled as a mixture of gaussians. This choice has the following rationale: To follow tempo fluctuations the observation noise variance R should not be too "broad". A broad noise covariance indicates that observations are not very reliable, so they have less effect to the state estimates.

In the extreme case when $R \rightarrow \infty$, all observations are practically missing so the observations have no effect on state estimates. On the other hand, a narrowR makes the filter sensitive to outliers since the same noise covariance is used regardless of the distance of an observation from its prediction. Outliers can be explicitely modeled by using a mixture of Gaussians, for example one "narrow" Gaussian for normal operation, and one "broad" Gaussian for outliers. Such a switching mechanism can be implemented by using a discrete variable c_j which indicates whether the j'th observation is an outlier or not. In other words different noise covariance depending upon the value of c_j. Mathematically, to write this statement as $w_j \mid c_j \sim N(0,R_c)$. Since c_j, a prior probability $c_j \sim p(c)$ and sum over all possible settings of c_j , i.e. $p(w_j) = \Sigma_{cj}\, p(c_j)p(w_j \mid c_j)$. In Figure 2 we can compare a switching Kalman filter and a standard Kalman filter. A switch variable makes a system more robust against outliers and consequentlymore realistic state estimates can be obtained. To summerize, the dynamical model of the tempo tracker is given by

$$\tau_j = \hat{\tau}_{j-1} + 2^{\omega_{j-1}} \tag{4}$$

$$\begin{pmatrix} \hat{\omega}_j \\ \hat{\mathrm{a}}_j \end{pmatrix} = \mathrm{A} \begin{pmatrix} \hat{\omega}_{j-1} \\ \hat{\mathrm{a}}_{j-1} \end{pmatrix} + \mathrm{v}_j \tag{5}$$

$$\begin{pmatrix} \tau_j \\ \omega_j \end{pmatrix} = \begin{pmatrix} \hat{\tau}_j \\ \hat{\omega}_j \end{pmatrix} + \mathrm{w}_j \tag{6}$$

where $\mathrm{v}_j \sim N(0,Q)$, $\mathrm{w}_j | c_j \sim N(0,Rc)$ and $c_j \sim p(c_j)$. c_j as a binary discrete switch variable. Note that, in Eq. 6 the observable space is two dimensional (includes both τ and ω), in contrast to one dimensional observable τ in Figure 2.

Tempogram Representation

In a real musical situation, however, the beat can not be observed directly from performance data. The sensation of a beat emerges from a collection of events rather than, say, single onsets. For example, a syncopated rhythm induces beats which do not neccesarly coincide with an onset.

A probability distribution which assigns probability masses to all possible beat interpretations given a performance. The Bayesian formulation of this problem is

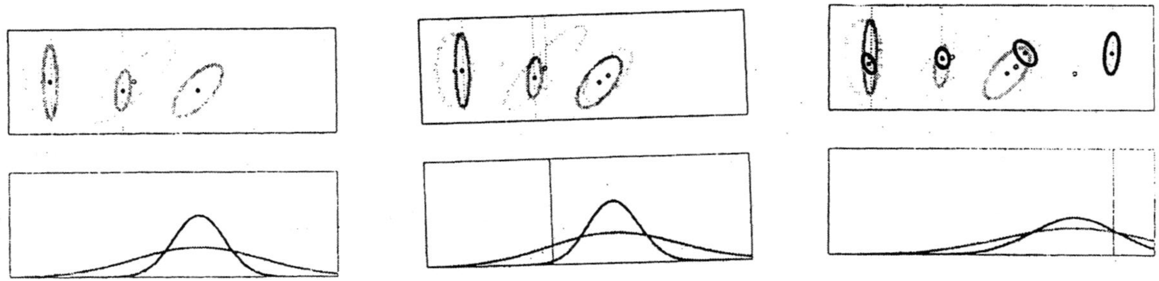

(a) Based on the state estimate $N(\mu_{2|2}, P_{2|2})$ the next state is predicted as $N(\mu_{3|2}, P_{3|2})$. When propagated through the measurement model, we obtain $p(\tau_3 | \tau_2, \tau_1)$, which is a mixture of Gaussians where the mixing coefficients are given by $p(c)$,

(b) The observation τ_3 is way off the mean of the prediction, i.e. it is highly likely an outlier. Only the broad Gaussian is active, which reflects the fact that the observations are expected to be very noisy. Consequently, the updated state estimate $N(\mu_{3|3}, P_{3|3})$ is not much different than its prediction $N(\mu_{3|3}, P_{3|3})$. However, the uncertainty in the next prediction $N(\mu_{4|3}, P_{4|3})$ will be higher,

(c) After all observations are obtained, the smoothed estimates $N(\mu_{j|4}, P_{j|4})$ are obtained. The estimated state trajectory shows that the observation τ_3 is correctly interpreted as an outlier.

Figure 2. Comparison of a standard Kalman filter with a switching Kalman filter.

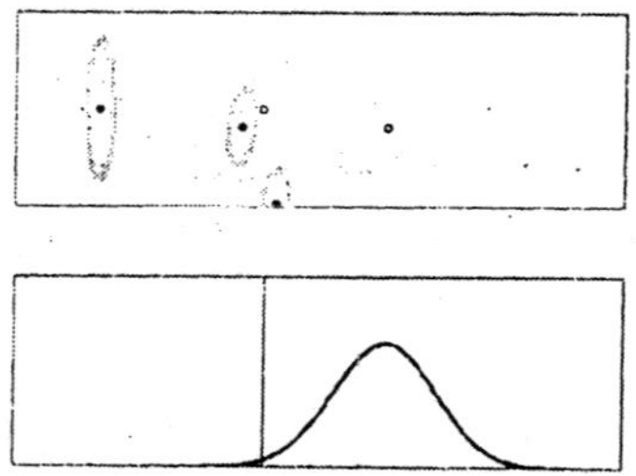

(d) In contrast to the switching Kalman filter, the ordinary Kalman filter is sensitive against outliers. In contrast to (b), the updated state estimate $N(\mu_{313}, P_{313})$ is way off the prediction.

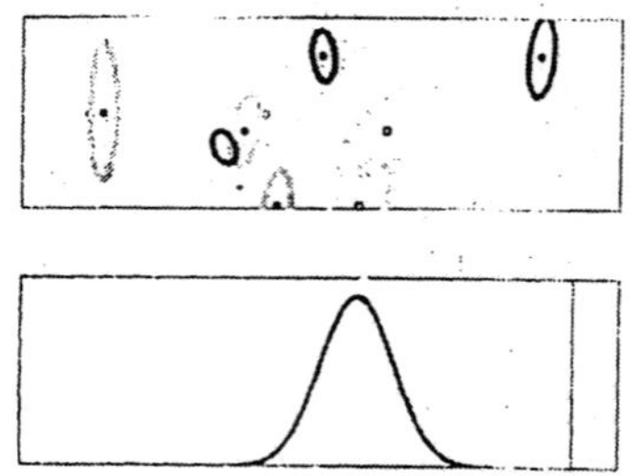

(e) Consequently a very "jumpy" state trajectory is estimated. This is simply due to the fact that the observation model does not account for presence of outliers.

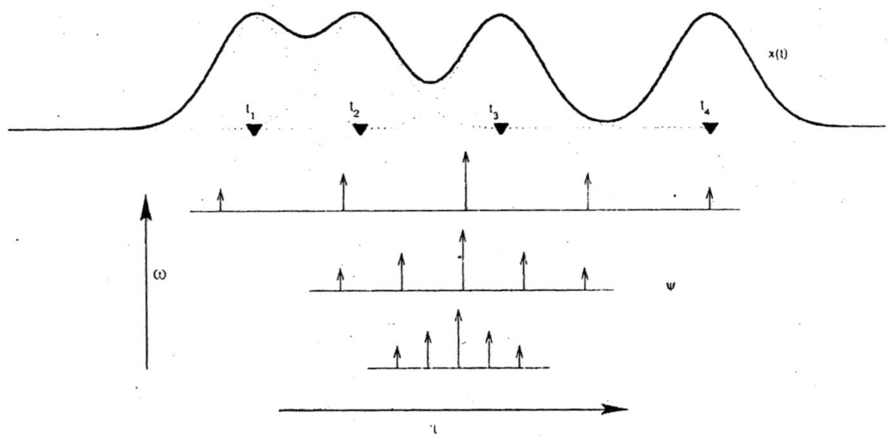

Figure 3. Tempogram Calculation. The continuous signal x(t) is obtained from the onset list by convolution with a Gaussian function. Below, three different basis functions ψ are shown. All are localized at the same τ and different ω. The tempogram at (τ, ω) is calculated by taking the inner product of x(t) and (t; τ ω). Due to the sparse nature of the basis functions, the inner product operation can be implemented very efficiently.

$$p(\tau, \omega \mid t) \propto p(t \mid t, \omega)p(\tau, \omega) \tag{7}$$

where τ is an onset list. In this context, a beat interpretation is the tuple τ (local beat) and *ω* (local log-period).

The first term $p(t \mid \tau,\omega)$ in Eq.7 is the probability of the onset list t given the tempo track. Since t is actually observed, $p(t \mid \tau, \omega)$ is a function of τ and *ω* and is thus called the likelihood of *τ* and *ω*. The second term $p(\tau, \omega)$ in Eq.7 is the prior distribution. The prior can be viewed as a function which weights the likelihood on the (τ, ω) space. It is reasonable to assume that the likelihood $p(t \mid \tau, \omega)$ is high when onsets $[t_i]$ in the performance coincide with the beats of the tempo track. To construct a likelihood function having this property, a similarity measure between the performance and a local constant tempo track. First we can define a continuous time signal $x(t) = \Sigma^{I}_{i=1} G(t - t_i)$ where we can take $G(t) = \exp(-t^2/2\sigma^2_x)$, a Gaussian function with variance σ^2_x. A local tempo track as a pulse train $\psi(t; \tau, \omega) = \Sigma\infty_m = \infty\ \alpha_m\ \delta(t\text{-}\tau\text{-}m2^{\omega})$ where $\delta(t - t_0)$ is a Dirac delta function, which represents an impulse located at t_0. The coefficients α_m are positive constants such that $\Sigma_m \alpha_m$ is a constant. (See Figure 3). In real-time applications, where causal analysis is desirable, am can be set to zero for $m > 0$. When α_m is a sequence of form $\alpha_m = \alpha_{m'}$, where $0 < \alpha < 1$, one has the infinite impulse response (IIR) comb filters are here. The tempogram of $x(t)$ at each (τ, ω) as the inner product

$$\mathrm{Tg}_x(\tau, \omega) = \int dt\ x(t)\psi(t; \tau, \omega) \tag{8}$$

The tempogram representation can be interpreted as the response of a comb filter bank and is analogous to a

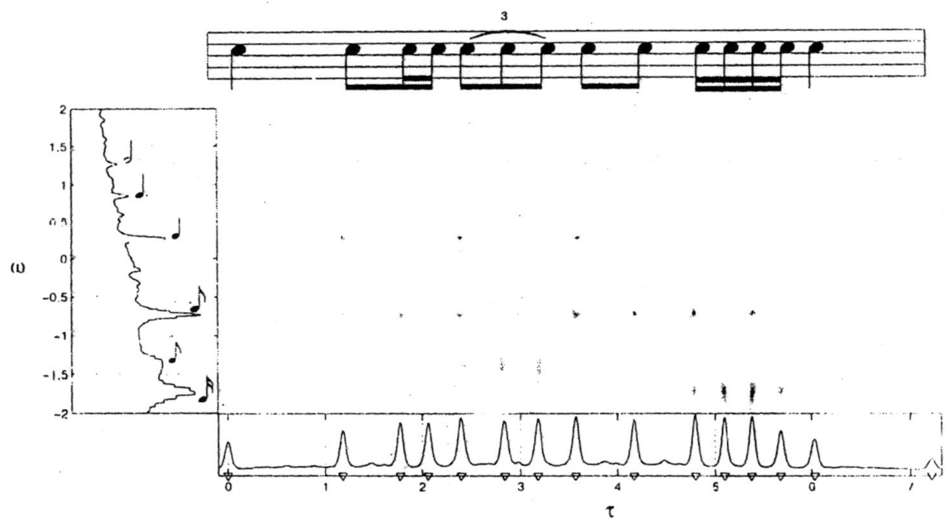

Figure 4. A simple rhythm and its Tempogram. x and y axes correspond to τ and ω respectively. The bottom figure shows the onset sequence (triangles). Assuming flat priors on τ and ω, the curve along the ω axis is the marginal $p(\omega \mid t) \propto \int d\tau \exp(Tg_x(\tau,\omega))$. $p(\omega \mid t)$ has peaks at ω, which correspond to quarter, eight and sixteenth note level as well as dotted quarter and half note levels of the original notation. This distribution can be used to estimate a reasonable initial state.

multiscale representation (e.g. the wavelet transform), where τ and ω correspond to transition and scaling parameters. The tempogram parameters have simple interpretations. The filter coefficient a adjust the time locality of basis functions. When a $\rightarrow$ 1, basis functions ω extend to infinity and locality is lost. For $\alpha \rightarrow 0$ the basis degenerates to a single Dirac pulse and the tempogram is effectively equal to $x(t)$ for all ω and thus gives no information about the local period.

The variance parameter σ_x corresponds to the amount of small scale expressive deviation in an onsets timing. If σ_x would be large, the tempogram gets "smeared-out" and all beat interpretations become almost equally likely. When $\sigma_x \rightarrow 0$, we get a very "spiky" tempogram, where most beat interpretations have zero probability.

In Figure 4 a tempogram obtained from a simple onset sequence. The likelihood as $p(t \mid \tau, \omega) \cdot \exp(Tg_x(\tau, \omega))$. When combined with the prior, the tempogram gives an estimate of likely beat interpretations (τ, ω).

Model Training

In this section, we can see the summary of conditional distributions and their parameters. First, we can summerize the relationships among variables by using a a graphical model. A graphical model is a directed acyclic graph, where nodes represent variables and missing directed links represent conditional independence relations. The distributions that we have specified so far are summarized in Table 1.

Table 1: Summary of conditional distributions and their parameters

Model	Distribution	Parameters
State Transition (Eq. 5)	$p(s_j+_1 \mid s_j)$	A, Q
(Switching) Observation (Eq. 6)	$p(\tau_j, \omega_j \mid s_j, c_j)$	R_c
Switch prior (Eq. 6)	$p(c_j)$	p_c
Tempogram (Eq.8)	$p(t \mid \tau_j, \omega_j)$	σ_x, α

The resulting graphical model is shown in Figure 5. For example, the graphical model has a directed link from s_j to s_j+1 to encode $p(s_{j+1} \mid s_j)$. Other links towards s_{j+1} are missing. In principle, we could jointly optimize allmodel parameters. However, such an approach would be computationally very intensive.

This observation effectively "decouples" the model into two parts (See Fig. 5), (i) The Kalman Filter (State transition model and Observation (Switch) model) and (ii) Tempogram. We will train each part separately.

Estimation of t_j from performance data

A score is always available, so we can extract τ_j from a performance t by matching the notes that coincide with the beat (quarter note) level and the bar (whole note). If there are more than one note on a beat, and take the median of the onset times. For each performance, to compute $\omega_j = \log_2 (\tau_{j+1} - \tau_j)$ from the extracted noisy beats $[\tau_j]$. The resulting tempo track $\{\tau_1, \omega_1 \ldots \tau_j, \omega_j \ldots \tau_J, \omega_J\}$ as $\{\tau_{1:J}, \omega_{1:J}\}$.

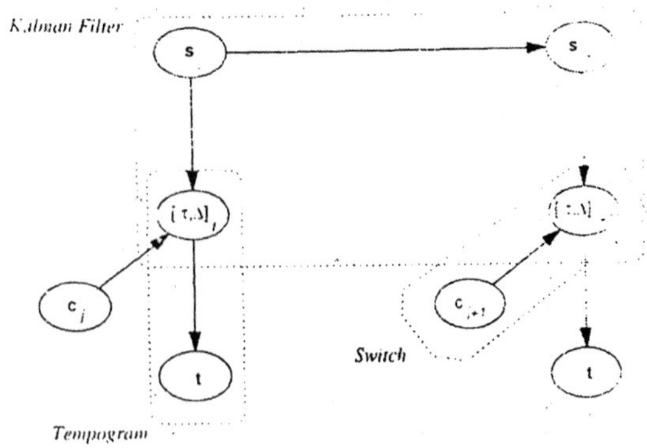

Figure 5. The Graphical Model will assume that we observe the noisy tempo track τ_j.

Estimation of state transition parameters

The state transition model parameters A and Q by an EM algorithm which learns a linear dynamics in the ω space. The EM algorithm monotonically increases $p(\{\tau_{1:j}, \omega_{1:j}\})$, i.e. the likelihood of the observed tempo track. Put another way, the parameters A and Q are adjusted in such a way that, at each j, the probability of the observation is maximized under the predictive distribution $p(\tau_j, \omega_j \mid \tau_{j-1}, \tau_{j-1}, \ldots \tau_1, \omega_1)$. The likelihood is simply the hight of the predictive distribution evaluated at the observation (See Figure 1).

Estimation of switch parameters

The observation model is a Gaussian mixture with diagonal R_c and prior probability p_c. R_c and p_c jointly with the state transition parameters A and Q. However, then the noise model would be totally independent from the tempogram representation. Instead, the observation noise model should reflect the uncertainty in the tempogram; for example the expected amount of deviations in (τ, ω) estimates due to spurious local maxima. To estimate the "tempogram noise" by standard EM methods, sample from the tempogram around each $[\hat{\tau}_j, \hat{\omega}_j]$, i.e. sample τ_j and τ_j from the posterior distribution $p(\tau_j, \omega_j \mid \hat{\tau}_j, \omega_j, t;Q) \propto p(t \mid \tau_j, \omega_j)p(\tau_j, \omega_j \mid \hat{\tau}_j, \hat{\omega}_j ;Q)$. Note that $[\hat{\tau}_j, \hat{\omega}_j]$ are estimated during the E step of the EM algorithm when finding the parameters A and Q.

Estimation of Tempogram parameters

The tempogramas a likelihood $p(t \mid \tau, \omega; \theta)$ where θ denotes the tempogram parameters (e.g. $\theta = \{\alpha, \sigma_x\}$). If we assume a uniform prior $p(\tau, \omega)$ then the posterior probability can be written as

$$p(\tau, \omega | t: \theta) = \frac{p(t|\tau, \omega: \theta)}{p(t|\theta)} \tag{9}$$

where the normalization constant is given by $p(t \mid \theta) = \int d\tau d0\omega \; p(t \mid \tau, \omega; \theta)$. Now, we can estimate tempogram parameters θ by a maximum likelihood approach. The log-likelihood of an observed tempo track $\{\tau_{1:j}, \omega_{1:j}\}$ as

$$\log p(\{\tau_{1:J}, \omega_{1:J}\}|t: \theta) = \sum_j \log p(\tau_j, \omega_j|t: \theta) \tag{10}$$

Note that the quantity in Equation 10 is a function of the parameters ω. If we have k tempo tracks in the dataset, the complete data log-likelihood is simply the sum of all individual log-likelihoods. i.e.

$$\mathcal{L} = \sum_k \log p(\{\tau_{1:J}, \omega_{1:J}\}^k | \mathbf{t}^k; a, \sigma_x) \tag{11}$$

where t^k is the k'th performance and $\{\tau_{1:J}, \omega_{1:J}\}^k$ is the corresponding tempo track.

Evaluation

Many tempo trackers described in the introduction are often tested with ad hoc examples. However, to validate tempo tracking models, more systematic data and rigorous testing is necessary. A tempo tracker can be evaluated by systematically modulating the tempo of the data, for instance by applying instantaneous or gradual tempo changes and comparing the models responses to human behavior. Another approach is to evaluate tempo trackers on a systematically collected set of natural data, monitoring piano performances in which the use of expressive tempo change is free. This type of data has the advantage of reflecting the type of data one expects automated music transcription systems to deal with.

A tempogram model used with a first order IIR comb basis. This choice leaves two free parameters that need to be estimated from data, namely a, the coefficient of the comb filter and sx, the width of the Gaussian window. The optimal parameter values by maximization of the log-likelihood in Equation 11 on the Michelle dataset. The optimal parameters are shown in Table 2.

Table 2: Optimal tempogram parameters

	α	ρ_x
Non-Causal	0.55	0.017
Causal	0.73	0.023

Initialization

To have a fully automated tempo tracker, the initial state s0 has to be estimated from data as well. In the tracking experiments, we have initialized the filter to the beat level by computing a tempogram for the first 5 seconds of each performance. By assuming a flat prior on τ and ω, compute the posterior marginal $p(\omega \mid t) = \int d\tau p(\omega, \tau \mid t)$. Note that this is operation is just equivalent to summation along the t dimension of the tempogram (See Figure 4).

For the Beatles dataset, all performances of a given piece, the most likely log-period $\omega^* = \arg\max_\omega p(\omega \mid t)$ corresponds always to the same level, i.e. the ω^* estimate was always consistent. For "Michelle", this level is the beat level and for "Yesterday" the half-beat (eighth note) level. The latter piece begins with an arpeggio of eight notes; based on onset information only, and without any other prior knowledge, half-beat level is also a reasonable solution. For "Yesterday", to test the tracking performance, we can correct the estimate to the beat level. τ^* using a similar procedure, however since all performances in the data set started "on the beat", we have chosen $\tau^* = t_1$, the first onset of the piece. All the other state variables $\hat{a}_0$ are set to zero. We have chosen a broad initial state covariance $P_0 = 9Q$.

Evaluation of tempo tracking performance

To evaluate, the accuracy of the tempo tracking performance

of the completemodel. The accuracy of tempo tracking is measured by using the following criterion:

where $[\psi_i]$ $i = 1 \dots I$ is the target (true) tempo track and $[t_j]$ $j = 1 \dots J$ is the estimated tempo track. W is a window function. In the following results we have used a Gaussian window function $W(d) = \exp(-d^2/2\sigma_e^2)$. The width of the window is chosen as $\sigma_e = 0.04$ sec which corresponds roughly to the spread of onsets from their mechanical means during performance of short rhythms.

It can be checked that $0 \leq \rho \leq 100$ and $\rho = 100$ if and only if $\psi = t$. Intuitively, this measure is similar to a normalized inner-product (as in the tempogram calculation); the difference is in the max operator which merely avoids double counting. For example, if the target is $\psi = [0, 1, 2]$ and we have $t = [0, 0, 0]$, the ordinary inner product would still give $\rho = 100$ while only one beat is correct ($t = 0$). The proposed measure gives $\rho = 33$ in this case. The tracking index ρ can be roughly interpreted as percentage of "correct" beats. For example, $\rho = 90$ effectively means that about 9C percent of estimated beats are in the near vicinity of their targets.

To test the relative relevance of model components, the tempo tracking performance under different conditions. We have varied the filter order and enabled or disabled switching. For this purpose, there are two filters, one with a large and one with a small state space dimension on beat level (using the Michelle dataset). Tested each model with both causal and non-causal tempograms. To test whether a tempogram is at all necessary, we can propose a simple onset-only measurement model. In Kalman filter prediction, there are no onsets in 1σ interval of the prediction.

In Table 3 the tracking results averaged over all performances in the Yesterday dataset. The estimated tempo tracks are obtained by using a non-causal tempogram and Kalman filtering. In this case, Kalman smoothed estimates are not significantly different. The results suggest, that for the Yesterday dataset, a higher order filter or a (binary) switching mechanism does not improve the tracking performance.

However, presence of a tempogram makes the tracking performance both more accurate and consistent (note the lower standard deviations). As a "base line" performance criteria, to compute the best constant tempo track (by a linear regression to estimated tempo tracks). In this case, the average tracking index obtained from a constant tempo approximation is rather poor (ρ= 28 ± 18), confirming that there is indeed a need for tempo tracking.

The same experiment with a causal tempogram and computed the tracking performance for predicted, filtered and smoothed estimates In Table 4 we can see the results for a switching Kalman filter. The results without switching are not significantly different. As one would expect, the tracking index with predicted estimates is lower. In contrast to a non-causal tempogram, smoothing improves the tempo tracking and results in a comparable performance as a non-causal tempogram.

Table 3. Average tracking performance ρ and standard deviations on Yesterday dataset using a non-causal tempogram. + denotes the case when we have the switch prior p(c)= [0.8, 0.2]. - denotes the absence of a switching, i.e. the case when p(c) = [1, 0].

Filter order	Switching	tempogram	no tempogram
10	+	92 ± 7	75 ± 21
2	+	91 ± 9	75 ± 21
10	-	91 ± 6	73 ± 21
2	-	90 ± 9	73 ± 22

Naturally, the performance of the tracker depends on the amount of tempo variations introduced by the performer. For example, the tempo tracker fails consistently for a subject who tends to use quite some tempo variation. The tempo tracking performance is not significantly different among different groups (Table 5). For different tempo conditions (Table 6) the results are also similar.

Table 4. Average tracking performance ρ on Yesterday dataset. Figures indicate tracking index ρ followed by the standard deviation. The label "non-causal" refers to a tempogram calculated using non-causal comb filters.

		causal	
Filter order	predicted	filtered	smoothed
10	74 ± 12	86 ± 9	91 ± 8
2	73 ± 12	85 ±	8 90 ± 8

This might have two potential reasons. First, the performance criteria ρ is independent of the absolute tempo, i.e. the window W is always fixed. Second, for slower performances there is more room for adding expression.

Table 5. Tracking Averages on subject groups. As a reference, the right most column shows the results obtained by the best constant tempo track. The label "non-causal" refers to a tempogram calculated using non-causal comb filters.

	non-causal		causal		
Subject Group	filtered	predicted	filtered	smoothed	Best const.
Prof. Jazz	95 ± 3	81 ± 7	92 ± 4	94 ± 3	34 ± 22
Amateur Classical	92 ± 8	74 ± 7	88 ± 5	92 ± 4	24 ± 19
Prof. Classical	89 ± 7	66 ± 14	82 ± 11	86 ± 11	27 ± 12

Table 6: Tracking Averages on tempo conditions. As a reference, the right most column shows the results obtained by the best constant tempo track. The label "non-causal" refers to a tempogram calculated using non-causal comb filters.

	non-causal	causal			
Subject Group	filtered	predicted	filtered	smoothed	Best const.
fast	94 ± 5	79 ± 9	90 ± 6	93 ± 6	39 ± 21
normal	92 ± 8	74 ± 9	88 ± 6	92 ± 4	25 ± 13
slow	90 ± 7	68 ± 14	84 ± 10	87 ± 11	21 ± 14

8

Changing Trends in Music Composition

Until the early half of 20th century, music has been totally dominated by regular measurements of time and rhythm, with up- and down-beats built into every measure. From the time of Scarlatti on, we have a standard formula for a four measure passage in which a phrase is stated, repeated, altered, and then "resolved". This becomes a lock-stepped four part "passage" which can be extended from the simple song to the symphony. This parallels the use in poetry of a classically measured poetic hexameter, but following the pattern of 5th century Latin religious poetry we have a tradition of rhymed couplets in infinitely boring sequence, which dominated English poetry until Milton and the poets of the 17th century restored blank verse by circumcising the rhymed line-ending.

Turn to Music for a moment. Should there not be a free and unfettered musical art which lets cadences flow forth like the words in a well written piece of prose, an art without measured paces, no repeating echoes like those of rhymed poetry, no pre-set structure whether sonata or symphony form filled in with one or two melody lines repeated and recast with variations in pitch ad pace? If we were asking this question in 1900, we would have had to say that much poetry had the kind of freedom we were asking for, while music had very little to show at that time.

But soon after the turn of that century things began to change. We find a vein of music which was emerging after 1910, stretching from early Stravinsky through Schoenberg and his Serials, past Bartok into mid-century Cage aleatorics, on into Electro-Acoustic music with synthesizers and finally computers with composing algorithms. Here the restrictions of rhythm, cadence, harmony and overall form have been totally revised, with the end result of producing something quite different from the musical tradition which comes down to us from the early Renaissance. What is the final result of all this change? Probably that only one percent of humanity likes or can even tolerate the New Music, and many of will go back in a hurry to what it can comfortably understand in the rich world of Classical harmony.

But there is another musical thread which has immense popular appeal worldwide, with the regular beats and measures of Country music, or the non-experimental style of Rock, or the thin three note Pop style with a mild voice wailing over a bass beat with a few stroke of the guitar. Popular and dance music now has the enrichment of available electronic sounds , a piece can revolve around a melody line to hold together an assemblage of factory preset sounds, with predictable meter to set hands keeping time or feet shuffling on the floor. But if you have been musically educated in the Western tradition, you find this popular music thin, so you can turn back to the world of Classical 19th c. music with its fine timbres, great instrumentation, to enjoy the comfort of measure, repetitions and repeated thematic material, the signposts of familiar musical experience.

We do have something more in mind. We want to hear music which is constructed like a well written art-prose, with fine micro-texture in every phrase, freely unfolding so each moment of sound generates artistically what follows in a perceptible and ineluctable order. Our whole musical background is available to us now for re-forming and re-shaping. We have the whole musical range from the fourteenth century to the present time, which we can mold like musical clay into any form and format we can imagine. We can have rhythm which is infinitely variable, pitch and timbre in unthinkable variety, and an overall form as free as a Fantasia to represent the shape of our musical thinking in unconstricted format. These are the tools of music in the new day.

Going into the future of new sounds takes daring and the risk of creating something which is unpopular, ahead of its time. For such a venture what we need most is openness and a fine sense of subtlety, taking time to watch the processes of thought as ideas configure themselves in an auditory montage within our consciousness. It requires mortar to be put things together firmly, and the mortar of music or of any other art is always the same.

Music Composiiton in Digital Age

Music always means lessons for thousands of young adolescents who were set down at the piano as the instrument of choice, learning to push the right buttons for the right black dots on the score page. How many people will remark that they used to play the piano, although it was hardly play in most cases, just hard discipline soon to be terminated as school days ended. For many parents Music Lessons were a matter of cultural prestige, the right thing to do for a child's education, and although the idea was sincere and educational, the process was often more disciplinary than artistic.

As the chain of music becomes longer and more indirect, starting from composer to score to beginning performer studying an instrument, and on to public performer for an audience in a concert venue, or to a recording session in a studio, followed by mastering and finally a CD which goes to market —— through all these stages music itself can become distant and somewhat impersonal. In a world where the Personal Computer has come into use everywhere, we need some new tools to access Personal Music for the good of our minds. The violin in its case in the closet or the piano gathering dust in the living room are often mere reminders of a pre-recording day when you had to play music yourself if you wanted to hear it. Now there is much more music everywhere, but less for your private personal use, much to hear but less for personal participation. Music like baseball has become a non-participating activity for the majority, a passive auditory activity.

So one might ask: Is there going to be such a thing in the new America as "Personal Music"? Following rock or country performers to crowded halls, or getting the newest popular CDs as soon as they appear - - - these things are musical experiences in a sense. But some of this is part of the human social instinct to participate in what everyone else does, to be in the au courant scene, following the musical crowd. We participate in Music as hearers, not as doers.

One might wonder if Jazz doesn't fulfill a creative personal function for many, not specifically those who listen but those who are engaged in making jazz music. Jazz is at this time the only place for musical self-expression, but some of us who have been brought up on a diet of Bach and Brahms feel somewhat distant from jazz because of its self-imposed restrictions. It is a group playing activity, which involves a healthy social sense , but with costs of self-adjustment to the group activity. Since Jazz is performance oriented, it involves an integrated group response, which sets it apart from the personal music we are talking about. The pre-set formats of rhythm and recognizable melodic thread do hold the group together so they can function musically, but this has real musical costs in scope and expression.

And Jazz has a history if its own, it is very conscious of its antecedents, and tends to work within an historical framework, even if much de-modulated as in the European Free Improvisation movement. Bach's Brandenburgs might be considered a written score evolving from something which was at an earlier time a free-form proto-Baroque Jazz, with measured cadences, instrumental leads in turns and a general group feeling not unlike the small jazz ensemble. Jazz and Baroque have been noted as sharing certain features in overall rhythmic regularity, the instrumental turns of the Concerto Grosso, and the lack of open-spaces and rests a la Mozart. Entirely different in sound and spirit are the unaccompanied Cello Suites which Bach wrote in the privacy of his home in virtual house-arrest; they are very intense and very personal. We suspect really personal music will be solo playing for a long while, but if you find a second or third voice to work with in real-time, that is certainly good fortune. But the start of personal music must be you and your instrument, and what the two of you can devise as you go.

Learning to play an instrument is self-defeating in a sense, since the Beethoven Sonata you have practiced for months is in fact played much better on any one of a dozen brilliant recordings, probably with much better sound than your half-in-tune piano can muster. And if you decide to go into things seriously and study the harmony, counterpoint and historical chains of musical threads, are you prepared for the details of immaculate phrasing and pedaling, the infinite splitting of analytical interpretational hairs? Whose taste are you following in playing, the original composer's, your teacher's. or your own sense of musicality? Is drill to a set pattern what music is really about?

Back to the beginning: Can there be a new interest now for such a thing as PM or Personal Music? Is there a possible relationship with music for you as a private person, working with a musical instrument which you can manipulate to your personal satisfaction. And if so how would you want to go about it? If you are one of the many who have taken piano lessons as a child for more than half a dozen years, you have a lot of musical phraseology stored in your mind, and your hands are familiar with scales, chords, arpeggios and much basic music theory. Since the piano has the largest pitch range of any instrument, a graphic layout in the keyboard, and is capable of independent voices with two hands, each to some extent capable of controlling two voices with practice the piano would seem be best a good vehicle for your private, personal experiments. Unlike violin or flute, the piano doesn't feel isolated when playing solo. So let's continue this discussion with the notion of "The Personal Piano"!

But there are no simple situations. When you play a piece, you are repeating the inventions of a "composer", doing faithfully now what he or she was once doing expressively. This is not your personal creation, it will always someone else's song or sonata, and if you are of a mind to read others' things this is quite enough. But if you have a yen for something of your own, something you design and execute yourself, then you find little help from your traditionally oriented schools, teachers and mentors.

Children have wonderful imagination, they tell personal stories and sing their own tunes — until the schools regularize them in the name of education. They don't have hands to play a keyboard scale yet, not enough grasp of the fingers and not enough practice. But one who goes through eight years of lessons and does have the necessary equipment to play a piano, has often lost a great part of the original child's imagination along the way. Notice the way Itzak Perlman plays violin: He closes his eyes, there is no score on his music stand, but it is all there in his mind down to the details. He has enough talent and training to make the music his own, and it shows in the performance. Of course Perlman is a talented musician, a man of rare ability. But is it only for the trained virtuoso to close his eyes and hear the music from within?

Putting together a personal sense of music is something which anyone can do. Hum your own tune rather than a popular one, think of sounds which come from your mind rather than from your CD player. And above all, select an instrument which you can learn to play with your own mental and digital equipment. Stay with that instrument year after year as you evoke its sounds at times when your mind needs quiet and comfort.

There are people who play music for fame or money, for ego or status, for friends' and family compliments......and this is perfectly reasonable in a highly social and competitive society. But there should be room for a personal reconnoitering with the self in a flow of musical sound, which you do for yourself, by yourself, and with knowledge that it is your own music property, something nobody else in the world will be doing exactly that way at that time.

There is innate individuality in music, and in a world in which the role of the individual is constantly shrinking, there should be some private retreat in which a person can be secure for a half hour a day in being alone musically with oneself. Formal meditation as an act of emptying the self of the self is a good way for many of us, but for those who rejoice in the fullness and richness of a vibrant life-experience, music offers another pathway. When you add personal music to your life you can speak to it privately and personally.

We often wondered why the cicadas which become so prominent in early August bother bowing their serrated little legs so persistently day in and day out, concertizing everywhere for that short season before the great cold comes. Some have suggested that it is an involuntary action of no great meaning, others have found that it is an accurate indicator of the ambient air temperature. But we are sure that the cicadas have found their way into the ancient art of music-making, and with all the energy their short lives can muster, they go about declaring with a vengeance that they are alive, that they are here and can, with absolute confidence in the process, make their very own music. That is in essence what personal music is about.

Realtime Improvisation

Improvisation in music means composing something new which has not been notated, something quite literally "un-foreseen". Any amateur musician in the 18th century could improvise, but as methodologies for music teaching developed in the 19th century, reading and playing complicated scores became the focus of the teacher's attention, to the extent of crowding out analysis of how music was constructed and how a student might put together a piece on his or her own. Reinforced by continuous practice, piano students became adept at pressing down the right keys at the right time, while the talented student could be further instructed about putting feeling and "expression" into the rehearsed product later.

Today, many who have never studied music can pick out a tune on an instrument by ear, some may develop a high degree of musical skill even at semi-professional performing levels. Here as elsewhere the personal learning curve is likely to be more important than being taught step by step by a formal teaching program. The complex music of non-Western "musical illiterates" (incorrectly defined as those who cannot read music as in the unscored Indian musical tradition), shows how music can come from the individual who has learned to express himself personally while working within the framework of a developed cultural matrix.

In America Improvisation was formerly a suspect word, often associated with musical amateurs who "play by ear" without reallly knowing what they are doing. But in this last half century the huge popularity of Jazz has given a seal of approval to the word "Improv.". Jazz performers have shown that it is possible to work without a written score, and many feel that Jazz musicians are the only real improvisers of our world. At the same time other kinds of improvisation, ranging from Classical to "new music" experimental, attract little attention from either instrumental performers or the musical listening public.

Improvisation at Close Range

A quick list of the range of Improvisers in our Western world is given below:

1) Unnotated music is generally is thought to be improvisory, but a great deal of it is firmly structured. The outlines are often well thought out and sections are roughly "in place", although some decoration can be applied in terms of cadenzas, changes of shifting rhythm, and the details of instrumental performance. As Jazz developed from a free improvisational base, much of it became fossilized rotating around melodic centers with increasingly virtuosic performance skills. Jazz performance is now part of a familiar style, which started out from peculiarly local American origins, but soon became a global musical phenomenon with performances and recordings heard worldwide. The thematic or melodic core in a piece can usually still be recognized, along with identifiable skills stemming from a list of well known performers and within the jazz realm there is a clear range of performance and historical styles.

2) Our current relatively structured Universal Jazz is now the main thread of the improvisatory spectrum. But the improvisatory process need not be Jazz oriented and a skilled performer can play within the framework of any interesting style which seems attractive and comfortable. Modern classically trained improvisers often do 19th century Schumann-like free variations which can be quite lovely. or one can improvise in a Baroque idiom on the harpsichord, which is well worth doing since it must be based on an understanding of traditional standard theory. And then there is a style of easy playing of the 1970's which is associated with a nightclub atmosphere, pleasant to hear as background and not overly hard to imitate. This cocktail club kind of improvisation which involves musical memory and imitation of a

certain cadenced style, can become trite and somewhat limiting as the process ends up by imitating itself. But it has an aura of freedom clearly different from mechanical playing out of a memorized score.

3) Improvising always was the testing ground for a new idea. and every major composer after 1750 could use instruments to try out and develop musical ideas. It would have been unthinkable for a composer to be unable to play several instruments reasonably well if not quite expertly. Improvisation was a critical part of music training, composers knew how to do live experimentation with complex configurations of pitch, dynamics and rhythm. Doors closed in the 19th century as virtuosic technique was demanded and taught under the hard hand of music programs designed to train professional performers. But as music in the early 19th century moved toward self-expression in the spirit of the literary Romantic Revolution, many new avenues opened. In the new spirit, music need not be considered merely a technique and a craft, it could become an "Art" and as such it would enter into the heady atmosphere of ideas, feelings and personality. In this atmosphere improvisation could be used to register personal impressions, emotions ranging from joy to anger to nostalgia, in a relaxed non-performance opportunity for experimentation.

4) It is not difficult to learn basic diatonic harmony. You start by picking out "by ear" with the right hand on piano or KB a melody line (your own or from a song), and filling in an "accompaniment" of solid or arpeggiated chords with the left hand. A great part of the music most people hear today is constructed this way, not only our popular music but much Baroque and Classical composition as well. Almost all

of the popular music we hear on records or radio today is constructed in this way with a Melody which gets our musical attention, riding acoustically above a background Accompaniment.

Before 1900 music in the colleges and conservatories was taught diatonically, with dissonances used mainly for color and texture. But after 1920 the sound of a new music appeared, and manuals of composition began to state flatly that triadic harmony was to be avoided, along with diatonic scales and anything that reeked of the last century's over-sweetened sound.

5) Authentic folk music that Bartok and others were recording at the beginning of the last century, has always been in good part improvisatory. Musical history is always present for the folk performer working in an established tradition, but there is enough elbowroom in the presence of his audience to define his personality, to say exactly who he is and why and how he is playing. Held in line by the echoes of his musical past, he has freedom despite a highly organized musical background in a conservative societal framework. This is why the folk singer or priest-seer is such an important person to his audience, as representative of live performance at a given moment, while yet tracing the thread of musical history back to his past.

6) A private person working with an instrument which is long practiced and well understood, can have a remarkable kind of freedom. Not having to please an audience as he plays alone in his private room, free to think his own thoughts and experiment mentally and manually, he has only one major concern: To please himself. All great art is done by people who, even if they were engaged in pleasing others, are

above all intent on pleasing themselves. The study of the endorphins bears exactly on this point, but there is more involved than our ultimate brain chemistry. Becoming enthusiastically involved in a process is the initial germ of artistic creativity, whether it is a child playing with clay or stones, or an established musical composer putting together the parts of a new quartet.

Improvisation in Wider View

But the improviser has to deal with other matters than hand, ear and instrument if his work is going to have real meaning to himself and to others. Music since the start of history has always been man's most basic means of expressing himself. But when much music after the Renaissance became the formal accompaniment to a sacred text, it could lose some of its imaginative individuality. Bach transcended this limitation by his intense personal religious devotion, coupled with his extraordinary ability at composing live keyboard music in evocation of new musical ideas. But much music of his time was conceived as background if not pure decoration, like the chairs tables and carpets of a salon, finally becoming "tafelmusik" for the pleasure of the educated rich, who as an educated class did appreciate craftsmanship in and for itself. Music became one of the costly ornaments of a high living standard for the sensitive and educated European upper class.

We don't like to think of Mozart writing music to pay for his living expenses, but funds whether earned of contributed are involved in artistic production one way or another. At the present time the greatest part of new music goes from electronic studios into the world of advertising or serves as backgrounding for TV and movies. There is a commercial need for disposable filler music to fill the needs of the recording and radio broadcast industry.

Since the beginning of the last century, all the arts have been faced with the cultural problem of tearing up everything that had been done before, in order the create something which would be entirely modern and "new". At the same time artists who were well trained in the techniques of their art were fully aware of what it was that they were ripping to shreds. All the arts were going through a similar reaction phase, as a way of defining themselves in their own point in time. Painting, sculpture, writing and music all faced this problem of "newness", sometimes outrageously defying public taste for half a century, before slowly gaining recognition and some tardy acceptance. As a reaction against this reactive mood, some artists reversed the process and ingeniously imitated the past in a NeoClassical mood redefined by their personal taste, balancing as it were an uncertain artistic future with the well understood and familiar past. The music of Stravinsky in 1910 as compared to his work in 1950 shows this shift of sensibilities.

In order to create something new, one has to go back into ones self. This can be done consciously and sometimes quite mathematically selecting parameters and algorithms to put sounds together in arranged ranks and orders. Schoenberg and the later serialists were doing something of this kind with the tone row, and in a different vein the development of computers music later in the century produced a new experience in ElectroAcoustic Music. Behind these new directions lay a deep dissatisfaction with the old notions of Established Art. In a time of fast moving change, artists felt a compelling need to open the doors of the mind, to let a lifetime of experience in, and then sort things out with the sifting processes of the complex human mind. All this upheaval could end up with something personally valid, something vital and really new. Or it could dead end in a cul de sac to be documented in the annals of the history of art.

Lendvai demonstrated with precision the many ways in which Bartok employed both the Fibonacci Section and the Golden Mean in his composition, but Bartok had much earlier remarked that in composing he relied essentially on feeling and intuition. Nobody can exactly define intuition, possibly because it is one of the more complex functions of the human mind, and the brain is not a good tool to auto-describe itself. But Bartok's remark is deep. How can we utilize the full capacities of the mind without a process like "intuition", which etymologically means a "looking within"? In making music, can we have half a dozen separate functions operating independently, without working with an overall architecture? How can we help ourselves do more than we can consciously think about doing, and still have the results of this mysterious pondering come out as organized musical thought?

In the new millennium we stand as heir to a complex musical heritage. We face a new kind of academically taught "serious" music, which is neither totally tonal nor yet atonal, where a musical line, which is not necessarily distinguishable as a melody, proceeds by motions of fourths leaps, while thirds and sixths are replaced by minor seconds. This neo-tonal "style" presents a style-sound of its own just as clearly as the 1970's cocktail lounge music had a recognizable sound of its own. This is not the first time that academic preferences have tried to define and regularize art. But it seems that public musical taste may be ready for some changes. However there are no sharp lines of cleavage appearing, no harsh breaks with the past like the upheavals of 1910.

Or it may be the moment for our public taste to turn backward to the established excellence of the Western Classical tradition, and enjoy the art of the past in preference to the uneasy artistic shiftings of the present age. There were recent painters who used only black or brown, with minor touches of brightness at the edges, but they soon went their way as history of art curiosities. Any art which is constructed on narrow or limiting parameters is going to be moribund in a generation, while art which selectively uses the full palette of available materials (if done by a person who has courage, craft and intuition of some mysterious sort), will have a chance of being appreciated a century later as still vital and vivid.

There is no reason to avoid tradition. Traditional Western triadic harmony has much value from a long history of development. It accords with the harmonic overtone series to which our ears respond naturally. Triadics can be mixed and matched with "dissonances" of all sorts and proportions, and the results will carry a variety of "beats" which enrich the acoustic texture of a performance. Beatless fourths, fifth and octaves were the inheritance of early church music singing drawn from Greek antiquity, but slowly abandoned by the 12th century composers as sole basis for composition, in favor of enriching intervals like the thirds and sixths with multiple beats per second. Tallis' 16th century "Alternating Hymns for Plainsong and Polyphony" contrasts timbrally dry and rich textures perfectly, while reminding us that parallel fifths octaves apart or sounds in unison are also usable and artistically valuable. Nothing in music is ipso facto un-usable!

We are in a sense products of our past, this is the inevitable burden of history both personally and culturally . But we are also the product of what we currently are doing, what we make and fashion and devise. The composer has a long list of interfaces between him and the final musical product, starting with his thought as it gets penciled or computed into score form, next finding and briefing a performer, who will find a manager to arrange a concert in a hall, with a given date and a paying audience. Considering all the requirements which a musical composition involves, it may be hard to see the importance of intentional artistic "newness" as a device to free the artist from part of the tradition of history. In fact some of our preoccupation with newness and the Cutting Edge may be a reflex from the Sciences which after 1906 have had to do much scrapping to make room for newly developing knowledge. It may be that the arts and the sciences both felt they were trapped in the attitudes of the past and needed to clear away certain mists if they were to see more accurately into the future.

Some of the historical interface between the artist and his music can be avoided by the composer of electro-acoustic music, who has only himself, the synthesizer and the generated sound tape recording to consider in shaping his final product. Modern synthesizing and editing possibilities are enormous, and the composer as "musical thinker" will have to be in some measure an audio-engineer before he is done with a piece. Much composition can be done by laying out procedures for assembling sounds as recorded or fre-abricating them into new ones. But there should be some hands-on improvisation on keyboard or electronic controlling instrument to give an idea of what the newly configured sound will be like. Electro-Acoustic music may sound different from what we have been accustomed to hear as Music. But most of the craft and technique implications still remain in the areas of traditional subharmony, in the shape of phrasing and in the dynamic variables, although the final result will have a very modern and distinct EAM flavor of its own.

But now there is a new twist for the Improviser who can record on tape what he is doing, listen to it, criticize and revise it, rework it, and if he likes what he hears, he can even have it recorded inexpensively on CD to sell or give to friends. This direct line from the improvised composition to a hearable musical artifact is something new in the history of Western music, which formerly had to be played by instrumentalists from score to be heard at all. Countless Jazz, rock and country groups record their music as they progress from their own sounds in a studio to a CD and on out to the world. Most don't fulfill their dream of making it big, most don't even break even, but the recording path is available and it has the ability of turning a stream of sound into a durable artifact. And for the private improviser recording is the only way to hear his own playing the way it sounds to someone else. For the improviser the recording is the best and ultimate Critic.

The Greek philosopher Epictetus said that what you have in the reach of your arms, you can control; from there on out it is less and less yours. Just so in this case. You are still for the major part personally in control as a relationship is being made between thoughts in your mind, the sounds which echo from your thinking, your hands on an instrument and the tape in your recording machine. This directness frees you for more work tomorrow, new thinking the day after, without waiting on other people's criticism or praise for your work. Writing music will come later, after and out of the live real-time experiments, and it will have more solidity of shape and more permanence. But it will have less fluidity overall.

An ancient Chinese thinker said that the best training for political life and the ruling of a country was MUSIC. He saw that if you have skill to regulate the multiple parameters of musical composition and performance, you can probably think fairly coherently about the polyphonic parameters of running a state. In this country we think of the Law as ideal training for a political career, since law teaches us to reduce a complex set of standards to operating rules to perform a finite job. However training in Music may have another ability to attune future politicians to multi-dimensionality, something which major societies require in order to operate simultaneously on many levels. Our world depends on processes and instruments of all kinds, which are often found to be difficult to harmonize among themselves. There is no political melody which rides above a background accompaniment, all parts must combine to make a properly resonant whole.

Music is one of the remarkable activities native in the structure of the human mind. Making music employs brain, hand, tool, ears and eyes, body rhythm, inner vision along with visual imagination guided by intuition and some degree of good luck. The human activity which best approaches Music in complexity and need for intuition, is found in the higher levels of our scientific studies. Science demands a lifetime of study, laboratories and high professional experience to operate effectively, while Music, operating at several parallel levels of complexity, is open by contrast to us all, it is completely in the public domain. It does demand study, practice, technique and a lot of patience, but the rewards can be counted in terms of health of the body and happiness of the mind.

Stages of Improvisation

Within the range of modern classical or simply modern

impromptu music, there is a wide range of musical activity called "Improvisation", some stages of which are these:

1) First is the original function of the toccata, named from the Ital. "toccare" or touching the keys/strings of an instrument, which may be called warming up, or testing out the instrument. This can verge unconsciously into a little piece, or it can be just warming up.
2) The composer tests out a series of ideas, improvised Studies or musical notions. For example the first volume of Bartok's Mikrokosmos which were originally improvised as composed live; these become Etudes/Studies when notated and edited.
3) The composer/performer casually goes to the instrument with a mood, a feeling which he wants to express. Like a poem, it may be something not sayable in the ordinary modes. When he finished playing, the the piece disappears.
4) He, or friends he is playing for, recall the piece, so it may get played again later. It becomes in partn part become by frequent use, and as such it becomes part of the composer's live-repertoire, often with variations. It may stay this ways for years, or forever...
5) The composer/performer decides to keep the piece un -notated, and uses it for performance regularly. It becomes fixed, actually edited with most of it left exactly "in place", but there is slight room for alteration in performance.
6) The composer decides to notate this piece. Now it is fixed, it can be played by others, or published, but it may still be called an "Improvisation".

7) The composer draws on improvised materials he had done at some previous time, makes sketches of these, and later uses them in a formal work. Beethoven has such famous sketch books.

8) The composer is notating a piece at his desk (Bach's son said he always wrote away from the keyboard...) he needs something new, goes to his instrument and tries out a passage, or contiunues or perhaps just lets it flow. Back to the desk, this goes into the formal piece he is writing.

9) The composer cannot or does not like to play an instrument, he writes on paper and waits for a performer to let him hear the sound of what he has written. This is the exact polar-opposite of the Improvisational Mode.

10) There is a relatively new type of serious musical composition, which is conceived and produced with the aid of a synthesizer , which must be mentioned as one of the most interesting directions for composers in the coming century. In this music, much can be planned in advance, or sections can be left in rought notation to be improvised live in performance.

11) For decades, popular musical artists have recorded their live performance on tape directly, often sequentially into simultaneous-play channels on the tape deck,. Songs have often gone from the microphone to the market without a score, unless a rudimentary score were needed for copyright protection. Jazz, pop, rock and country have been able to use this semi-improvisatory technique easily, their live music directly being converted directly from the recording into a saleable CD.

12) A new development for the individual composer which has become practicable only in the last ten years, is the use of electronic keyboard or an electronic musical instrument, which uses the MIDI format to communicate with a computer employing a music reading and annotating program. With this system, improvisation of all sorts can be converted into a notated score with some adjustment and jiggling . As of now, the programs work well for hand-notation, but there are many problems with recording complex music in real-time, from wrong notes, wrong durations and rests and imperfect "quantization" or regularization of the notes. But in the near future, the gap between the Improvisor and his finished score may be much less, and this will change the role of "improvisation vs. score-composition" greatly.

13) A great mass of commercial new music is being recorded in hi-tech music studios for use directly as recorded. It can be either digitally recorded and put on CD, or composed with a synthesizer. Some of this music is worked out in detail before playing, some is clearly improvised and edited for use later. Much of music you hear on TV ads, TV shows and cinema soundtracks is produced by this route, since it is economical and offers a wide range of sounds and effects.

One step further along for piano Improvisation, is to have installed a pitch and velocity sensitive sensor strip underneath the keys of the instrument, so recording of the actual instrumental sound can be done at the same time as electronic signaling is being fed to a MIDI program for editing and notation. Piano sound can be recorded and MIDI sounds on any combination of instruments at the same time p[rovided that we are using the same pitches.

Do all these things make composition overly facile and automatic? Not at all! We are now able to tune in on the neglected improvisational art, and use an original, intuitive flow of music which the mind feeds to the fingers, as the original-source for composition. This avoids the various interfaces of stop-and-start pencil writing, of transfer to paper for reconstruction by a performer at a later date, since the acoustic original is being simultaneously taped.

What is required is a composer whose hands can develop in real-time musical thoughts as they sequence themselves in the composer's mind. For composers in the classical tradition of "new-music", this is difficult, sinceacademic training does not go in this direction. But the gains working faster, more intuitively while self-monitoring composition at real-time pace, are significant indeed.

Improvising with Electronic Equipment

There is much more to be said about traditional improvisation, but we are going to turn to the less well known world of Electronic Music generation, which offers unusual opportunities for improvisers as well as carefully scored compositions written for electronic sounds. Working with Electro-Acoustic instruments which put the music directly on tape as the final medium, we incidentally solve most of the problems of the Traditional Jungle which we have described above. This is new so we want give it some additional delineation and space.

You can use electronic orchestral instrumental sounds and devise trios, quartets and even add orchestral ambiances as you wish. The sounds may not be as convincing as the sound of a professional orchestra, but there is plenty to work with and the sound are getting much better all the time as the industry develops.

Electronic music instruments using MIDI or digital recording, are these days is quite accessible, with the development of the compact, electronic musical instruments we call Synthesizers. Since these are keyboard based to begin with, they offer a novel way into creating personal, improvised music to anyone who has a modest sense of how the piano keyboard works. Now you can have the sounds of any instrument, of many instrument together, with more options than you can shake a baton at. Given an improvisational penchant, the electronic Synth is an inviting piece of equipment, and it can operate in two dimensions:

The really good synthesizers have ways to alter sounds away from the traditional timbres, and some like the Kurzweil can generate entirely new sounds in a world of their own. This world is taught in the Universities, and it is called Electro- Acoustic-Music or EAM, and it has generated in this last half century a wholly new approach to music and sound. EAM music is not easy to get into, there are lots of technical terms and functions which a person who hasn't pulled back the Computer Curtain would find impenetrable. And EAM music is not to everyone's taste. Some EAM composers incline toward squeaks, raps, sirens and musical moans, but in the hands of the new generation some really lovely music is coming forth. You may have heard a lot of it already without realizing the source in cinema and TV musical scoring, where it has made a strong inroad since is it new, different and also economical as studio produced work.

Electro-Acoustic Music may not be the final word as this century comes to an end, but it can solve most of the above "Sins". Now for the first time, Sound can be manufactured and manicured to be whatever the composer wants, and it can be spread over a time sequence in any way the composer wishes. There are no bars, measures or downbeats needed, problems of what goes with what, and what goes where, can disappear. The idea and concept come first, and almost everything can be adjusted and rearranged in the composing process or on the digital editing screen. In short we have in EAM at last a musical carte-blanche, on which we can write the musical ideas of the moment into the library of the future.

There have been enormous musical shifts of taste in this last hundred years. Arnold Schoenberg was breaking new ground in the piano Opus 11 of 1909 with his Little Piano Pieces, as he turned his back, with something of a wrench, on the 19th century harmonic music he had been writing just a year before. These short studies are wonderfully imaginative and new, they explore the pan-tonal possibilities of sound. But in a dozen years Schoenberg had replaced much of this hard-won freedom with the twelve-tone serial concept, a rigid notion which persisted in academic circles until it wore itself out by mechanical over-use. The promise of the 12 tone Row did not offer a great deal for the musical future of the West, after all.

When John Cage after WW II brought back from Zen philosophy notions of fortuitousness, the aleatory process in the moment of swift-passing time, this seemed to point to new ways indeed. But brilliant as Cage was, his work ended in self-repetition, and development of a style (which was the very thing he was avoiding). After 1970 there has been a swift succession of New Styles following the Cagian Fortuitous, the Minimalist, the "experimental" and notions borrowed from the world of Ethno- Musicology. But these tend to be of concern to relatively narrow ranges of academic persons, while Electro-Acoustic Music on the other hand has grown systematically as new electronic digital equipment develops with our New Electronic Age.

In just the last three decades we have started to open up new worlds, unknown realms of musical sound, with EAM. Not all of it sounds as great as the above tout, because EAM composers are generally schooled in university programs which teach the state-of-the-art composition of a given date. Much EAM music sounds alike, much has not got out of the academic groove. Some is designed as a style which will best get acceptance in EAM competitions. Some pieces are academic "exercises" like the tens of thousands of student fugues written a hundred years ago in the Conservatories of the world. But these are human problems likely to occur in times of social flux, they are certainly not musical problems.

Aims of Electro-Acoustic Music

Somewhere around 1906, just when Einstein was publishing his important work on Relativity, a general process of "dematerialization" began to take place in the arts. It may have had little or nothing to do with Relativity, other than the fact that two activities in the same ambiance are likely to have some relationship. Almost simultaneously with the changed ideas about time and space and as early as Schoenberg's six little piano pieces and Ives piano work after he left Yale, music began to lose its traditional harmonic shape. Change suddenly occurred in all the arts, painting had changed shape and attitude almost before Duchamp's Lady had finished descending the staircase, while international Poetry started to unravel and knit itself up again during the great war. Nothing was going to be the same ever again. Why this all occurred at the exact time when men of science began to look at the world in radically new ways, we do not know. But looking back we recognize a radical and persistent change in all the varieties of taste and perception.

When in the 1920's Vareze assembled new displays of analog sounds from acoustic instruments, ranging from the sound of the platinum flute to clicks and fire siren wails, he was doing something that was perfectly new as music. And it was clearly music. Those new sounds couched in startling rhythmic matrices must have seemed far more shocking then than now, when we can listen to a remastered CD of his once-recondite pieces with more appreciation than surprise. Many were trying out new musical ideas in those days, but it was Vareze who seemed to announce the future landscape best in his tightly constructed, odd little pieces.

When Vareze titled a piece Poeme Electronique in the 1950's, it was more than a reworking of what he had been doing for years. It was a grand demonstration of what could be done with Electronic Music in a vast public performance with amplification sufficient to fill a great hall. Those clear and clean and specially designed sounds echoing in an airy auditorium space did catch the ear of young composers like Davidovsky by 1950, and gave a new generation of composers one of the musical thrusts which were to develop as Electro-Acoustic music in the coming decades.

Two new antithetical threads appeared after the war. Cage had been meditating in the Zen garden of discovery, and came out with another set of startlingly new " designed-sounds" to be used in a chance world of aleatory music. At the present time the prepared piano and aleatory techniques are stock terms in a college music introductory courses and we can hardly imagine how unthinkably new and advance guard these notions seemed then.

The other thread was less obvious and would take more time to develop. When transistors appeared in 1952, the giant tube computers of the wartime period vanished as the computer became smaller, more electrically efficient, and finally ended as a desk-size machine. Soon the smaller personal computer had become a a familiar piece of equipment on every university campus. By the mid 1950's plans were laid to get music into the computers, with two aims. First aim was to be able to totally modify existing sounds, even to create entirely new sounds from sine and square waves, and even design new sounds from mathematical specifications. This was an entirely different avenue into new acoustics from Cage's wires and bolts fastened between the piano strings. A second aim was to be able to organize sequences of sounds in a rhythmic time-frame with a mechanical design, or as we now say with a computer-program. This goes back to the pioneering work of Max Matthews, culminating later in programs like Music V in Europe and Opcode's MAX here. Structures could be rigid and repeating, or they could be designed with randomizing patterns to become aleatory in Cage's sense. But of course they were not aleatory in the same sense as Cage's word, since they were random-designed rather than evolved by a process of pure chance.

By the 1970's "synthesizing machines" which could make up sounds, had appeared. These were analog devices like the Arp, Moog, Prophet, some early Rolands and the great and remarkable Synclavier, all producing real-sounds in the auditory spectrum from oscillators with a battery of modifying stages. Here could be constructed an infinite library of "Electro-Acoustic Sounds", from clicks and pulsating grunts to sighs and wails, as well as imperfect imitations of flute and trumpet. Some compositions of the period sounded more like an early short-wave radio being tuned than Music, but many were surprisingly reminiscent of what Vareze had been doing decades earlier.

This kind of musical composition was new and to be found only in a few dozen universities in 1975, but it would become part of the fabric of a musical education in every college twenty years later. Most people applying for college teaching positions in music at the present time have extensive experience in electro-acoustic techniques, which are found in all music graduate programs and of course in myriad commercial recording studios which prepare material for TV and film use. On the one hand electro-acoustic music leads to degrees in college programs and to a scattering of concerts around the country for the EAM cognoscenti. On the other hand it flourishes as an industry, effectively and efficiently producing most of the sound one hears on the sound tracks of film and TV programs. It is no longer surprising to hear the hybrid use of synthesized sounds coupled with live instruments in an effects-drenched and hugely amplified concert of music by Yanni or John Tesh, which the public enjoys live even more than on the ubiquitous TV and CD. This is a different strain of music from the university-based work of the Seamus composers, but much of the underlying concept and electronic base is identical.

This brings up the matter of what music in the 21st Century really is. We still go to concerts to hear artists' personal interpretation in performances of Bach and Brahms, but this is not the performance based world of 1900. The musical world has changed much more than we have noticed. Virtually all the music heard in today's world is electronically involved in some degree. There are many intervening electronic stages, from microphones through digital processing to remastering, and finally to performance on a theater set or in your home theater on sound reproducing devices. The luxury of hearing a symphony orchestra of a hundred pieces in a good hall is restricted to those who live near cities and can afford tickets, while performances by large orchestras are disappearing under impossible financial burdens. Music is no longer the business of a grand hall in 1800 featuring the new symphony of Herr Haydn. It is everywhere, it is cheap, and it is electronic.

Only a minute percentage of our population can enjoy non-harmonic, non-diatonic music, while the rest of our world reclines on the soft couch of jazz, pop and country music in various denominations. Some popular music very rich and well constructed, but much is weak and thin from a classically trained composer's point of view. But the new musical aesthetic and new sounds which come from groups of the electro-acoustic composers are beginning to find their way into the general music culture. In 1952 Kurosawa had in his sound track of the Seven Samurai a virtual preview of analog synthesized possibilities, long before synths were commonly in use. We hear on commercially produced TV many segments of well constructed electro-acoustic work, partly because there are available trained composers who produce interesting sound sequences, partly because this can be done inexpensively in a commercial or private studio as job-contract work synching frame by frame a video tape. The old way of using a written score with a group of recorded instrumentalists has become prohibitively expensive in a commercially driven world.

If composers in Mozart's time were seen as craftsmen, later to become searchers of the soul and deep thinkers in the wake of the Romantic Revolution, what are composers supposed to be in this new century? For many practitioners in the arts, the only righteous way seemed to tear up everything that had gone before, and construct again from scratch. Atonality at one point seemed likely to scrub the notes out of the harmonic diction, just as painters dripped or splashed paint on nude canvases while sculptors inclined toward blobs or assemblages of unknown objects. For the first time around in the show and museum circuit, the key word seemed to be totally new and unique . Working in a artistic tradition was out, and those who could not devise absolute newness generally retired from the field. The less scrupulous were content to copy the old with some new twist, content with a footnote in the academic history of their art. Of course this "destroying the past" attitude toward art is a self-defeating process. In the final analysis you carry your impressions of the past with you always, old work (whether yours or theirs) all gets recycled in the course of time and when it comes out it will always be somehow different, without proclaiming its newness as Cutting Edge of the new age.

We live in a new world of musical engineering, with blaring and bewildering new devices which can shape and organize sound plastically beyond belief. But it is not just a matter of what you can afford to buy, or what you can get access to in your school or university studio. Everything is available to look at and much to download from pages of url addresses on the expanding horizon of the net. We realize that we do not have the time to check all the things culminating right now, to read all the exciting new pages on the net, to update on all the new programs and hardware constantly flowing out of the cornucopia of the electronic engineering salesmen. If success is the art of being able to keep on-top-of everything - - - gadget-wise program-wise and module-wise - - -then many of us might well admit failure to keep up and at least have some peace of mind. A lot of new work is reminiscent of some of the rich sounds of the synth experiments of the 1980's, and behind that one can hear many of the ancient transients of Vareze even more clearly. This may be in part coming from the teaching of electro-acoustic music in graduate education, which was shaped in large part by the role of computers in making music. There may now be a trend toward partly unconscious imitation of the tonal sounds and sequences of the past, just as hundreds of highly competent 19th c. composers imitated the standard harmony of the classical period as a base for their new music..

With the ubiquitous availability of the previous analog and now digital synths, there is a general range of sounds promoted by the nature of the instruments, so the results naturally will sound like synthesized music. We need a careful and cautious vision with which to approach our electronic composing machines, lest music sounds specifically synthesized. New programs are constantly striving toward the full sound of traditional Western instruments, but there is a fine degree of control which a performer with a well understood instrument can provide beyond the capabilities of a finely programmed musical sound. It may be that the fusing of traditional and synthesized sounds will reach a new level of musical acoustics suitable to the age in which we live.

Rhythmic simplicity has always been the weak link in Western music. Ultimately rhythm can have extremely complex patterning, based on large odd numbered series, or on Fibonacci numbers, or on the other hand it can be very simple. But the pattern must be variable in toto, it must not be slave to a polka beat or the number of quanta in a stock measure. Our present danger is inattention to rhythm, which must not be an side-issue which surfaces incidentally while we are busy monitoring our carefully manicured timbres.

Leaving diatonic notions to the side early in this century, we were quickly open to whole-tone and chromatic options, with tempered scales as well as a total portamento. Our word "scale" is merely the Latin scala "ladder", which is used for progressing somewhere in terms of pitch, while not inviting rhythmal variations automatically. It is only in a closely arranged sequence of Pitches and Rhythms that you have the heart of melody-line.

In a highly mechanized, engineering society, it is most important that we do not lose contact with the hand-made object. In furniture making, house building, pottery and cuisine, we seem to have sensed the danger and re-discovered the value of what is devised by the mind and shaped by the hand. Someone said that the hand is the cutting edge of the mind, certainly something any serious instrumentalist knows well.We find live-composing or improvising as it is often called, the natural medium for hand-worked music, but someone else can do it in a different way with the hand guiding a pencil on paper or nowadays on the computer screen. As we use mechanical systems for putting together music, we can lose the ancient hand-crafted feel, thus missing the sense of musicality which distinguishes a Mozart from a very similar arranger in Mozartean style. The human brain is a much more complex designing machine than the best music program, since it responds with complete memory to all sounds ever heard, while it combines them with "today".

Perils of Musical Inventiveness

On any piece of fertile land in a warm climate, a jungle is a natural happening. Parts of it are old and ancestral, other parts are competing for the light, and some is destined never to make it successfully. In a society which has lived a thousand years, the there will be comparable jungles — impenetrable, self- perpetuating and very confusing. Music since the twelfth century has developed just such a jungle of overgrowth. We can try to sort it out as social development in what we call Music History. But for a student of music or a composer it is still very confusing, all the more so because we learn music from the early stages of life, and absorb along with the beauty and delicacy of the music of each century, the formal notational characteristics of the music of that age. Step by step we move through the jumble of time, into the morass of a set of musical layers, remembering every detail in our unconscious mind, until we begin to invent our own voice, our own sound, under the burden of a long past. Rigidified patterns from the ages become the perils of musical inventiveness, and we note a short list of such perils as symptomatic:

1) Rhythmic repetition and rhythmic evenness, come from ancient use of music as accompaniment and regulator of the steps for popular dance. As workers move better to a chantey, or soldiers march to a drum or song, so dancers need a beat for their feet. This persisted into Classical musical forms as the Gigue, the Allemande and all the elements of the Baroque Suite (which was finally no longer a dance mode). Rock, Country and Jazz music still lockstep to the beat of the measure, creating the symmetrical sound to which our society is attuned. For peoples of the world who have complex and subtle metrical cadences, our Western music seems altogether too measured and tight.

2) In the Westereners have developed large instrumental ensembles which have the problem of the voices sounding exactly together. If you are going to have Harmony and an Orchestra, you will have to synchronize. In the 18th century the Conductor tapped the beat out with his baton and that was his primary function, although smaller ensembles could follow the bow of the first violin as a baton of sorts. This need

for multi-instrument synchronizing lies behind the modern teacher's insistence that the young student count out "ONE and TWO and..." evenly. And if there is question, that instrument of musical torture, the Metronome, can be brought out. Recordings in the last fifty years have become increasingly firm about exact timing, often to the extent of sounding mechanical. The great pianist Alfred Cortot in his wonderful recordings of the four Chopin Ballades in the 1930's, used subtle rhythmic variations as part of his interpretation, possibly following Chopin himself since he studied in his youth with the last of Chopin's students. Or consider the way Casals played the Bach Cello Suites, with their subtle and meaningful off-time variances. The term Rubato is literally "robbing" some time from a measure at one end and restoring it in synchronization at the other end of the phrase. If one wonders why we have become so mechanized, just take a look at the hundred piece Symphony Orchestra,. a little music making factory where everything must fit perfectly. One can even compare the Orchestra with a well run office of a major insurance company, precisely integrating a host of varying functions.

3) It is not just in popular music, but everywhere there seems to be a need for the regularity of an Upbeat and a Downbeat in each Measure. First count out the measures according to a set timing, then divide each measure into parts with a strong dynamic on the first note, a weak one half way through. Now count these out evenly "ONE and..." as a student, or add them all up arithmetically as a composer. They must all "come out right" in our musical arithmetic. If you can't do the complex math and guarantee results for

publication, let a modern Notation Program do it with its better computational abilities.

4) Harmony is certainly the notable characteristic of Western music. The piano keyboard invites and then demands Harmony. You can play it as a solo instrument with eight synchronous notes if you want, or three or four voices can be monitored with a little care. The white notes once represented the basic series, the scale or "ladder" which you climbed up or down fingerwise. But it is an odd-runged ladder, with uneven spacing, so between the larger intervals were put smaller ones as half-tones, which appear as the smaller (black) keys on our keyboard instruments. All composers have, by their musical training, something of this piano Graphic-Layout in mind, it is a basic part of music training and of harmonic thinking. But as piano is now taught, from traditional examples with a right hand melody and left hand "accompaniment", it becomes monophonic in spirit and a foe to the intelligent leading of voices.

5) Form has been so codified that the musically aware public looks automatically to the familiar "form" of the Sonata, the Symphony, the Suite as a necessary part of music expression. What is a Fantasia but something "fantastic" and unreal, in a world which rewards accountants more than dreamers? Doesn't the barebones outline of the Sonata seem a little like the pre-drawn canvases with numbers for fill-in painting? Aren't the sequences of a symphony as expectable as the scenario of a cowboy Western?

6) In closer view, we must note the ubiquitous four measure phrase, with its repeat, its variation, its resolution. This might have been a clever notion at the start, but running through two centuries of

compositions as a cliche', it has become trite and boring. Good for a song with many stanzas, good to remember and sing along. But it is bad when it gets into the uniform fabric of musical thinking, which is what has happened If a phrase is found good, why repeat it, why repeat a section, why do variations at all? Would we repeat lines of poetry to get the message through to the casual reader ?

7) There is a standardized set of timbres which goes with orchestral expectations, another one with country music, another with jazz. In developing with great skill the musical instruments in the 19th century, we standardized a lot of our thinking about sound.The classically trained singing voice became a formalized sound, which weonly begin to hear as a Western style, when we hear the Chinese operatic voice or the many voices out of Africa.

8) In this jungle where is the MUSIC? Does it become music only when played by highly trained performers reading marks on scores and supplying the musical remainder through intuition? Scores contain less than 40 % of the composer's intentions. Some believe that the score in black and white (like the office ledger) is really the hard, musical bottom line, the real reality, and that the Sound is a variable which is added by "artists" in performance. Others would go further and see musical reality in social notions of the History of Music, the true mycelium from which music appears incidentally like mushroom buttons.

9) As soon as you study an instrument a while. you have to confront that historical bugbear which we call "Notation", which is the accretion of times long past, needs long forgotten, instruments gone to dust and crude approximations of sounds in time reduced to

> tight formulae which we teach our children. If we are taught early to hold the hand or the bow in a certain "acceptable" position, and count out automatically "One...and...TWO....and....", that will do a great deal to form the mechanical musical taste which we will live with for the rest of our lives. Why say more here?

We all remember the old lady on the TV ads who quizzically looked at a hamburger and asked to our delight "Where's the meat?. That's soon forgotten, but the situation remains for the tens of thousands of kids who do their traditional music lessons traditionally only to ask later "Where's the music?"

In this jumbled jungle the greatest effort with the sharpest machete will not get you through to the open and quiet place where you can attend to the sounds of your own mind and generate your own personal notions of sound. To write or play music out of this maze of historical layerings, groping for a disappearing musical heaven, is not a healthy business for a sane mind.

Bibliography

Alden, Raymond M., English Verse. New York, 1903. *An Introduction to Poetry*. New York, 1909.

Alexander, Hartley B., *Poetry and the Individual*. New York, 1906.

Aristotle, *Theory of Poetry and Fine Art*, edited by S. H. Butcher. New York, 1902.

Bernbaum, Ernest, editor. *English Poets of the 18th Century*. New York, 1918.

Bosnquet, Bernard, *A History of Aesthetic*. New York, 1892.

Bradley, A. C. *Oxford Lectures on Poetry*. London, 1909.

Clark, A. C. *Prose Rhythm in English*. Oxford, 1913.

Drink Water, John. *The Lyric*. New York (n.d.).

Fairchild, Arthur H. R. *The Making of Poetry*. New York, 1912.

Hayes, Alfred. "Relation of Music to Poetry," in Atlantic, January, 1914.

Holmes, Edmond. *What is Poetry*? New York, 1900.

Neilson, William A. *Essentials of Poetry*. Boston and New York, 1912.

Rhys, Ernest. *Lyric Poetry*. New York, 1913.

Saintsbury, George, *History of English Prose Rhythm*. London, 1912.

Santayana, George, *Interpretation of Poetry and Religion*. New York, 1900.

Schelling, F. E. *The English Lyric*. Boston and New York, 1913.

Shackford, Martha H., *A First Book of Poetics*. Boston, 1906.

Shelley, Percy B., *A Defense of Poetry*, edited by Albert S. Cook. Boston, 1891.

Sidney, Sir Philip, *The Defense of Poesy*, edited by Albert S. Cook. Boston, 1890.

Stedman, Edmund C., *The Nature and Elements of Poetry*. Boston and New York, 1892.

Untermeyer, Louis, *The New Era in American Poetry*. New York, 1919.

Watts-Dunton, Theodore. *Poetry and the Renascence of Wonder*. New York, (n.d.).

Whitmore, C. E. *Article on the Lyric in Pub. Mod. Lang*. Ass., December, 1918.

Index